THE RED AND THE BLACK

The Red and the Black

Glory and Uncertainty at Saracens Ltd

MICHAEL AYLWIN with Matt Singer

MAINSTREAM
PUBLISHING

EDINBURGH AND LONDON

First published in Great Britain in 1999 by
MAINSTREAM PUBLISHING COMPANY (EDINBURGH) LTD
7 Albany Street
Edinburgh EH1 3UG

ISBN 1 84018 194 X

A catalogue record for this book is available from the British Library

Typeset in Berkeley Book
Printed and bound in Great Britain by Butler and Tanner Ltd

For Tommy Jobisselleat.
And Gower.

'It is now proved beyond doubt that for 50 years Saracens have consistently supported the Rugby Football Union, but the greatest difficulty with which they have always been confronted is that of a suitable ground. Once this difficulty is removed there can be no doubt that the Saracens Club will continue for another 50 years and more, and it is hoped that the efforts of the club officials to acquire a permanent ground will meet with the success they so richly deserve. As the Saracens Club proceeds to the commencement of its second half-century, may present and past Saracens keep in mind what a fine heritage has been handed down to them, and may they strive unceasingly to keep the game a pure sport for leisure hours, so that as amateur Rugby Football prevails, the Saracens Club may prove its most uncompromising supporter.'

O.R.G. Williams
Saracens: The First Fifty Years, 1926

Contents

Acknowledgements

Books like this can only be written with permission. Thanks must go first then to Nigel Wray, who has never been anything other than enthusiastic about the project and adamant that it not be a mindless glorification of Saracens. His resultant support has been liberating, as has his happiness to let us get on with it without interference. It would have been so easy for him to insist that he monitor the project carefully and control its output. That he, François Pienaar and Mark Evans agreed that we should tell the story as it unfolded is tribute to their strength, honesty and integrity as men.

Similarly, the myriad characters in the Saracen story, be they players or management, committee or marketing, past or present, have all been most accommodating. The players and management at Saracens, in particular, deserve special thanks. In a time when suspicion of the media is worryingly well placed, their trust has been richly appreciated. Thanks to them all for letting me intrude and for living a storyline of which Shakespeare would have been proud. Humble beginnings, superstar names, sun-drenched glory, professional pressures, financial worries . . . they even managed to have a few arguments to add extra spice. I hope I have depicted it all fairly. I have certainly tried.

Another thing that books need is a publisher. Many thanks to Bill Campbell at Mainstream for not knowing us from Adam yet still taking the punt. I hope it proves worth it!

Allison, I apologise for the interminable telephone calls with your husband while you were watching telly. I can assure you I did not enjoy them any more than you did. You also devoted many hours to the thankless task of selling (or not selling) *Year of the Fez*. Thanks to you for that and, of course, to the rest of the Singer clan, Andrew and Liz, Ben and Dan, as well as Ross Whightman and Harriet Bryce-Morris for the cold, lonely hours on the *YOTF* stalls. While on the subject of *Year of the*

9

Fez, many thanks also to Bill Edwards, whom we inexcusably forgot to credit for providing us with the player statistics for the magazine. Apologies for that and for stealing from your personal collection of match-day programmes in the following season.

Renowned for my wordiness, I rely implicitly upon impartial readers to review my work and tell me to shut up and get to the point. Thanks here are due to my parents, John and Angela (I shall cut down on the commas), and to Dan Morrish, the venerable intellect. And thanks to Angus Peterson for reading the odd chapter when he could be bothered and for not doing the washing up.

Finally, thanks go to Matt for having the idea. Once again I doubted the project was feasible, once again you appeared not to hear me and left me with little choice but to continue. Having finished it, I am grateful. It was another good idea.

1

Striking the Pose

The black tassel on the fez hat bobbed mischievously as Tony Diprose hoisted the cup towards the clear blue sky. It had been a definitive season for Saracens. It was a season now crowned by the heavy trophy in Diprose's hands, which had itself been coronated a few seconds earlier by the cheeky fez hat that seemed to transcend all on a glorious May afternoon.

Diprose's face struggled to contain a smile so animate it threatened to take leave of his weary body. From his perch high in the West Stand, he nodded his head with a victorious swagger at the scene below him, reflected in the convex polished base of the Tetley's Bitter Cup.

It was a brand new trophy. It was a brand new team. It was a brand new scene in English rugby. The old cabbage patch at Twickenham had seen many images and dreams come and go, but here was another series of twists with which to contend. The ubiquity of the strange fez-hat uniform. The raucous strains of an American rap artist that shook the cabbage graveyard to its core: 'Here come the Men in Black, the galaxy defenders.' The presence of players, familiar to the downtrodden cabbages in their international colours of green, gold and blue, now strutting in the black of an unfamiliar team from Southgate. The thousands of befezzed supporters, some now spread across the turf, over whom the new trophy hovered triumphantly.

The uplifting sunshine had ushered a new wave of rugby club into Twickenham and with all its radiance it tried to convince Her Eminence that such populist scenes were worthy of her dignity. The emerald temple had herself been renovated in recent years, but her walls presided in puzzlement over the joyous pageant as her afternoon shadow crept slowly across the floor. The name Saracens was a new one in the visitors' book and yet, from nowhere, they had come in their thousands to pay ecstatic homage. Something unusual was happening to her religion.

Diprose knew Twickenham well, but he knew Saracens even better. Introducing them to each other under such happy circumstances brought him considerable release. He savoured the moment as he finally lowered the trophy from its giddy height.

Suddenly his serenity was disrupted as the cup was seized from him by Gregg Botterman. The replacement hooker knew Saracens even better than Diprose. This was the end of his tenth season at the club. He had made damned sure he would not miss out on any of the glory. He had followed Diprose closely up the steps to the royal box and now snatched the cup from his young captain's grasp as soon as was remotely appropriate. To say he was grinning would not do justice to the look on his face. His aspect managed to incorporate allusions to ecstasy, aggression, relief and apparent physical pain as he shook the hapless pot above his head, egged on by the affectionate roar that swelled the stadium. The lid of the cup and the gimmicky fez hat that clung to it were shaken loose by his vigour, fell from their perch and were dashed on the skull of this true club man.

Oblivious to the mementoes of new glamour and consumerism that had hit him on the head, Botterman turned and passed the cup to another colleague from the old days who had been called through to the front by his team-mates. Steve Ravenscroft stepped up next to feel the unfamiliar spoils of success, before in turn handing over to another Saracen institution, Andy Lee, who had been at the club as long as Botterman.

It was poignant that these four stalwarts should be the first to handle the symbol of victory. They represented the roots of the club that reached back into the friendly poverty for which Saracens had long been renowned. It was a poverty that knew nothing of the exhilaration of achievement, other than the exhilaration of surviving against the odds. This was the exhilaration of triumphing with the odds in their favour. It was a different thrill. The fruits of achievement had now become tangible, while those of the old days had resided in the intangible of small-town defiance.

The four club stalwarts derived a peculiar sense of fulfilment as they looked down at the scene below. Meanwhile, amid the jostling mêlée that bounced their celebration back up to them, the injured Richard Hill stood and smiled. Hill and Diprose had been among the first players to go full-time in 1995. As back-row forwards of peculiar talent, they had joined Saracens fresh from school in the early '90s, and the club had moved swiftly to secure their services as soon as the game went open.

In the stalls near Hill, Mark Evans also enjoyed the realisation of a Saracen dream. Evans had joined Saracens as a player in 1981 and had been a coach at the club since 1989. He now found himself at Saracens as the director of rugby, a grand title that, depending on your interpretation, constituted a promotion, demotion or step to one side from his beloved role of first-team coach. No more than a respectable player in his youth as a Saracen hooker in and out of the first team, his ambitions had never been of the 'I want to play for England' variety. But he had always had his eye on the cup, a goal which might have been considered equally fanciful not so long ago.

Now, however, the cup belonged to Saracens, and as Evans's four charges proudly demonstrated as much to the thousands before them, the committee-room aficionados watched from the royal box behind. Mike Smith, the chief executive, allowed himself a grin and a clap. Along the line from Smith, Bruce Claridge, the portly president of the club, heartily shook the hands of the players as they began to file past. On the other side of the royal box from him, the tall, angular figure of James Wyness, the chairman of Saracens Ltd, joined the celebratory fray.

Wyness's Oxbridge elegance was nicely set off by Peter Deakin, Saracens' marketing director, looking dazzling in the same designer suit and shades with which the playing squad had been issued and which had been designed for them by his friend, a bloke called Jonny Hamburger. Having transformed the Bradford Bulls into the biggest-supported rugby league club in the country, Deakin had within nine months of his arrival achieved the seemingly impossible at Saracens. He and his marketing team had in April attracted a crowd of 20,000 to a home game.

And then, somewhere out in the middle of the crowd, surrounded by his family, Nigel Wray, the multi-millionaire tycoon whose money had facilitated the show, laughed out loud and applauded as he watched each member of the squad feel the cup and milk the applause. Wearing a large Saracen rosette on his lapel, he had by now slipped into the smart-casual mode that he favoured on match-day. His Saracen tie had been removed and his shirt collar lay open under his black suit while he brushed back his thick, tousled hair, whose unruly behaviour merely served to reflect the afternoon's excitement.

Meanwhile, the cup had been passed down the line. George Chuter, a symbol of Saracens' youthful future, took it from Lee, before Paul Wallace and Ben Sturnham held it aloft together. With each hoist of the trophy the stadium reverberated with a renewed cheer. The cup continued down the line: Paddy Johns, Marcus Olsen, Kyran Bracken and then Philippe Sella.

The 36-year-old Frenchman was bringing the curtain down on a glorious career that boasted a world-record 111 Test caps for his country. A long, lingering cheer distinguished Sella's turn with the cup and unwisely encouraged him. Getting the cup out of the ebullient Frenchman's hands was now to prove as hard a qualification for lifting it as winning it had been. Alex Bennett, the young flanker, was the first to try. Succeeding at the second attempt, Bennett transferred the trophy further down the line, where youngsters and experienced internationals alike handled it. Richard Wallace, Gavin Johnson, Matt Singer, Adrian Olver, Ryan Constable, Roberto Grau and Danny Grewcock all had their turn before the cup arrived in the soft hands of another world great taking his bow on the big stage: Michael Lynagh.

Lynagh was the man upon whom Wray and the Saracen committee had first alighted as the superstar to set the ball rolling. Having scored a world-record 911 points in international rugby, he was, in retrospect, the obvious target. When his signing was swiftly followed by the recruitment of Sella, resplendent in possession of the other world record in international rugby, a simple if absurdly ambitious logic to Saracens' strategy had begun to emerge.

From Lynagh the cup passed to Brendan Reidy, the big Samoan front-row forward, before resting in the hands of Brendon Daniel. The winger's father had died two days before, back home in New Zealand. He looked up at the trophy with some feeling as he raised it above his head.

Daniel then turned to the last man in the line. 'Listen to the roar,' advised Miles Harrison in the Sky Sports commentary box as the cup neared the completion of its journey, making its way into the 23rd pair of hands.

On cue, the roar came as François Pienaar let the trophy dangle effortlessly over his head. He wore the contented grin of the father enjoying with his sons the realisation of all their efforts. Pienaar was the third component of the celebrated trinity that Wray had enshrined at Saracens and he had been invested, the preceding season, with the duties of player-manager. A man of iron will and fearsome presence, Pienaar had captained the South African team to victory in the 1995 World Cup final in Johannesburg. It was an achievement that had united a previously divided and tortured nation. Pienaar was a figurehead who had transcended sport and experienced a sense of achievement that is denied to all but a handful of sportsmen. In the light of such achievement, his recruitment a little over a year later to the Saracen cause in the wake of Lynagh's and Sella's smacked of that same simple logic.

With the various photo calls negotiated, the cup gravitated back into the hands of Sella as the team walked along the front of the royal box and down the steps. Diprose led the way and headed back for the expanses of the pitch to soak up more of the atmosphere. His path was intercepted by a steward, who thrust a rude arm across his chest and attempted to usher him down the tunnel. The prosaic reception of the Twickenham dressing-rooms awaited. Diprose, however, preferred the sun-drenched reception of the open-air auditorium. With a devastating look of contempt for the steward, he brushed past the arm and set off to enjoy the lap of honour.

Following their captain's example, the rest of the team followed. Botterman and Lee took to the field with their arms around each other. Sella walked down the steps with the cup held out in front of him, like a child showing off a new toy. Now the ever-growing cavalcade of players, friends and fans slowly made its way around the pitch, waving to the factions of 15,000 Saracen fans scattered throughout the stadium's 75,000 seats. Lynagh was chaired on the shoulders of Brendan Reidy and Richie Wallace. Sella ran around as excitedly as his little six-year-old boy, the cup in his grasp. Social secretary Singer and captain Diprose, arms entwined, strolled around the pitch and wondered whether they shouldn't plan some sort of celebration that evening.

Pienaar stood tall and strong in the north-west corner and pointed both index fingers in triumph towards the chanting fans stretching up towards Twickenham's ceiling. As he turned to walk back towards the tunnel, he spotted Nigel Wray, who had now come down from the crowd to enjoy the party. Pienaar immediately approached Sella and gently prised the cup from the Frenchman's clutches. He then turned and marched through the swarm that separated him from Wray, carrying the cup just beyond the reach of the many clutching hands. In a scene not dissimilar to any number of Hollywood climaxes, he eventually broke through to Wray and handed over the spoils that he had won his governor. Wray now had his hands on the first tangible return from his £4.5 million investment. He too held it aloft, and if a Hollywood camera had been present at that moment, it would have circled him and panned away while the credits ran and the music played.

It seems that it had been destined to be Saracens' day. More or less everything had followed the same perfect course and had culminated in an ending so happy that even the most shameless Hollywood mogul might have blushed before incorporating it into his script. Peter Deakin, who had seen a lot in the way of spectacular success stories, shook his head in amazement as the cup was taken on its lap of honour. For a club that even three years earlier had still been playing its rugby on a patch of north London parkland in front of the proverbial three men and a dog, the scenes at Twickenham on 9 March 1998 indeed beggared belief.

The colourful pageant finally moved on, however, and left the interred cabbages to their peace. The emerald temple that enshrined them was soon left deserted once more. She stood in a stunned and eerie silence. Somewhere to the north she could still hear the retreating strains of the party.

2

Bramley Road

Wedged inauspiciously into the south-east corner of the junction where the busy Bramley Road meets the busy Chase Side, there resides a nondescript patch of parkland. A tarmacadam footpath stretches from the northern reach of the park to the southern, upon and around which members of the Southgate community in north London idly walk their dogs or play with their children.

To the north of the park there is a small squash and bowling complex. Across Chase Side to the west is Oak Hill Technical College, to the east a primary school and to the south, and all around, the residential repetition of a typical London suburb.

As you drive along Green Road, which runs along the south side, a tight gate opens into the pockmarked driveway of the pavilion that stands on the park. A featureless wall greets you immediately, but to its left it turns a corner and runs back to the small red double door that constitutes the pavilion's principal entrance. To the west and north of the pavilion, the parkland houses a series of rugby and football pitches in winter, cricket pitches in summer. The pitch caught between the western side of the pavilion and Chase Side is honoured with a primitive grandstand that sprouts uncomfortably from the ramshackle pavilion wall. It might accommodate a couple of hundred people on its rude benches.

Since the Second World War, this has been the home of Saracens Football Club (RFU). Known as Bramley Road, it had become famous throughout the none-too-flash circuit of British rugby for its friendly poverty. As had the club that calls it home. Saracens were founded in 1876, when F.W. Dunn led a group of old boys of the Philological School, Marylebone, in a game on Primrose Hill playing fields, wearing black shirts with red star-and-crescent badges. Perversely amalgamating with a neighbouring club called the Crusaders in 1878, Saracens gradually developed their fixture list as the fledgling sport of rugby football grew. Their early years were spent searching for a suitable ground, until in 1939 they finally alighted upon Bramley Road – but not before they had experimented at nine other residences.

'Friendly' and 'family' are the words with which Saracens proudly associated themselves, and it was an image that the rest of rugby was only too pleased to endorse. Not all were so keen, however, to endorse that image by turning up to play there. First-class rugby players all over Britain viewed the trip to Bramley Road as the one to avoid: a debilitating trek into the back of beyond to roll around in mud and dog turds in front of three men and one of the many defecatory culprits.

Saracens' history is defined by the perennial struggle to improve their fixture list. By the early '50s, voices in rugby were beginning to suggest that Saracens would soon have to be recognised as fully first class. It was not until 1971, however, that Blackheath (the oldest first-class club) deigned to include them in their fixture list and not until the '80s, when rugby in England became more structured and formal, that the aristocrats at Harlequins did.

For decades, as they strove to improve their status on the field, Saracens would labour under the primitive conditions at Bramley Road. Training would be conducted two evenings a week by the light of the street-lamps on Chase Side, players wantonly tearing into each other in the murk. A powerful solidarity between the players grew from the perpetual fight against the odds. Saracens were always the poor relations of rugby's big names, ceaselessly trying to cling on to the coat tails of first-class rugby.

They did, however, manage to squeeze out three internationals in their first 100 years. John Steeds played for England five times in 1949 and 1950 and Vic Harding six times in the early '60s, before George Sheriff completed a remarkable rise to the top in 1966. A stevedore from Bristol, Sheriff casually arrived at Bramley Road in 1962 to try out this game called rugby for the first time. Aged 24, he was given a run-out in the fourth XV. Four years later, aged 28, he made his debut for England in the back row against Scotland and turned out for them again the following year against Australia and New Zealand. It was an extraordinary achievement by a charmingly self-effacing man and one that neatly captured the romantic ideal of survival against the odds that Saracens guarded so jealously.

By the early '90s, Saracens were still the Cinderella club of rugby. In

1987, English rugby initiated a league system for the first time. Saracens were placed in the second division but won promotion to the top flight two years later. They gained a reputation for producing young talent and for rising above themselves through the astute management of limited resources, and the 1989–90 season saw their stock reach its highest yet. Another England international, the fleet-footed outside centre John Buckton, was in his prime, ably supported by youngsters like Jason Leonard, Dean Ryan and Ben Clarke. As the season reached its climax, mighty Bath visited Bramley Road chasing the title. Saracens produced the definitive ambush performance, beating them 9–7 with a late penalty that effectively ended Bath's interest in the championship race. Under the directorship of Sheriff, who was now president, a legion of amateur members pulled together to organise temporary stands and marquees for a massive day in the club's history that saw an attendance of approximately 3,000. The next and final game of the season saw Saracens lose at Wasps, and with favourites Gloucester slipping up at Nottingham, Wasps thus snatched the title at the death. Saracens finished fourth and, as the old committee will remind you, misty-eyed with pride, they would have won the title themselves had they beaten Wasps by 55 points on that last day.

Jason Leonard toured with England to Argentina that summer, earning Saracens another international player on their register. But Leonard never returned. Will Carling et al. got their teeth into him on tour and, needing to develop his international career, Leonard joined Harlequins. Ryan had joined Wasps and at the end of the following season Clarke moved to Bath. Saracens, always the homely club of top-flight rugby, were now developing a reputation for being the nursery. Talented players would be nurtured in the humble school before the big names lured them away. More powerful clubs could woo them with the possibility of enhancing their rugby careers, something that Saracens, as the unfashionable paupers, could simply not provide. Big clubs were also offering extremely generous expenses as rugby's profile grew and grew on the back of a newly powerful England team.

Saracens, despite keeping company with the big boys, still retained the sort of qualities with which any common-or-garden rugby player will be familiar at his local club. The big teams thus hated travelling to Bramley Road as much as ever, despite the much-acknowledged friendliness of the simple pavilion bar. Players would have to queue for the toilet with the public before kick-off. They would also have to hope the subsequent game was not too close. If it was, nobody would drag themselves away to turn on the hot water. Correspondingly cold showers would await. Yet the Saracen players were perfectly used to such primitive conditions and when they walked into the bar after the game they knew everybody. The team would traditionally move into the annexe off the bar and settle down with a barrel of Abbot's Ale and a barrel of Harp lager. They would start with the bar packed with committee members, families and supporters and finish several hours later when they had seen the bottom of both barrels. The bar would be deserted. As changes in the game of rugby were gathering apace all around them, Saracens remained in a charming time warp, the missing link between the top clubs and those famously seedy legions below them that constituted the ranks of junior rugby.

The top rugby clubs gradually became more organised as the '90s wore on (the very fact that a club like Saracens survived in their company for so long was as much a reflection of the disorganisation in English rugby as it was a tribute to Saracens' canny management). In the 1992–93 season, however, Saracens' inadequate resources caught up with them and they were finally relegated after finishing third from bottom in the first division. That year saw an exodus of seven first-team players, one into retirement, the others for pastures new. Down in the second division, the team would have to rebuild and the club rethink if it wanted to retain its unlikely seat at the top table.

The nucleus of a new team did start to materialise in that first season back in the second division. A supremely gifted 20-year-old in his final year at Loughborough University established himself in the first team at number eight. Tony Diprose anchored the Saracen scrum from the beginning of that season and in the following six years (that is, until the time of writing) was to miss only two league matches for Saracens, one because of the Hong Kong Sevens, the other in 1998 because of England commitments. The man who was to become his partner in crime in the back row in the years that followed also broke into the first team that season. Richard Hill, a 20-year-old flanker from Brunel University, formed a dynamic alliance with Diprose that extended off the field, where the two shared a flat. Also in that flat was Andy Lee, who was becoming the most consistent of goal-kickers at fly-half, and Craig Yandell, a young lock forward. Elsewhere in the team, Steve Ravenscroft formed the solid complement to the evergreen speed of John Buckton in the centre, Gregg Botterman grew in confidence at hooker, Andy

Tunningley, John Green, Mark Langley, Mark Burrows and Richie Andrews all lent a blend of experience and talent, and scrum-half Brian Davies, commuting from Wales, lent astute direction as captain.

In 1994, Saracens finished third in the second division but by common consent were not ready for a return to the top flight. That was to be achieved the following season, when, with Diprose and Hill beginning to attract those all-too-familiar overtures from other clubs, Saracens won promotion at a canter under the guidance of Mark Evans.

Evans had been appointed head coach at the beginning of that promotion season. An accomplished technician and a combative competitor, he had played in every one of Saracens' many teams, including the first team. But, with his short, compact physique, he never wielded the physical presence to make a lasting impression as a player. Supremely competitive and with the intellect that brought him painfully short of a first-class honours degree from Cambridge, Evans's inability to be the best on the field sat uneasily with him. He quickly recognised, however, that his affinity for teaching and intellectualising might assist him more handsomely as a coach. At the age of 28 he retired from playing and a year later he started coaching the second team in their unbeaten season of 1989–90. At the end of that season the first-team coach, Tony Russ, invited him to look after the first-team forwards when Mike Yates left to coach his son, Matthew, who was forging a career as a successful middle-distance runner.

Evans was nervous. Having retired young, he had played with most of the current first-team players. Most of them had been better than him. His second game coaching the first team was the 9–7 victory over Bath, after which Russ left for Leicester. Evans thus had total charge of the first team for that final game against Wasps. When Bruce Millar, the chairman of playing, then started looking for a new head coach, Evans ruled himself out, not feeling ready for the position. The Welshman John Davies, another schoolteacher, took over the first team for the following four years and formed an uneasy partnership with Evans, who continued as assistant coach.

Evans is commonly described as having been a strident dictator in those years. He possessed an acerbic and brilliant mind, and his qualities were very different from those of the big-hearted Davies. And Evans had never been a great player, which further sharpened his attitude. But he was brilliant. His career as a teacher was already progressing at a precocious rate. A deputy head at an 1,800-pupil state school in Essex,

THE RED AND THE BLACK

he was now being courted for headmasterships in his mid-thirties. On the rugby field, meanwhile, he was finally given his headship with the first team when Davies left to coach Cork at the end of the 1993–94 season. Evans had never enjoyed being number two and now his astute analyses and game plans were given full rein. By March, they had helped Saracens to secure the 1995 second-division title, and in the early part of the following season they were to do for a healthy number of high-flyers in the first division as well.

As the 1995 World Cup approached, the face of world rugby was poised to mutate as Kerry Packer's rugby circus drew ever nearer to reality with hundreds of players across the globe ready to sign. It was becoming clear that the game was on the verge of a revolution and Saracens, as ever, were intent on sticking with the big boys. James Wyness was now the president of the club. A former captain at Saracens, Wyness was also the senior partner of Linklaters and Paines, making him one of the foremost international lawyers. He and the newly formed forward-planning committee identified three objectives for Saracens' future prosperity: a new ground, a team that would be successful in Europe and, of course, money.

Wyness, because of his work, was unable to devote sufficient time to move the project on but quickly came to realise that Mike Smith, another former player and a successful property developer who had started showing up at the club after a long absence, represented Saracens' best chance of progress. Smith was a ferociously single-minded character with an unashamed contempt for the concept, as prevalent at Saracens as anywhere else, of the rugby-club committee. He would scorn their propensity to spend hours debating which washers should be used on which taps and how best to remedy the uneven heights of the goalposts. Smith was largely a free agent and Wyness was keen for him to take control. He became Saracens' minister without portfolio.

Wyness was also alerted to the floating talents of another free agent, who had moved over from Canada specifically to explore the possibilities thrown up by the imminent boom in rugby. Angus Stewart had captained Cambridge University in the Varsity matches of 1975 and 1976. He had played for Scotland A in 1977 before returning to his native Canada, where he did a great deal to develop the commercial stature of Canadian rugby. When he returned to attend the Varsity match of 1993, he was astonished by what he saw as an explosion of interest in rugby. He resolved to bring his family to England, where he intended to tap into this burgeoning resource. His former club, London Scottish, did not seem to have any genuine plans for the impending revolution, but on his arrival he identified the charm of Saracens as having potential. Stewart had an interest in licensing and noticed that the Saracen crescent and star was one of the readily recognisable logos in English rugby and 'Saracens' one of the most romantic names. He asked a common acquaintance to introduce him to Wyness, and Wyness put him together with Smith.

The pair immediately got on. Smith would shake his head in amused disbelief that Stewart should have travelled 8,000 miles for a dream. Yet this was the quality that Wyness liked so much in Stewart and that he saw as the perfect complement to Smith's qualities. If Smith was the no-nonsense hard man, Stewart was the dreamer. One of Stewart's first undertakings was to develop a screenplay inspired by the situation at Saracens. Set in America, the story detailed the rags-to-riches rise of a team called Saracens. Stewart lost patience with the project and it has yet to see the light of day, but the idea was symptomatic of the lateral vision that he brought to the club.

Both Smith and Stewart were comfortable from their previous commercial adventures and Wyness granted them a roving brief to advance the club's cause. Working from their homes, they set up a company called Vision Sports Management and laid out their conception of the future for rugby. They went out and about, knocking on doors. They registered Saracens as a trademark and looked into building revenue out of the merchandising. Smith engaged his experience in property to try to push forward his plans to redevelop Bramley Road. That in itself was a missionary task that culminated in the death of the Labour councillor Pat Horridge. In 1995, he collapsed following a heart attack during a particularly heated forum of the Southgate residents, who were bitterly opposed to the development plans. Permission was finally won but the Saracen project would soon outgrow Bramley Road altogether.

Stewart, meanwhile, whose radical imagination accepted no frontiers, had struck upon a somewhat mightier target. He had noticed that there was a star and crescent in the crest of the Sultan of Brunei and suggested to Smith that they attend the forthcoming Saudi Day at the Saudi Embassy with a view to securing the financial input of the richest man in the world. The template for Saracens' mind-dislocating ambition had been set. Smith, despite the reluctance of some of the Saracen committee, who were seethingly distrustful of him, appropriated some club memorabilia from the clubhouse and put together a brief history of Saracens. He and Stewart then made a presentation to the Saudi ambassador, which included a mock-up of Tony Diprose with the Sultan's crest emblazoned on his Saracen shirt. In addition to the obvious Middle Eastern connection with the Saracens, the Sultan had a vaguely local connection, owning houses on Bishop's Avenue in north London. 'You are here and we are here!' ran the salesman's line. 'Just a stone's throw away! Bring the whole family!'

Notwithstanding the affinity of the club's name, however, the concept of a party of sheikhs patrolling the touchline at Bramley Road avoiding the dog turds was too incongruous even for the new adventure that Saracens would embrace. Stewart later received a polite letter declining the offer.

The pair soon alighted upon a more realistic proposition closer to home. Local rugby club Old Millhillians had been benefiting from the sponsorship of one of its multi-millionaire members. A man called Nigel Wray. With plenty of links between Saracens and Old Millhillians, Stewart and Smith soon got wind of this and noticed in the recently published list in *The Sunday Times* that Wray was indeed a wealthy man, with a personal fortune estimated by the paper to be in the region of £100 million. He had a history in the game, having played county rugby for Hampshire in his youth, and he lived ten minutes from Bramley Road. It was perfect. Stewart immediately drew up a letter to Wray on 9 March 1995, sending him VSM's blueprint for the future of English rugby and inviting Wray to become involved with Saracens.

Wray's company, Burford Holdings, had bought the Trocadero in Piccadilly a few months earlier and it was a correspondingly busy time for him. Nevertheless, Wray replied the following day, thanking Stewart for his letter and the 'details of the very enthusiastic way you propose the funding of rugby clubs and rugby itself'.

'I think that for my part,' Wray went on in his letter, 'this is a venture that today is too early for me to get involved with. However, I would like to be kept in touch and perhaps I can help at some more advanced stage.'

This was not a gentle refusal. Wray was serious about the prospect of becoming involved but had no interest in sponsoring the players' kit for a few thousand pounds, which at the time was all that was permitted under the amateur regulations. He intended to wait until the imminent professional revolution that everyone in rugby expected, whereupon he might actively invest in Saracens rather than merely sponsor them. In a month, however, rugby union began to wake up as Rupert Murdoch underwrote rugby league's Super League in Britain. With Kerry Packer's rugby union circus also looming to add to his interests in Australian rugby league, Wray decided the time was approaching to consider the proposal from Saracens. Through Lee Adamson, recently retired captain of the club and then player-coach at Old Millhillians, the link between Wray and Saracens was resuscitated.

On Thursday, 29 June 1995, Wray and his partner, Wayne Lewis, met with Angus Stewart, Mike Smith and Mark Evans for lunch at a restaurant around the corner from Burford's offices in the West End. Wray had decided beforehand what he was going to say. They chatted harmoniously over the meal and, when the dessert came out, Wray suggested that he invest £2 million in the club. With a mouthful of soufflé at the time, it was all Mark Evans could do to prevent an embarrassing incident ensuing. A sum of £2 million would be of considerable assistance in the club's perennial struggle to survive.

With initial agreement secured from the first Saracen envoy, Wray next visited Wyness at Linklaters. The venerable president thought it the most exciting thing he had heard and the long drawn-out process of ratification began.

Wyness was the ideal man to have as president at that time. He was steeped in the traditions of the club he had joined from Cambridge University 34 years earlier, yet he had the clearest appreciation of the need for a radical transformation if the club were not to fade away into oblivion over the next five to ten years. Armed with his credentials as one of the country's leading lawyers, he began the meticulous procedure of ensuring that everything was done by the book. Wyness's experience and position were such that he was not at all fazed by the magnitude of the transaction and Wray had as much respect for him as Wyness and the rest of Saracens had for Wray.

Nevertheless, both sides checked each other out first. One of Wyness's old friends from his Middlesex playing days was an Old Millhillian and Wyness asked him about Wray. The reply was effusive and Wray was confirmed as a genuine rugby man rather than an opportunist businessman. Likewise, Mike Salinger, Wray's personal accountant, investigated Saracens and discovered a bundle of nothing but a name in the first division. The club was valued at £500,000 by its treasurer, Chris Sneath (second senior partner at KPMG, another leader in his field whose tough treasury had helped to keep the club solvent on an annual turnover of £200,000).

Most of this valuation, however, consisted of good will. In terms of tangible assets, an independent accountant assessed Saracens as worth nothing more than £100,000. Wray would invest a further £2 million (and would later underwrite £500,000 worth of shares to the members) and the club would be reversed into a public limited company. Saracens would retain 20 per cent of the equity and hold a 51 per cent veto. Wyness was insistent, as his firm prepared the relevant documentation, that the old club should not be left behind by the new plc. In a meeting with Wray and Wyness, Salinger advised Wray that they did not need any more of the old club than they wanted and that agreeing to the veto arrangement was an unnecessary compromise in view of the level of investment Wray was making. Wyness suggested, however, that the continuing importance of the club would be a strength not a weakness, and Wray, keen to distance himself from the image of the domineering tycoon, readily agreed to settle for just 49 per cent of the vote. As the summer drew on, the terms of the takeover were minutely drawn up, with select members of the old club taking an active role.

In August the inevitable came to pass. The International Rugby Board announced that rugby would become a professional sport. A year's moratorium was set. In early September, Sir John Hall declared his purchase of Newcastle Gosforth, who were struggling at the foot of the second division. One of the truly flamboyant and abrasive characters had been let loose on English rugby and the gentle intentions of those hoping to ease their way into professionalism were blown apart. Sir John would sit outside meetings of the first-division clubs, demanding to be let in. He would harangue the leading clubs with horror stories about football, television revenue and UEFA. He vowed to ruin the top clubs if they would not listen to him. And he quickly set about buying a team that could threaten to do just that.

Saracens, however, had still to put the issue of Wray's involvement before the club membership. Nevertheless, every detail was prepared before that final clearance was sought. Issues of recruitment were addressed. Names such as Damian Hopley, Nick Beal, Tony Copsey, Simon Geoghegan and Andy Gomarsall were bandied around, but a truly enormous name was needed to set the ball rolling. Mike Salinger suggested Michael Lynagh as just such a name. Stewart immediately fired off a letter to Lynagh, who rang him back on the eve of the special general meeting that would determine the future of the club.

Over 350 people crammed into the bar at Bramley Road on the evening of Monday, 6 November 1995. It was clear that the meeting was of momentous significance, but no one bar the select few knew what it was about. Mark Evans had told the players just to stick their hands in the air when they were asked to vote. Released from training early, they were happy to vote for anything.

Wyness, as president, stood up and addressed the gathering that spilled into every last cranny of the pavilion bar. In his soft but assured manner, he set out the motion before the club as the incorporation of Saracens as a plc and the issuing of shares for cash to raise funds. Having drawn attention to the club's survival to date on an annual revenue of about £250,000, he strongly urged the members to embrace the proposals or face the overdue and irreversible slide into oblivion that they had managed to avoid for so long. In the professional era their romantic defiance would soon be unceremoniously crushed as their bigger competitors started to exploit the new possibilities.

Wyness informed the members of the interest of a local businessman who was prepared to invest £2 million in the club and, at a later date, to underwrite a further £500,000 worth of shares to the club members. Mindful of the uneasiness that many of his old friends would be feeling at the news, Wyness went to great lengths to explain the terms of the deal and the veto that the club membership would retain. The investor would remain anonymous until such time as his offer was accepted for fear of the damage a rejection might do to his reputation. It was, after all, Saracen representatives that had approached him and not the other way round. Wyness nevertheless fully endorsed the character of their investor.

'For myself,' Wyness volunteered, 'I remember him saying, "The last thing I want is anyone saying 'rich bugger takes over Saracens'. I want to join the Saracens team." He is a rugby man who lives not far from the ground, who played for a local club and a neighbouring county. He is, like us, mad about the game. On the other hand, he is a hard-nosed businessman who would like to see Saracens be successful, not only in the playing sense but also in making a good commercial return on shareholders' money. On relatively brief personal acquaintance, although at the moment I seem to talk to him rather often on the telephone, I find I like and admire him and, personally, I would very much like to see him join the Saracens.

'That is why I strongly recommend this proposal. It is a unique opportunity and we must not miss it.'

Wyness threw the debate open and a stunned silence prevailed. To the disbelief of the more progressive members of the club, some of the inner sanctum had had powerful reservations about the idea when it had first been mooted. Inevitably, there was the deepest affection for the small, cosy club as it had always been. The prospect of million-pound investments and professional eras, although exciting, would probably mean the end of that integral part of their lives. Saracens was to many a nourishing community centre, the place where everybody knew your name. No one anticipated just what was in store for the club in the ensuing years, but everyone appreciated that, if the motion were passed, the place would never be the same again. Some were invigorated at the prospect, some were wary, to others it was anathema, akin to the demolition of your lifelong cottage home for the construction of a spangling new leisure centre. There are times when the march of progress can trample over the lives of those who are blissfully happy in the intimacy of pre-modern simplicity. As the game of rugby itself was riven in two between those who loved it as it was and those who welcomed its progress into a corporate machine, so the split echoed throughout the clubs as each one wrestled with the dilemma of professionalism.

A corresponding air of wary division pervaded at Bramley Road that night. There was no riotous conflict of opinion, but the eagerness with which many itched to embrace the new era was tempered by the cagey reticence of many of the members. The principal concern was the issue of control: the members did not want to cede possession of their beloved institution. Several objections were voiced, despite the veto arrangement, over the concept of the club being placed in the hands of one outsider. An equal fear was the decline of the rest of the club: what provision would be made for teams outside the first team? All objections were fielded smoothly by the committee, who assured all present that Saracens would remain theirs and that the deal would not be signed if adequate control were not rendered to the members.

Another major sticking point was to emerge. In his speech, Wyness had praised Smith highly for the proactive work that he had carried out on the club's behalf in recent years and Smith had been applauded by the assembly. Angus Stewart was mentioned in dispatches. But Wyness had also drawn attention to the wish of Smith that his company, VSM, be credited with a 1 per cent broker's fee for securing the input of the investor. It was stressed that the £20,000 fee would be paid by the investor, not the club. Nevertheless, it created seething suspicion. The first overt implications of the professional era were beginning to creep in: it would be money that talked. If Smith was on the committee, he was there to look after the club's interests, so why was he being paid for this? The objections were so strong to this rider that some people, including players, did not vote for the motion.

Before the vote was carried out, Bruce Claridge, the president elect, stood up to endorse the motion whole-heartedly before Bruce Millar, the chairman of playing, whose biggest playing budget had been £80,000, insisted that the proposition had to be embraced. In recent years, Millar had co-ordinated the playing side and had overseen its shoestring survival, but each year it had become harder to stay in touch with their competitors. The motion had to be accepted if a terminal decline was to be averted. Wyness finally called for a show of hands, expressing his hope that there would be no cause for any further discussion or vote. The motion was duly carried unanimously.

The wheels turned in earnest. Stewart wrote another letter to Lynagh, informing him of the successful outcome of the special general meeting, and preparations were made for the weekend's game against champions Leicester while Wyness's men got to work on the relevant paperwork.

Meanwhile, a fascinated press swarmed over the latest bizarre twist in the new era. Wray outlined his vision to them. 'We need to invest in players, the ground, spectators,' he said, before remembering the club he was discussing, 'and absolutely everything.' Unperturbed, he continued to elucidate his goals.

'I want Saracens to be playing against Toulouse in the quarter-final of the European Cup under lights in front of a capacity crowd.'

The press took one look at Bramley Road and laughed.

Saracens, however, were laughing at Bramley Road that weekend. Despite the dizzy feeling induced by the uncertainty of their future, the news had invigorated the players. None of them had been able to appreciate fully the implications of the takeover, other than to feel an innocent excitement that their years of struggle would now be eased with the new funds. With Wray watching in delight, that Saturday's game was to see another classic Saracen ambush at Bramley Road. It was to prove the last one that season. And it will almost certainly prove to be the last one ever.

Although it was only November, Bath and Leicester had already put daylight between themselves and the rest at the top of the table, while Saracens were third from bottom. The Saracen team to face Leicester was an archetypal patchwork outfit, with a 20-stone chap called Dave Brain called up from nowhere to answer an SOS call in the second row. All the expertise and experience of Dean Richards, Rory Underwood and the infamous ABC club came to nought. With Diprose and Hill in inspirational form and Andy Lee unable to miss at goal, Saracens won 25–21. Lee scored 20 points with his boot, and after his hour of glory playing for Saracens Brain embarked upon the mother of all piss-ups and was never seen again. Saracens were still third from bottom but they had four wins under their belt already. Gloucester and the relegation zone were six points behind them. It looked like Saracens would defy predictions by avoiding the drop and enter the first season of professional rugby in a very powerful position in the top flight.

That weekend, the vibes continued as Lynagh came across from Italy for a productive meeting with Wray, Smith and Stewart. Meanwhile, Smith started up a new company called Ebbswift, effectively a promotional body acting on behalf of Saracens. The game was still under the moratorium and therefore amateur, so Saracens plc could not pay their players any money. Nevertheless, Diprose and Hill, who had remained faithful to the club for so long in the face of such temptation, were immediately rewarded. They resigned from their jobs and, after Mike Catt, became the first full-time rugby players in England. Ebbswift paid the pair, technically for the promotional work that they carried out for the club, and Diprose and Hill began the lonely business of full-time training without any team-mates.

An unrest, however, began to grow among the other players as developments gathered pace around them. Smith and Millar went scouting for players and over the course of the season squad members, one by one, were called in for a chat about staying on, while others waited on tenterhooks. It did little for building team spirit. Players were told nothing until the club had decided to keep them on. Steve Ravenscroft, Andy Tunningley, Andy Lee and Tony Diprose formed a players' committee to try and safeguard the players' rights within the club and with relation to the RFU. Yet cagey fencing became the order of the day, mixed with the occasional burst of excitement.

At the beginning of January 1996, Lynagh was unveiled to the press as Saracens' next major acquisition. With a hat on his head and a scarf wrapped around his face, not just to protect him from the seasonal chill, he was smuggled into the league defeat against Wasps at Bramley Road on the Saturday under the very noses of journalists and future team-mates alike. The following Monday, with rumours abounding that Philippe Sella was to join the club, Saracens bowled a googly by calling a press conference at the French café opposite Wray's offices. The sheer enormity of the press interest meant that the conference had to be staggered over two sessions lasting a total of four hours as Lynagh was presented. Some of the players attended to meet him, palpably excited at the prospect of Lynagh joining the effort next season. Yet it amounted to the first step in the beginning of the end. It now appeared that Andy Lee, one of Saracens' most popular and effective players, would be relieved from his berth as Saracen fly-half.

Ever the chirpy optimist, Lee tackled the news with characteristic humour: 'It's great news for the club. Lynagh is an amazing player. Doesn't he also play centre?' Lee was as excited as anyone but, while he knew that Lynagh's presence would be a great help to the club, he also realised that the team he loved was not going to be his team for very much longer.

Further transfer news materialised, prompting players at Saracens to continue looking over their shoulders. As every big-name signing was announced, each member of the squad would wait with trepidation to see whether it was his number that was up next. Irish flanker Eddie Halvey had signed in December and Tony Copsey signed in February. Rob Howley's pen was also poised and the plc made no secret of it. Howley was persuaded to stay in Wales, but soon the worst-kept secret in rugby was confirmed when Saracens called a press conference in the Rugby Club of St James. With the press sitting comfortably, a bowler-hatted Philippe Sella walked into the room and, in an amusing attempt at a cockney accent, asked if anyone was looking for a centre. The world's most-capped player would be joining the world's highest international points-scorer at the humblest of first-class clubs the following season. With that absurdity established, Wray also announced that they would all be playing their rugby at nearby Enfield football club. The plans for developing Bramley Road had been shelved and for the 11th time in their history Saracens would be moving home.

That last piece of news was received particularly badly by many members at the club. The reaction among the discontented ranged from disapproval to sheer horror. Their worst fears were being realised. At the general meeting in 1997, a lady called Gill Coburn would stand up and tell Wray that in one year he had single-handedly ruined a club that had been around since 1876. Gill and her husband Bill had been devoted to Saracens for decades and had given tea to the young Jim Wyness on selection nights when Wyness was captain in the '60s. The move to Enfield signalled the end of an intimate part of their lives as Bramley Road, their local community centre, effectively closed down. The Coburns were never to see Saracens play again after the move to Enfield and the consequent loss of the club's homely atmosphere. If theirs was an extreme, though not isolated, reaction, it was nevertheless a reflection of a general mood of discontent that spread among much of the old club as the irresistible pistons of progress drove the plc forward into the professional era.

On the field, too, the relatively rosy outlook after the Leicester victory quickly turned sour. Saracens did not win again until 30 March, at bottom-placed West Hartlepool in a game that saw Lee, whose kicking that season had been Saracens' principal lifeline, break his collarbone. Gloucester, meanwhile, had started to string a few wins together since the New Year and a victory over Bath in April drew them level on points with Saracens and ahead on points difference.

As the realisation gradually dawned that relegation was a distinct possibility, threatening to compromise all that Saracens had achieved in the previous two years, Mike Smith, now installed as chief executive, began a contingency crusade. There was still a possibility that the first division would be extended to 12 clubs and that relegation would therefore be abolished. Smith now set his unshakeable sights on ensuring that outcome.

For the team, the aim was clearly to avoid relegation in their own right. Yet the defeats kept coming despite some sterling performances, and the relegation issue boiled down to the last game of the season. Gloucester would host Saracens at Kingsholm. The loser would be relegated. Faced with the inconceivable horror of relegation, the local clubs in Gloucester cancelled their fixtures and Kingsholm was consequently packed with 12,000 baying West Countrymen.

Saracens lost 17–10. It was a black day. The dressing-room was like a morgue. Mark Evans, mortified, drowned his sorrows at the bar. Wyness gathered his old mates around him and did likewise. On the surface, Wray appeared sanguine, accepting that it would just take an extra year, but he was in fact to find it as bleak a moment as any in his involvement with Saracens. Smith, meanwhile, stood with his calm smile and assured Wyness, Sheriff and Claridge, the new president, that they would not be going down.

A month later, at the end of May, his confidence was borne out. Smith had relentlessly lobbied the first-division clubs in an attempt to convince them that they could not afford to be without the riches that Saracens would be offering the following season. Having got the clubs on side, he then had to take his case to the RFU. On Friday, 24 May, he made a presentation to them at the Hilton hotel during a day of talks between the clubs and the RFU concerning the future of the game. The next morning, the details of a co-operative future between the clubs and the RFU were announced. One of the lower points of the resultant agreement gave notice of a first division expanded to 12 teams the following season. Northampton and London Irish would come up from the second division and Saracens and West Hartlepool would not be going down.

As one, the administrators at Saracens breathed a sigh of relief, and Mike Smith, unusually, was the toast of the club. On this occasion, his strident deal-making had paid dividends with which they could all be happy. James Wyness had long argued that it was morally unacceptable, in the context of the moratorium, for anyone to be relegated. You could not expect clubs to be given a year to make provisions for a professional future only to have those futures compromised, or even jeopardised, by their subsequent removal from the top table at the end of that year. It was an argument that Smith also drew heavily upon in his crusade. Yet, amid the elation, there remained among the playing side a sense of embarrassment at the decision. On the field they had not been good enough to stay up. Fortunately, however, off the field Saracens had rapidly become very serious competitors indeed.

Further fruits from that department were harvested over the summer as the Saracen recruitment machine went into overdrive. The original plan back in November had been for Saracens to secure the services of just one or two stars and with their help bring on players of their own. Lynagh and Sella would nurture the young talents which Saracens had become renowned for producing. Now, however, having produced them, they would also be holding on to them. An early memo from Mike Smith to Angus Stewart is illustrative of the kind of economics that were being considered. In it, Smith detailed how he believed they could get away with paying players for league and cup games only. 'Some might require a retainer, say £50 to £100 per week plus £150 for *matches played*,' Smith conceded. 'The signing-on fee, however, may need to be £7.5k to £10k, rather than £5k. We can build in a bonus for league position, cup run, etc.'

VSM's five-year financial plan, drawn up in November 1995, made provision for the recruitment of four or five key players on the above terms, setting aside a £65,000 match-fee and expenses budget. An extra £150,000 to £200,000 was to be set aside for a big signing in the mould of a David Campese or a Michael Lynagh. Meanwhile, average gates were projected to rise from 2,500 in year one to 5,000 in year two and 10,000 thereafter, helping to generate, along with sponsorship and advertising, a turnover in excess of £2 million by year five, when the projected profit would be £1.5 million.

With Sir John Hall in the vanguard, however, this level of economics was to be blown sky-high in the coming months by the reckless recruitment upon which English rugby embarked. In the summer of 1996, Saracens played their full part. In addition to Lynagh and Sella, Kyran Bracken was signed from Bristol. Irish internationals Paddy Johns and both Wallace brothers came over from the Emerald Isle. Lynagh's fellow Australian World Cup winner Tony Daly was recruited to play at prop and was to be joined in the front row by Argentinian Christian Martin, who was afforded a three-month trial.

Already, within nine months of Wray's arrival, Saracens were all but unrecognisable from the homely and plucky club to which it had become fashionable to condescend. With a new stadium and a new team, along with the unwieldy residue of most of the old one, Saracens prepared for the most eagerly awaited season in English rugby's history. The professional era had finally arrived.

3

Enfield

New seasons at Saracens had always been greeted with the first-day-at-school excitement that one might find at any common-or-garden rugby club. Players would arrive at pre-season training in T-shirts and trainers, with the sun still out and the ground firm. Not even Bramley Road was muddy at this time of year. People would eagerly ask each other what they had done over the summer, how many beers they had drunk – that sort of thing. And normally there were a couple of new faces to add spice to the atmosphere, one or two players looking for a trial.

The atmosphere for the pre-season gathering in 1996 was different from that of previous years. Suddenly there were quite a few players looking for a trial. Numbered in their ranks were Michael Lynagh and Philippe Sella, two of the greatest figures in the history of the game. Kyran Bracken, rapidly superseding Will Carling as the face of English rugby, was another of the 'nervous' new boys. To add to the unusual air, nine of those gathered were now full-time professionals. Two of them, Hill and Diprose, were familiar faces, but Diprose was now invested with the responsibility of captaincy, a position that he had filled with distinction for an unbeaten England A team the previous season.

But some things had not changed. Most of the previous squad were still around on the same arrangement as ever, although now with the prospect of the odd match fee and win bonus. The lifestyle of the club was not appreciably different from that of the old days. Training was still to be in the evenings, twice a week, with a couple of daytime sessions for those who could make it, i.e. the full-time professionals. Even the full-time professionals were not entirely full-time, however. One of the attractions of the Saracen package for Michael Lynagh had been the prospect of developing his career in property, and in the early days he was working during the week with Wray at Burford. Although that was to change before too long, professional rugby at Saracens was at this stage similar in its format to the amateur rugby that it had so recently succeeded.

At the first training session of the season, nobody quite knew how to handle the sudden presence of some of the world's finest talent. The British are reserved in such circumstances, waiting for the stranger, and certainly the world-famous superstar, to make the first move. There were no open arms to greet the likes of Lynagh and Sella. In Sella's case, this stand-off quickly dissolved as the Frenchman threw himself whole-heartedly into the fray and became one of the focal points of the squad. Bracken, another socialite who knew a few of the key Saracen players from various England squads over the years, was also quick to settle. Lynagh, though, by nature a quieter man, took a lot longer to work his way into the squad spirit.

At that first training session, a crude exercise saw Lynagh, in front of the assembled squad of about 40 players, have to tackle Charlie Olney, the bristling boulder of a hooker, in full flight. The old hands in the squad nudged each other as Olney careered towards him. 'Now we'll see if he's just come for the dollars!' they whispered. Lynagh passed that unofficial test, but a sense of embarrassment was creeping in among some of the newer members of the squad at the schoolboy treatment being meted out to all and sundry.

The first game of the season, however, saw any niggles put aside. Tackling Leicester at Enfield, Saracens put on an imperious display for the shirt-sleeved crowd of 6,000 who basked in the August sunshine. At the first game of the season, the record for a home gate had been smashed. The next thing to tumble was mighty Leicester. Although the final score was 25–23, Saracens had led 25–9 with four minutes of normal time remaining. This was no backs-to-the-wall triumph against the odds. Copsey ruled the line-out, Diprose had a platform upon which to parade his remarkable skills, Bracken and Lynagh struck up the most eloquent of partnerships at half-back and Sella and Richie Wallace cut up the Leicester defence at will. Two late Leicester tries, however, had brought the Tigers to within two points, and an even later penalty attempt to win them the game was sent wide. Nevertheless, the game marked a radical departure from the norm for players like Ravenscroft, Tunningley, Diprose, Hill and Botterman. Suddenly they realised they had beaten a top team while playing at only 75 per cent. Gone were the old days of 110-per-cent defiance: this was a relatively gentle stroll. They had even been able to concede 14 points in the dying minutes and still win the game. Things were changing.

That opening victory was an early triumph for the new money and new marketing that was taking hold of rugby. The 6,000 gate constituted a particularly promising start by the commercial team of Smith and Stewart. But their relationship was becoming strained. Smith had been installed as chief executive and it was becoming increasingly clear to Stewart, who had been given the role of commercial manager, that neither Smith nor Wray considered Stewart's contribution integral to the game plan. The hard man was in the driving seat and he now had the investor's money. The dreamer was no longer required. Stewart and Smith grew apart, and when only 1,500 turned up for a meaningless midweek fixture against Newport, in the light of the Leicester crowd inevitable fingers were pointed at Stewart. Stewart had been hired as commercial manager in April, but the commercial wheels had turned and he had been gradually emasculated by the mounting corporate momentum of the project. By November, he had left the club.

Meanwhile, Mark Evans and Mike Scott were the only two full-time administrative members of staff on the playing side. Evans had accepted the post of director of coaching over the summer and resigned his deputy-headmastership to take the post. Scott similarly accepted the role of team manager. In what Bruce Millar describes as one of his best signings, Scott had been seconded to work for Saracens as playing administrator in 1992 while talking to Millar on a supporters' train to West Hartlepool. Scott's busy efficiency immediately endeared him to the club, as did his unstinting commitment, and in the professional era he was to remain an institution at Saracens.

Scott and Evans worked out of the small Enfield office that Saracens had acquired. It was a ludicrously hectic time for the pair of them that was symptomatic of the half-baked nature of professional rugby that season. Tasks that were to be completed by several members of staff two years later were left at their doorstep. Evans was assisted on the training and playing field by Rob Cunningham, whom he had recruited as a forward coach in the 1994–95 season, and Tim Wright, an assistant coach whom John Davies had recruited in the early '90s to look after the second team.

Cunningham was a hard Scotsman from the old school of rugby coaches and had precious little time for the fancy techniques that were shaping top-class rugby in the modern era. Wright was an Essex boy who had fallen into rugby at a late age and risen to his prominent position through coaching local junior sides with considerable success. He was a sharp man with an eye for detail, but, like Evans, he did not have the safety net of a glittering playing career to fall back on should his authority as a coach be doubted.

An uncomfortable air quickly developed in the squad and was exacerbated when that early victory against Leicester was discredited by Saracens' erratic form in the games that followed. A principal problem was the awkward mix of the old and the new within the squad. The responsibility of Evans, Cunningham and Wright was now to strike upon a game plan that might incorporate the sublime vision of the likes of Lynagh and Sella with the more limited ability of the club men that remained from yesteryear. And the coaches themselves were still adapting. Evans's schoolmasterly approach on the training field was still in evidence, while Wright would coach Lynagh as if he were one of his charges at Barking. 'There's Wrighty teaching Mike how to kick again!' would be the amused banter among the squad as Wright pulled Lynagh aside to offer a few observations, as was his remit. It was an uncomfortable situation for those on both sides of the fence.

The situation was further complicated, however, on Tuesday, 3 December 1996, by the unveiling of probably Wray's most outrageous coup. On the day that the teams for that year's Varsity match were announced at a London lunch, a memo had been sent to the press advising them of a Saracen press conference at the Trocadero afterwards that should not be missed. Without even a rumour to be called upon – a rare situation indeed! – the press and some of the players awaited the impending news in total ignorance. Just before the news was announced, however, Diprose suddenly twigged. Amid all the jostling and excitement in the Trocadero, he caught sight of an elegant lady sitting quietly in the corner of the room. He recognised her from a gala dinner that he had attended a few months earlier. The hairs on the back of his neck stood on end as he realised whose wife she was. Before he had time to react, a cacophony of clicks and gasps bounced off the shiny metallic walls of the virtual-reality arena. Standing strong on the escalator that brought him up to the assembled press, François Pienaar was heralded into the English game.

The arrivals of Lynagh and Sella had made English rugby sit bolt upright. The concept of them playing for Saracens took some getting used to. But the pair of them were in the autumn of glorious careers that had hit their heights some years before. Pienaar, however, was still an enormous figure. The memories of the 1995 World Cup were fresh in the mind. The images of Pienaar holding the gold trophy above his hard, grinning features and of the colourful and united country that looked up to him were ones that still wielded unprecedented power in the rugby world. Pienaar was more than just a sportsman; he was an icon. He had galvanised into world-beaters a disjointed team that was still coming to terms with its recent re-admission into international rugby. In so doing, he had helped galvanise a nation that still nursed a bleeding and tortured history.

Within months of South Africa's historic triumph, however, he had been dropped by the controversial coach, André Margkraaff, who had taken over the reins after the World Cup. It had caused public outcry in South Africa. There were television programmes devoted to the subject and death threats issued to Margkraaff. Yet South Africa's loss turned into Saracens' gain. Personally handling the deal from start to finish, Wray had flown Pienaar and his wife, Nerine, to England the previous weekend. Having found Wray to be 'a scholar and a gentleman' and having sought the blessing of Nelson Mandela himself, Pienaar agreed to the deal there and then. He and Wray decided to announce it immediately.

In what was becoming a familiar scenario, English rugby was once again aghast. But no quarter was more shocked than members of the playing staff at Saracens. At the time, Diprose was particularly stunned. Like many other young players, Diprose was in awe of Pienaar's unparalleled presence in world rugby. His immediate concern was how on earth he was going to be able to captain such a figure. Technically, Lynagh and Sella also fell under his captaincy, but they, at least, were out in the backs, directing play with the independence and autonomy that is required of players in their positions. Pienaar, however, would be right next to Diprose in the back row.

Wray, meanwhile, was adamant that his new purchase should be given the captaincy. Diprose, at that stage, was a young, uncapped forward of great promise who was on the verge of becoming a full international. Pienaar, on the other hand, was one of the great captains in the game who had achieved the highest honours. But, despite considerable pressure from Wray, Pienaar declined the captaincy. He was not physically fit and, like Wray when he had first arrived, he did not want to take over the club. Diprose was a popular member of the squad who represented the roots of Saracens, and Pienaar was sensitive to that. It was also felt, by Evans in particular, that the captaincy should not be changed in the middle of the season.

Tensions grew and festered in the coming months. Pienaar spent much of that time on the injured list with Lynagh and shared the Australian's misgivings over the coaching set-up. He had little time for Cunningham's old-school approach and was appalled at the archaic conditions under which Saracens were training. The mud, the flickering floodlights and the bitter cold were as far removed from the purity of conditions on the high veldt as Pienaar could conceive. And Wray was itching to invest his prize possession with the power to exercise his gifts effectively.

Matters came to a head during a ludicrous run-in to the end of the season that required Saracens to play nine games in 34 days. With the club chasing a place in Europe, their run of games started promisingly with a 50-point hiding of West Hartlepool at Enfield but then nosedived with defeats at Gloucester and Harlequins before soon-to-be-crowned-champions Wasps became the first side to win at Enfield. With those three defeats suffered within eight days of each other, Saracens' faltering hopes of a place in Europe were terminated the following week on a bleak Tuesday evening in Sale. Having lost 33–23, the players sat morbidly about the hotel in the evening, playing spoof to see who had to ask the painful new press officer for a game of pool. Elsewhere, the machinations were taking place that would move Saracens on to the next stage of their march into the future.

Bruce Millar called Diprose away from the high-stake game of spoof and informed him that there were to be changes. Rob Cunningham was going with immediate effect, Mark Evans was moving into a new role as director of rugby while also overseeing the backs, and François Pienaar was to become player-manager. Diprose's immediate concern was how he could possibly captain the side now, with the boss and world-renowned captain playing alongside him in the back row. His next concern, like those of several others, was over the future of Evans, who had reared him as a player and was one of the central figures at Saracens.

Cunningham left in a storm. The forwards had been performing well during the recent run of defeats; it had been the backs who had not been firing. Lynagh had been out through injury and Andy Lee was facing a tortuous schedule as his replacement, with a new job as a teacher around which he was trying to fit his rugby. His form had suffered accordingly. With Wright coaching the out-of-form backs and Evans overseeing the entire operation, Cunningham felt something of a scapegoat.

Evans himself was as uncertain and disillusioned as anyone, having thrown in his job as a teacher to concentrate on coaching. Although the proposed role of director of rugby was to prove an enormous one, Evans, at the time, felt it spurious compensation for losing control of playing matters. He received a lot of support from the longer-serving players and Diprose phoned Wray to tell him that he felt it important that Evans be retained. Wray, who liked Evans personally, was only too pleased to oblige. Evans had mellowed since his earlier fiery days as a coach and, like Wright, had adapted to the changes in personnel at the club with commendable flexibility over the course of the year and was to continue to do so in the one that followed. Cunningham had gone because he would not change from his old ways, but Evans and Wright managed to ride the shifting tides and consolidate their positions within the club. This latest development, however, further knocked the confidence of both men.

The following morning, before the players left to prepare for that weekend's game against Leicester, Pienaar told them the news of his appointment and gave the first of many inimitable addresses. 'This ship is going forward,' he said. 'You can either get on board or jump off now.'

Pienaar's uncompromising reign had begun. Lynagh, who was by now close friends with Pienaar, felt nervous for the man. A thick atmosphere had greeted his appointment, waiting for him to fail. There was particular tension between Pienaar and Evans, the former none too convinced of the latter's credentials, the latter none too enamoured that he had lost control of the coaching. James Wyness felt moved to write to them both to sort their differences out, while the likes of Tim Wright, who had also been moved aside into a technical role, and Mike Yates, who had returned as fitness advisor, were continually mopping up the fall-out from Pienaar and Evans's relationship.

Nevertheless, matters on the field showed a marked improvement. Pienaar immediately simplified training, moved it increasingly towards daylight hours and drastically reduced the heavy contact upon which Cunningham had placed such emphasis. That weekend at Leicester Saracens lost narrowly, having been dominant throughout the game, but thereafter the season finished with three straight wins. Pienaar scored a try in each of them. Things looked like they were starting to go his way.

For things to go his way, however, it meant Saracens jettisoning more ballast from their past. There had been a growing unease among the squad. New players who arrived that season had been afforded a less-than-warm welcome by the famously friendly club, while the retained members of the old squad recognised that the Saracens they knew and loved had gone. Enfield may only have been a halfway house between the homely past and the shiny future, but it was far enough for most of the old guard to know that they did not want to travel any further with new Saracens. Nor were they wanted.

The final match of the season was against Bath at Enfield. Lynagh was fit and back in place and masterminded a convincing 36–29 victory. It was an emotional day. There was optimism in the camp, with several players involved in forthcoming international tours that summer. Lynagh and Sella had pledged themselves to the cause for another year. But there was an undercurrent of heavier emotions too. For many, it was goodbye. Before the game, John Buckton, the definitive club 'legend', was presented with an award for his services over a long career. Sella, his replacement, who had lined up with the teams to applaud Buckton (who was not playing), instinctively broke rank and ran over to Buckton to shake his hand.

If that gesture had been handled sensitively by Saracens, a public ceremony in the marquee after the game was far clumsier. Tony Daly, the Australian prop, was leaving after less than a year at the club. Daly had been a huge disappointment on the field and, although he had a wicked sense of humour, had not made much of a contribution to the team effort. Nevertheless, the presentation of an award was organised for the former World Cup winner on this, his last game for Saracens. As Daly collected his award, a legion of long-serving Saracens who were also leaving stood in mild disbelief. It was a staggering oversight to have ignored the contribution to the club of such stalwarts as Andy Tunningley, John Green and Mark Langley, to name but a few, while recognising the token efforts of a big-name player from the other side of the world. It left a very sour taste in the mouth and prompted people to question the integrity of the new regime's much-trumpeted commitment to preserve the club's family values.

After the ceremony, however, traditional rugby customs were honoured in the end-of-season court session. Judge Tony Copsey was in fine form, ably assisted by counsels Andy Lee and Steve Ravenscroft, the latter putting his experience as a lawyer to good use. Indeed, Ravenscroft had also believed that this would be his last game for the club. In view of his legal commitments, he did not feel that he would be able to carry on as a full-time rugby player. An emotional and passionately honest Yorkshireman, Ravenscroft had come off the field after the game and gone straight to the changing-room in tears. Pienaar had gone in after him and asked him what was wrong. Ravenscroft replied that he thought it was the end of his time at Saracens. Pienaar assured him that he would be involved the following year and proved true to his word. Ravenscroft was to be the only senior player allowed to continue on a part-time contract.

Among the many amusing penalties handed out during the high-spirited court session that followed behind the marquee, Pienaar was punished for mutiny. He and Mark Evans carried out a duel. Each had to down a beer and spin around a broomstick and then, sufficiently dizzy, complete a prepared assault course. Both supremely competitive yet now directionally incontinent, Evans proceeded to charge uncontrollably into the fence that ran along one side of the course, while Pienaar crashed into the marquee itself on the other. Trying to keep a curious public inside the marquee from spying on them proved increasingly difficult.

A season of mixed results and mixed emotions thus ended on a day of excitement for the future and nostalgia for the past. But any lingering compromises between amateur and professional rugby were finally swept away that summer. Wray pumped another £2.5 million into the venture. Pienaar embarked upon an overhaul of the set-up at Bramley Road, which was extensively modernised and improved, making it a more sophisticated base for training. The changing-rooms were revamped and offices for Evans, Scott and Wright (now full-time) were installed, as well as physio rooms and offices for other members of staff. In the annexe off the bar, a lounge was created for the players, who were now all to be full-time bar Ravenscroft and a few youngsters. Training was to be conducted entirely during the day. And, having failed to get the required planning permission to develop the Enfield stadium, Wray had decided to move the first team to another new ground.

Nestling just inside the north-west stretch of the M25, within easy reach of London and the surrounding Home Counties, Vicarage Road Stadium, the home of Watford Town FC, was identified by Wray as the perfect base from which to spread the gospel of new rugby. It was another unpopular move among the old members as it represented yet another leap from Saracens' roots, but the developments that were to follow would render those old members increasingly superfluous. Wray recruited the rugby-league missionary Peter Deakin as the head of a bold new department that would take rugby to the people. Deakin, in turn, recruited an entire team to fill it. Setting up camp in the shadow of the Watford stadium that summer, they embarked upon an energetic campaign predicated upon the headgear adopted by a small band of hardcore fans.

The year of the fez was imminent.

4

Fizzing

Matt Singer is one of those people that rugby prides itself on producing. Or certainly used to.

On the field, he strikes a pleasing balance between flair and application, while off it a sensible work ethic and responsibility are offset by an effortless charisma. He is universally popular. Not only does he delight in and healthily contribute to the inimitable banter that reverberates throughout any number of rugby clubs, he also brings boundless enthusiasm and a raft of fresh ideas to any institution that benefits from his membership.

He is, I confess, one of my best friends, which may suddenly instil a certain cynicism in readers with regard to matters concerning Singer as portrayed in this book. We are going to have to get over this, however, because his case will be considered closely in the following pages. I hope I can be relied upon to deal with the subject impartially. He has his faults and he has his weaknesses, which I hope will become as apparent in my treatment of him as his prevailing qualities and strengths. I think his credentials as one of the truly good guys in life can be recorded as objectively sound whether they are acknowledged by one of his friends (of which there are many) or one of his enemies (an example of which I have yet to encounter). The reasons for his popularity lie in the many diverse qualities that he brings to a cause. I like to think he is my friend precisely because of those qualities, rather than that I have exaggerated those qualities because he is my friend.

Now that I have attempted to justify myself, I will next attempt to justify Matt Singer as a poignant subject for a case study within this case study. He is representative of a large body of players whose circumstances receive little attention yet whose fortunes will act as an accurate barometer in coming years of the viability of professional rugby.

He was in his mid-twenties when, along with several others, he embarked upon a full-time professional career with Saracens at the beginning of the 1997–98 season, their first season in Watford. He had had a distinguished but not glittering rugby career that had encompassed two Varsity matches in the light blue of Cambridge, first-class rugby at Neath as well as at Saracens, and representative honours with England at Under-16 and Student levels. He was not a star name, but occupied that uneasy vortex between well-paid international and part-time professional. Too good not to embark upon the unknown adventure of full-time professional rugby, he had yet to break out into the arena of the high-profile performer, where security, such as can be found in professional sport, embraces the individual more firmly and lends added justification to one's involvement in the escapade. We can read all we like about the lifestyles of the Will Carlings and the Jonah Lomus of this world, the superstars, but the truest measure of the success of professional rugby as a going concern will be to consider the case of the Matt Singers, the guys one rung off the very top.

It is a perennially uncertain existence. Always striving to reach the top rung, they are trying not only to satisfy that innate urge to be the best which is common to any first-class sportsman worth his salt but also to prepare for a future of some kind after the game. In his first contract, Saracens paid Singer a comfortable salary (after appearance fees and win bonuses) in absolute terms for a man in his mid-twenties. But when one considered that he would certainly be pensioned off from that particular line of work within ten years, and possibly a lot sooner than that, things suddenly looked a little less rosy. He was also to marry Allison and, although she was bringing in a salary too, they would want to start a family before long with all the attendant overheads.

With the dawn of rugby's professional era, every first-class player was confronted with the same dilemma. Do I throw everything into a full-time career in the game, about whose future I know nothing? Or do I continue in a career outside rugby, playing on a part-time basis but with the security of continued employment beyond my playing days? If I do throw myself into rugby and I make it all the way to the top, it will be lucrative. If I go for it but fall short, what will I do afterwards? When will that afterwards be? Will I be made redundant before I want to be? Will the game be able to support people like me for the foreseeable future?

For the players who are already established internationally, the decision is reasonably straightforward. The biggest names, as we know, make an awful lot of money, and even the merely big names make enough to make most people their age green with envy. For the player on the fringes of the big time, however, the decision is more delicate, but the proposition no less seductive. Most, quite rightly, succumb to the prospect of being a professional rugby player. It is an opportunity available to only a tiny élite and the prestige is at worst intoxicating and at best life-making. Once she has been embraced, however, professional rugby can be a cruel and fickle mistress. Like marrying your childhood sweetheart, what had always hovered above you as a dream now sits with you as a reality that requires a lot of hard work and conjures no small amount of heartache.

Matt Singer's dream took a little longer to crystallise than some. Or, rather, it took longer to mutate into the one that drives most rugby players. Singer's dream started life in the red shirt of Nottingham Forest Football Club.

Singer spent his youth in Porthcawl on the south coast of Wales, where his parents had moved in 1973 when he was less than a year old. Why, then, he should alight on Brian Clough's Nottingham outfit as the object of his homage was not immediately apparent as they swept their way on an all-conquering crusade through Europe in his early years. Many an hour was spent in the small but picturesque Singer garden emulating the feats of a wide variety of sporting heroes, from Botham to Becker. Football and Forest, however, were the primary beneficiaries of Singer's adulation. Rugby, though, did get a look in, particularly when Dusty Hare obligingly gave Singer something with which to celebrate his Englishness. It proved valuable ammunition for him as he strove for validation in that hotbed of Welsh rugby which constituted a trying cradle for an English boy.

'Matt Singer has this chance to kick England to victory against Wales in this year's Five Nations,' the commentary used to go. 'He steadies himself with two deep breaths, before attacking the ball in his inimitable way. The Welsh jeers are ringing all around him as he approaches the plastic ball that his dad gave him for Christmas. Years of practice have culminated in this dramatic moment. He strikes the ball beautifully. Has it got the legs to clear the garden fence? Yessss! It's there! The ball clatters into the dustbins as Matt Singer completes his victory lap of the garden.'

The plastic ball that Singer's father, Andrew, gave his son was a little later in its bestowal than he might have liked. Andrew had thrust a rugby ball in the hands of his eldest son, Ben, almost as soon as he could walk, but Ben had shown little or no interest in it. Andrew's wife, Liz, not quite as infatuated with the game as her husband, put her foot down when Matt was born and insisted that he be left untouched by such rugby harassment. It was to prove but a matter of time, however, before the oval religion began to cast its spell over their second born.

Having first emerged at St John's Prep School in Porthcawl, Singer's taste for rugby rapidly developed when he went to Wycliffe College, a public school in Gloucestershire, at the age of 13. Singer, now gaining in stature as a left-footed fly-half of some confidence, made the Under-14 team for the first match at his new school. The whole of his year travelled on a bus to watch the game at one of the local schools. It was one of those impossibly big occasions for a young lad. The game kicked off and Singer fielded the ball on his twenty-two. He danced his way through the opposition and promptly scored under the posts. Rugby was beginning to take on considerable appeal. Singer then made another break that led to a score in the corner. As he prepared to take the conversion from the touchline in the midst of his cheering contemporaries, the thrill of the occasion rather got the better of him. As the words of his personalised commentary ran through his head, he launched himself at the ball and belted it with all his might. It skewed off feebly to the right, while the muscles in his left leg seethed in agony. He retired from the field, unable to return for another six weeks.

But, if he incurred damage to his precious left leg that day, the damage was also now done to thoughts of a life not captivated by rugby. His love for football began to wane. Played in the Lent term, football was of lesser prestige at Wycliffe than rugby. Singer played football at county and district level, but by the time he reached the Upper Fifth rugby had grown to dominate his life. It was in that year that he progressed through the ranks of representative rugby at Under-16 level.

The Under-16 Divisional Championship in 1989 came to a head when the South-west played the South-east in the decider, both having won their games against the North and the Midlands. Singer captained the South-west at fly-half and played opposite Paul Burke, who went on to play fly-half for Ireland. A 6–0 victory for the South-west, with Singer kicking the points, heralded his call-up to the England Under-16 tour to Italy.

Wherever he had gone, Singer had never had difficulty asserting himself on the field of play. And with each successive step up the ladder, his aim had been the same: to play as well as he could. The fact that he now found himself playing as well as he could for a place in the England Under-16 team had not really registered. His was just a hearty desire to get out and play for the team of the moment, whether it be St John's Prep School or England. Not being able to do that had never hit home as a possibility.

The England selectors wanted Paul Burke to play fly-half and so Singer was considered as a full-back in the trials. He was picked for the week-long tour but was informed by the selectors that they wanted to try another lad at full-back for the first match against Italy B because they were not too sure of this lad's defence and wanted to see what it was like. Singer would sit on the bench.

It was one of those moments familiar to many, when the butt of exclusion is dressed up with the words of placatory reason. It provides the excluded with a spark of hope but, at the same time, sets a chain reaction of doubt fizzing throughout his brain. The game duly arrived and Singer watched from the bench, alongside Matt Dawson and Richard Hill, who was to become a soul mate on the tour, as England posted 40 points on the Italians, who, in turn, did nothing to test anyone's defence.

With the results of the full-back experiment inconclusive, Singer anxiously awaited the announcement of the team for the following Test match against Italy. They would surely pick their best side for that. There could be no excuses of the 'we just want to have a look at someone else' variety. Singer's worst fears were confirmed, however, when he was duly left out again. The case for the defence had not been answered, yet he was still being overlooked. Had they never intended to play him? It had been his first real introduction to the dreaded exclusion speech and on this occasion the words had been of the hollow variety.

The experience left him mortified. Although he later attempted to rationalise things himself by considering the standard he had reached and the number of boys across the country he had superseded to get there, nothing could override the pain of what he saw as a rejection. He had wanted to play in the team and all he could see was that, for the first time in his life, they had not wanted him. That it was at the highest level did not come into it.

It took him three years to recapture his enthusiasm for rugby. Like so many other competitive sportsmen who cannot understand their exclusion, he put it down to the politics of selection and became seriously disillusioned with representative rugby. The England tour did have another impact upon his life, however, for he then moved properly to full-back, where he was to play most of his rugby for the following six years. For the next two he was very happy playing with his mates in an excellent Wycliffe College 1st XV but could muster little enthusiasm for representative rugby, and he did not trouble the England selectors for the rest of his schooldays.

It was in his gap year, when he went to play in France, that Singer started to rediscover his confidence and his appetite for the game. After leaving school he had returned home to Porthcawl, where he spent the first half of his gap year teaching and playing rugby, before he left to spend six months in Narbonne. Playing for their liberated Under-20 team, Singer re-established his affinity for adventure and bravado on the field. The Frenchman who coached the side infused him with inimitable Gallic abandon. 'Matt, what are you doing?' he would say. 'You're so boring, so predictable. Do something different. Play!'

It gave Singer the licence to do what he wanted and he revelled in it. A coach from Neath, who had heard of him while he was playing at nearby Porthcawl earlier in his gap year, came out to watch him play in Narbonne and liked what he saw. Singer was invited to tour Florida with Neath upon his return from France in August 1992, a daunting prospect for a young Englishman but one that he seized with his characteristic combination of flair and deference. He also managed to improve his selection prospects somewhat. While enjoying Florida's marine facilities with the rest of the team, his control of a jetski proved less than adequate and, in the subsequent accident, Paul Thorburn, Neath's international full-back, was left with a nasty injury. It led to Singer's selection for the first two games of the season at Pontypridd and Bridgend. His perform-ances were of such quality that he was asked to play for the rest of the season, but his attentions were now turning to Bristol University. Bob Reeves, Bristol University's rugby coach and a man with a ravenous approach to player recruitment, had worked wonders to secure Singer's admittance to the university despite some disappointing A-level results, and Singer was profoundly grateful. He had never liked to spread himself thinly and he knew that he wanted to give his whole-hearted commit-ment to either Bristol University or Neath, not half-hearted commitment to both. He opted for Bristol.

I had already been at Bristol for a year when Singer arrived. I was a player of inconspicuous ability at the university rugby club. In September 1992, as the bedraggled masses gathered for pre-season training and swapped stories about the summer, talk, as always, turned to whom we should look out for among the freshers. Matt Singer was the name that emerged. Apparently, he played for Neath.

The event that invariably began to weed out the stragglers from the 150-odd that turned up to pre-season training every year was that infamous measure of fitness: the beep test. As usual, we all lined up for the start of this year's test with the silent bewilderment of those who are about to die. But we, the hopeless, always had the same tactic that was designed for only one purpose: to avoid the embarrassment of dropping out of the test first. We would keep going up the successive levels of speed until one of the big props dropped out (as they are invariably the first to do), and with our only criterion thus satisfied we would then start to wind up ourselves. I shall not reveal the level we usually reached – it would mean nothing to those unfamiliar with the beep test and I would not want to lose any more credibility in the eyes of those who are. Suffice it to say, we were not going for any Olympic performances.

A few minutes later (I could not say how many), we were sitting on the side of the field in contented exhaustion, watching the efforts of those who chose to continue. Long after we had stopped, the keen ones who had eyes on the 1st XV and maybe even the England Students squad also started to accept that enough was enough. The field dwindled as successive players collapsed into a defeated walk and joined the vanquished on the side. But one man, dressed in a black training top with a red trim that was reminiscent of a Duracell battery, just kept on and on. We, taking our well-earned break on the ground, began to fidget as, now alone, he remorselessly continued to move up through the levels of difficulty. This was getting embarrassingly ridiculous.

When Duracell finally called it a day, probably more out of sensitivity to our acute ridicule than any genuine fatigue, the fitness coach turned to the rest of us as we sat still on the ground. There was a rigid silence among the troops that needed breaking.

'That's first-class rugby for you, guys.'

Oh, so that's what it was. And this, presumably, was Matt Singer.

One of the first things that one noticed in Matt Singer was his humility. He always had a ready smile on his face and would appear to listen to every word you were saying as if you were speaking from Mount Sinai. He seemed to show us wizened cynics in the second year a healthy level of respect, which is always nice to see in a fresher.

Such levels of respect were not honoured on the rugby field, however, where Singer soon claimed his place in the 1st XV. The incumbent 1st XV full-back when he arrived was the English Universities full-back who was in his final year. The welcome extended towards Singer at the university was not entirely warm. When Singer said his position was full-back, some of the final-year students made a point of telling him that we already had a full-back in the 1st XV. Singer confined his response to the field and duly played himself into the side, pushing his rival out on to the wing.

The 1992–93 season was a very successful one for the club and culminated in the final of the Universities' Athletic Union Championship at Twickenham. Kyran Bracken was in his final year and at the peak of his powers as a student scrum-half. Having overcome the Durham University side of Will Greenwood and Tim Stimpson in the semi-final at Welford Road, Bristol met the might of Loughborough in an epic final. Bracken, to this day, relates with pride how the alickadoos at Twickenham said afterwards that it was one of the finest games they had ever seen at the stadium.

My recollections of the day are fairly hazy, enjoying the game, as I was, in the company of my inebriated student companions. I just remember the spring sunshine, the enormous Loughborough forwards who tore Bristol apart in the set-piece, the 15 Bristol athletes who tore Loughborough apart in the loose, the unbridled joy when the last-minute Bristol penalty took the game into extra time, and the agony when Loughborough were awarded a five-metre scrum in the last minute of extra time with the scores still level. Tony Diprose was Loughborough's number eight that day and after the irresistible drive of his pack he duly scored the try that broke our hearts.

Most of the plaudits in the press the next day went to the inspired Bracken (he was to make his full England debut before the year was out), but the promising young Bristol full-back also caught the eye of the seasoned hacks who attended the match for the national press. Indeed, a move that went down in Bristol University folklore was the 'Neath ball'. It was unnervingly straightforward. Bracken would receive the ball at scrum-half from his forwards and launch a 30-yard miss-pass that would cut out the entire back division and hit Singer on the hoof out wide. It created havoc in the Loughborough defence that day.

After the successes of that first season in student rugby and the continuing prestige of his association with Neath, for whom he played during the university holidays and from whom he received some very useful boot money, Singer's representative career began to revive. He played for English Universities before the season was out and won his first England Students cap.

Rugby was causing sufficient distraction, however, for him to fail two of his first-year exams and pass the others only by a whisker. He was in serious danger of not getting a degree and his sensible head made changing this his priority. Despite further overtures from Neath, he therefore elected to stay at the university rugby club, taking over the captaincy in his second year. Although their fortunes on the field would dip in the ensuing two years, the club never received anything less than Singer's undivided attention and enthusiasm.

In his final year, he launched an innovative competition in the university's student newspaper that was based on the popular 'fantasy football' idea. But this one had people selecting fantasy rugby teams from the pool of around 120 players that constituted the playing ranks of the university rugby club. It was a project that did much to boost the profile and the morale of a club that had been struggling that season. Singer had managed to secure a week for two in Lanzarote as the glittering first prize and the competition culminated in a hugely popular awards dinner that he had gone to great lengths to organise. He had committed himself to the university rugby club because he had not wanted to jeopardise his chances of getting a degree, but, ironically, that commitment nearly had the same effect. His enthusiasm for Fantasy First XV, as the competition was known, consumed his energies considerably more than his enthusiasm for his academic work. In the end, he came away with a solid 2:2 in Economics, but not before his colleagues voiced serious concerns that his interests in the rugby club might prove fatal to his degree.

Before he left Bristol, Singer entertained approaches from Gloucester, Harlequins and Saracens for his services the following season. He was also offered a place at Cambridge University for a teacher-training course in Maths, which he accepted. With that much resolved, Singer opted for Saracens. Geographically, it was convenient for Cambridge, and the friendly reputation of the club appealed to Singer's temperament.

He signed his registration forms in the summer of 1995 before he joined Cambridge, but he had no involvement with the club for the first half of the season. In the months leading up to Christmas, the student rugby players in the running for that fabled mantle the Oxbridge Blue devote all their energy towards their varsity rugby club, and Singer was no different. But his term had consisted of indifferent displays on the rugby field, and a leg injury from a day-long kicking session with Dave Alred two weeks before the Varsity match placed his selection for the game in serious doubt. A smoothly taken try against Leicester, however, in his last chance to prove his fitness for the Twickenham showpiece convinced the selectors to pick him.

Players at Oxford and Cambridge Universities are in a fairly unique situation in that their entire season is geared towards and justified in one match. Players channel all their energy into their varsity club so that they can play in that one game in December against the enemy. Players are also students, operating in that heady environment of carefree youth and carousing camaraderie. It generates a singular bond between team-mates, the upshot of which is the most fervent desire to be on the pitch on the big day at Twickenham. At all costs.

Singer was not really fit for the Varsity match but was not going to miss the occasion if they were happy for him to play. He was, however, unusually nervous as a result. On the day, with Cambridge the favourites, he had a torrid game on the big stage. He dropped balls and sliced kicks as his team struggled to overcome a David Humphreys-inspired Oxford. But, with the game ticking to its conclusion and Oxford holding a well-deserved if slender lead, a towering high ball went up on the Oxford defence with Singer chasing it. As the ball careered down on the Oxford twenty-two, Singer leapt high above the defenders and cleanly claimed the ball, which was then spun to the left for the try with which Cambridge stole the match. Singer, like Cambridge, had managed to atone for a ragged performance with a late flourish and the Light Blues' celebrations began in earnest.

A couple of weeks later, with his Varsity match commitments complete, he attended training at Saracens for the first time. Although Nigel Wray's acquisition of the club had been announced, the dark ages of Bramley Road had still not passed. He arrived early on the kind of black and miserable evening with which Bramley Road seemed to be perennially cursed. On arrival, he met Richard Hill, who took him through the rickety dining hall to the manager's small office, where the powers that be were presiding: Mark Evans, Bruce Millar, Mike Scott and Rob Cunningham.

Hill knocked on the door and told them that Matt Singer was here and did they want to meet him. The gruff Scottish tones of Rob Cunningham growled back, 'Yeah, get him in here and tell him to explain why he played like such a wanker in the Varsity match!' It was the sort of tactic employed by any number of old hands in welcoming a new boy to the fold, but it made Singer furious. The Varsity match was still a sensitive subject and this was not the sort of reception he had expected from a club with such a friendly reputation. He awkwardly entered the small office and paid his respects to the assembled cast, pointedly ignoring Cunningham.

Singer's temperament, however, had developed since his schooldays, and rather than stride out on a defeatist sulk, he tempered his reaction with determined anger, a humour that he carried into the subsequent training session. Invested with the edge that anger can instil and which can often raise the performance of the nice guy up a notch, he cut a swathe through the muddy darkness of that evening's training exercises. But he made his way back to the more forgiving bosom of Cambridge that night with little inclination ever to return to Bramley Road.

He was to return soon, though, but this time on his own terms. Andy Tunningley picked up an injury shortly afterwards and Saracens needed a full-back, so Singer was summoned. He soon picked up an injury himself, but he played an impressive role in Saracens' fight against relegation that season. Saracens were beginning to display a genuine appreciation of his talents. Mark Evans had considered him the man of the match in the relegation decider against Gloucester and was impressed with the unflustered way in which he had handled the torrent of high balls that had rained down on him at Kingsholm that day. The enormity of his left boot was also beginning to impress.

Indeed, I can testify to the power of his left boot through painful experience. At Bristol, in the summer after the exams in my third year, a large party of us was playing football on the grassy expanses of the Clifton Downs. During the game of football, Singer wound up his mighty left boot with clear intent to give the ball one of his Wales-defeating wallops. I was standing a few yards away and noticed that the ball could conceivably strike me. As one does in those situations, I instinctively raised my hands in front of my face, but sadly without much conviction. Rather than try to protect myself, I simply allowed my hands to fill the space limply in front of my face. Having left the boot of Singer a split second earlier, however, the ball struck the palm of my complacent right hand with rather more conviction and sent the knuckle of my right fist thumping with a corresponding force into the left-hand side of my jaw. The game continued apace as I stood in the middle of the field, confusedly trying to work out what had just happened.

The nearby ice-cream vendor had no ice cubes to hand, so I purchased a lolly from him and held it against my throbbing face until it melted, hoping it might rectify the situation. It did not. I was unable to eat for the rest of the evening, although drinking remained perfectly within my compass. When I was then unable to open my mouth the next morning, I visited the hospital to discover my jaw had been fractured, and I was forced to remain on a liquid diet for the next few weeks. I had effectively punched myself in the face. Friends inevitably delighted in the accident and drew many a comparison between my jaw and various glass ornaments. And they still do. Nevertheless, I prefer to draw attention to the enormous force with which Singer kicks the ball, and when Mark Evans later described to me in the wake of Singer's second Varsity match what a tremendous left boot he had, I nodded with a knowing smile.

Singer returned to Cambridge for the final year of his teacher-training course. He was now playing outside centre for the university and Evans kept tabs on him during the build-up to the Varsity match. Before the big game came around, Bruce Millar offered Singer a full-time contract with Saracens with effect from January 1997, once his Varsity match commitments were complete. Singer was reluctant, however, to give himself over entirely. He still had a teaching course to complete, which would occupy most of his time, and he also wanted to remain a free agent to enjoy to the full his last few months as a student. An arrangement was arrived at for the rest of the season that would see Singer paid a monthly retainer and additional fees for training and playing appearances. With his confidence still low from the previous Varsity match, Saracens' interest in him had progressive implications for his form on the field and that year's Varsity match was to belong to him.

The build-up to the match had been dominated by the tragic death of Ian Tucker, the Oxford centre, who had died from a head injury earlier that season in a friendly, coincidentally against Saracens. The game itself was an emotional and fractious affair, but was illuminated from a rugby point of view by three flashes of class from Singer that secured Cambridge their third consecutive victory against Oxford. The Dark Blues had taken an early lead, but shortly afterwards Singer broke from midfield and went in under the posts for a sparkling first try which handed the advantage to Cambridge. Thrilled at the roar that went up in the Twickenham stands, the excitable boy in his parents' garden suddenly got the better of him and he turned away and ran along the edge of the advertising hoarding in celebration, pointing at the crowd like a demented footballer. It was a moment his friends and team-mates would not let him forget in a hurry.

A few minutes later, a majestic 35-yard drop-goal from that left boot gave Cambridge further security, but it was not until the final minutes of the game that Cambridge were able to finish Oxford off. Singer was again the executioner. He was fed the ball on Oxford's twenty-two, came off his right foot twice and sprinted for the posts to beat four defenders for the match-securing try. There was no chance to indulge in any theatrics this time – he was mobbed by his jubilant team-mates before he could get to his feet. After the game, Singer handled the lengthy press conference with a characteristic blend of enthusiasm and humility. Not one to look for the camera, he nevertheless enjoyed it to the full when it found him on that cold December afternoon that would always lie in the shadow of a broader tragedy.

Singer's stock had risen further with his eye-catching display, but he stayed at Cambridge for much of the following term, busy with his teaching commitments and embarking upon the odd jolly with the university rugby club. He returned to Saracens in March, as the Lent term drew to its close, and played in the league game against Bristol at Enfield. He played a full part in their run-in to the season under François Pienaar before the summer arrived and, with it, the issue of contracts.

Saracens were paying an agent a finder's fee for every player whose contract he helped negotiate and, without an agent of his own, Singer took up the offer of his services. When he met him, all Singer's preconceptions of the archetypal agent were reaffirmed. Along with a characterless accountant, the agent arrived late for their meeting at an Enfield pub on the day of Singer's contract talks. He wore sunglasses, which he never removed while talking to Singer, and it was agreed that he would negotiate for him in the forthcoming talks. There was no fee to be paid (Saracens would be paying the agent the finder's fee), so Singer signed the relevant piece of paper. The ensuing negotiations must have been fairly one-sided. Mark Evans had told Singer what they were going to offer him and, after his champion's negotiations, that was exactly what he got. The agent apologetically described to Singer what a hard negotiator Evans had been and, with that, jumped into his Suzuki jeep and drove off into the sunset. Singer never saw him again.

The plunge had been taken, however, and he now found himself a full-time professional rugby player on a two-year contract with a one-year opt-out clause. He had his qualifications as a teacher to provide a reasonably secure back-up if his adventure backfired. He and his girlfriend, Allison, had been together now since their first week at Bristol, where they had been in the same hall of residence five years ago. Moving into a small flat with her in Radlett, near Watford, that summer, Singer prepared himself for his new career.

5

The Ghosts of Christmas Past

How perverse professional rugby can be. Christmas, as we all know, is the season to be jolly. We, the good, humble folk of Britain, in due deference to the Christmas ethos, tend to take the foot off the pedal and allow the festive spirit to wash over us as our carousing gradually builds over the season into a liberating crescendo of revelry. The price of the professional rugby career, then, is truly great at this time of year.

For the professionals at Saracens, barring those involved in the internationals, the four weeks preceding the Christmas season of 1997 had been ones of inactivity. The four pre-Christmas England internationals had required a total shutdown of the Premiership and, with their decision not to partake in the Cheltenham and Gloucester Cup, what little scope there was available to the Saracens for relaxation and revelry fell during those mundane weeks of November. How cruelly out of sync with the rest of us, for just as we started to wind up for the festive season, Saracens went back to work in earnest. Their commitments over the period were to host Bath and Leicester, two notoriously demanding houseguests probably not coming to quaff mulled wine and exchange presents around the tree. Saracens' first Christmas in their new home was to be one of intense examination.

Saracens sat proudly on top of the Allied Dunbar Premiership as dawn broke on 14 December 1997, unbeaten in the six league fixtures they had completed at that point. Today, however, was the visit of Bath, perennially at the top of the domestic game.

There had always been an intimidating mystique surrounding Bath, the club that for a decade had been lauded as the first truly professional outfit, albeit in an amateur game. The irony of their relative demise since the game itself had officially turned professional had not been lost on commentators. The 1996–97 season was the first since 1988 in which Bath finished empty-handed. Yet they succeeded in retaining much of their diminishing aura by finishing that season in breathtaking form. A series of astonishing victories against some of the top sides saw them propelled from mid-table obscurity to finish the season in second place, albeit a merely respectable achievement by their unforgiving standards. They had qualified for Europe and put 40 points past Leicester, 70 past Gloucester and 80 past Sale, but, perhaps ominously, they had lost the last match of the season against Saracens, when they conceded a record number of points in a 36–29 defeat at Enfield.

Nevertheless, Bath started the 1997–98 season as most people's favourites, but the sense of awful invincibility that the club had for so long exuded was yet to settle fully. As it continued to fluctuate, newly promoted Newcastle, in yet another foreboding omen of things to come, neatly picked their way through the imperfect outer shell to inflict a debilitating defeat upon them at the Recreation Ground on the opening day of the season. The aura seemed on the wane once more.

On the morning of 14 December, that aura wielded little thrall over the Saracen camp. Mark Evans was in no doubt that his team would win the afternoon's clash. He justified his eyebrow-raising confidence with disarming simplicity: 'We've got better players than them.'

A cursory glance around the breakfast room of the Hilton hotel in Watford, where the Saracen squad members were tucking into a brunch of pasta, vegetables and boiled chicken in a mood of studied relaxation, quickly confirmed the situation at which we had unwittingly arrived. There were two more internationals making their full debuts in the Saracen line-up. Roberto Grau, of the famously destructive Argentinian front row, was to pack down at loose-head, while Gavin Johnson, a prolific points-scorer for the Springboks, was finally given a proper run-out at full-back. Richard Wallace, meanwhile, was returning from injury for his first game in two months, allowing Ryan Constable to switch to his preferred position of outside centre and Saracens to cover seamlessly the loss of as influential a player as Philippe Sella.

After brunch the players gathered in a conference room where a large-screen TV was replaying the 80-point hiding that a Saracen side shorn of ten internationals had administered to the touring Tongans a fortnight earlier. It had been the club's only match of vague significance during the four-week lay-off for the pre-Christmas internationals. The video, an all-singing, all-dancing cabaret with seemingly choreographed lines of running, represented appropriate fare for a squad that needed to pick up that sort of form to retain their lofty position in the league. The inspiring team display then gave way to a team meeting fronted by an uncompromising François Pienaar.

Uncompromising, indeed, was Pienaar today. The team meeting ran late and the tardy team bus was repeatedly thwarted in its attempts to pull out from the hotel car park into the nose-to-tail traffic that barred its way to the stadium. Decisive in his concern for the team's preparation and blessed with the inimitable self-confidence of a South African, Pienaar leapt from the bus, strode purposefully into the oncoming traffic and, as fearlessly as he would in the forthcoming match, laid his body on the line to create an opening that his team-mates could exploit. His impromptu performance as traffic-policeman duly completed with this summary domination of the Watford motorists, the small matter of the Bath forwards remained.

Vicarage Road at 1.50 p.m. was already simmering with anticipation. The defiant chant of the hit single 'Tub-thumping' had reverberated throughout the coach as the stadium approached. DJ Mike Scott then turned the Saracen tape over for the now-ubiquitous signature tune 'Men in Black' as the team bus backed into the narrow passage alongside the East Stand to the players' entrance. Will Smith's triumphant strains soon gave way to the shouts and cheers of the excited children who had gathered outside the entrance to catch an early glimpse of the afternoon's combatants.

As the players slipped determinedly into the mind-focusing sanctuary of the changing-room, the atmosphere continued to build in the arena above them. There had been tentative whispers of a gate in excess of 10,000. As the game neared, it became increasingly obvious first that it would be a record crowd for a Saracen home game, and second that the final tally would indeed break five figures.

Further exciting evidence was shortly to emerge. An announcement came over the tannoy, interrupting the strident rock music that aurally occupied the expectant and fast-growing crowd in the stadium. The match would have to start five minutes later than scheduled in order to give those still outside a chance of admittance before the battle commenced. As Mick Cleary drily observed in his article in the *Daily Telegraph* the next morning, there was a time, not so long ago, when Saracens would only delay kick-off in the hope that a crowd might turn up. Here they needed extra time to shoehorn all the punters through the turnstiles before the game started. The delayed kick-off had crept into international rugby of late, but at Saracens it was truly unprecedented.

In the end, the final attendance figure of 10,658, which was announced midway through the second half (although it was later upgraded to over 11,000), seemed disappointing. It was difficult to see where the other 11,342 would have gone, had the stadium been full. Attendance figures are notoriously unreliable and in many ways quite superfluous. To look around the stadium at kick-off was to see three stands (North, East and West) to all intents and purposes packed. As always, the South Stand was closed due to lack of demand, and a huge awning covered the vacant rows. 'Welcome to Saracens' was the predictable headline on the awning, followed by the previously ludicrous subscript of 'World-class rugby at Watford'. The South Stand accommodates 7,000, but elsewhere in the stadium it was necessary to investigate carefully the banks of supporters in order to pick out the empty seats, allegedly numbered in their thousands, that were sparsely scattered among them.

Schools had been targeted and there was a large number of children present, with all the attendant excitement and enthusiasm that they bring. Getting from tunnel to pitchside, a brief jog of ten yards, for example, was a disproportionately time-consuming journey for anyone clad in Saracen attire. A frenzy of fluttering programmes, with accompanying pleas of 'Excuse me!', greeted those prepared to negotiate the hazardous trek. Countless schoolchildren thrust their eager arms from behind the railings, indiscriminately imploring the intrepid for autographs, be they most-capped player of all time or anonymous hack researching a book, the former proving by far the more obliging.

As the minutes ticked on, however, the players wound up their on-pitch warm-up and drills and retreated into the bowels of the stadium for their final preparations. The crowd, meanwhile, were simmering nicely and further brought to the boil by the elastic gyrations of the mandatory troupe of dancing girls, the Saracens Crown Jewels. Having worked through a couple of routines on the halfway line in conditions of compromising chill, they finished off by throwing mini rugby balls into the crowd. Two of the balls were marked in a specific way and the recipients of the marked balls would take part in a half-time kicking competition on the pitch. With that unfamiliar duty performed, the girls took their places at the mouth of the tunnel to welcome the players.

The atmosphere was at a suitable pitch by the time the Bath players were obliged to run out to the gloating anthem 'Nowhere to run to, nowhere to hide'. The home team followed shortly afterwards to the rather more forgiving chorus of 'Here come the men in black (the galaxy defenders)'. In the ensuing 40 minutes, despite losing Paul Wallace to an early calf strain, the galaxy defenders, with Pienaar particularly astronomic, proceeded to take their game to a dimension they had yet to explore.

By half-time, Saracens were 28–9 ahead. Something unusual was in the offing. As Saracens returned for the second half, Pienaar exhorted them with a demand for the registration of 50 points. Fifty points against Bath? Did he realise what he was saying? He had not, of course, had experience of English club rugby over the last ten years or he would clearly have choked on his Lucozade as he suggested such a thing. Mr Pienaar, however, has no respect for reputations. Not so long ago, even a fifth of that against Bath would have represented a small triumph, but Saracens had moved on, and, in a sparkling blur of running rugby, fulfilled their player-manager's directive with some aplomb. 50–23.

Bath had lost games of rugby before, but this defeat seemed to open up a fresh avenue of ideas for pioneering philosophers in rugby-think. Bath and 50-point thrashings are two concepts that have long sat comfortably with each other: for example, 'Bath regularly administer 50-point thrashings' is one of the more established maxims in the science, with a healthy catalogue of empirical evidence to support it. Here, however, was a development that sent the laws of rugby-think spinning into pole-reversing chaos. 'Bath receive a 50-point thrashing.' Things were no longer as they seemed. This was an X-file.

The truth that was out there was felt no more painfully than by Andy Robinson, Bath's coach. As a player, he was an integral component of the machine that had routinely demolished teams up and down the country throughout the last decade. He was well acquainted with the 'Bath-50-point-thrashing' theorem. Having played such an important role in the team that formulated the equation, the implications of this latest development were overwhelmed in him by the emotional implications. Robinson was gutted.

A ferociously proud man, he poked his head into the Saracens changing-room after the game to explain, with some economy, that his team would not be staying. Then, in the post-match press conference, he was even less generous with his words. The pressroom, meanwhile, was alive with scientists enthralled and excited by a new discovery. Very few of them sharing Robinson's emotional involvement with the subject, yet all of them sensitive to it, they awkwardly probed him for normal, or paranormal, explanations. Robinson repeatedly countered investigations, normally with a pause of several seconds followed by a terse mono-syllabic reply. The atmosphere was peculiar, nobody really knowing where to look in the presence of one so manifestly traumatised.

Mark Evans, however, bounced into the pressroom a little later in rather better spirits. He seemed more than happy to analyse the day's events and fielded a number of enquiries, most of which concerned the dubious origins of his trusty custard overcoat. He lauded the arrival of his team as title contenders to be genuinely respected. While paying tribute to the achievements of Bath over the previous decade, he wel-comed an end to 'the most boring duopoly in the land. If Bath did not win something, then Leicester did. Now we have the likes of ourselves and Newcastle, to name just two, all capable of winning things. It can only be good for the game.'

With one half of the dispossessed duopoly thus accounted for, the other half rumbled into town 12 days later. Twelve days later than 14 December is 26 December. Boxing Day, no less. Or, more to the point, the day after Christmas Day. Orange juice and pasta had replaced champagne and turkey in the players' festive diets.

Rugby matches on Boxing Day are not unheard of, the most famous being Leicester's annual frolic against the Barbarians. For that particular fixture, however, hangovers from the previous day's debauchery were welcomed as healthy confirmation of one's adherence to the spirit of the game. It was poignantly symbolic, then, to have that Corinthian tradition replaced by something so austere as the struggle for two points.

The hardships of the few, however, often facilitate the pleasures of the many. Having enjoyed a feast of rich indulgence the day before, there was yet more animation among the growing hordes in the stadium. Ten minutes before the scheduled kick-off, the queues outside the gates practically ringed the stadium. This time, kick-off was delayed by 15 minutes. A ten-minute improvement on the Bath game.

Yet another milestone was soon to fall on Saracens' trek towards their brave new world. It was with some excitement that the coaching staff looked towards the South Stand to see the carpet under which 7,000 empty seats had been swept rolled up and taken away. The awning welcoming one to Saracens was deemed superfluous today, being replaced by the far more responsive decor of a couple of thousand people. The final count was a mighty 14,291, by far the biggest crowd in the club's history, but again you needed to engage your imagination to see where another 7,500 might be squeezed to bring the crowd up to capacity.

Out on the pitch, meanwhile, only Joel Stransky, Leicester's South African international, remained. Stransky is a friend of Pienaar, a bond that was no doubt strengthened when the fly-half dropped the winning goal in extra time in the 1995 World Cup final. Like Pienaar, Stransky had been controversially jettisoned from the Springbok squad soon afterwards and he also embarked upon an adventure in England. Stransky, a cool-headed architect of the game, had invigorated Leicester's play almost immediately upon arrival.

As the cacophony of rock music and expectant cheers cascaded around him with minutes remaining before kick-off, Stransky's unflappable concentration was channelled into some place-kicking practice. From over the halfway line, he fired a succession of conversions that soared majestically over the goalposts in front of the South Stand. He looked to be on form. He operated in a bubble of his own, his focus total, his technique immaculate, the mounting waves of noise incidental. Nothing could disturb him.

Nothing, that is, but the Saracens Crown Jewels, who, with a rasping introduction from the master of ceremonies, suddenly came skipping on to the turf. Their kinky Santa Claus hats bobbing with every stride, they launched into a sparkling routine set to the thumping 'I wish it could be Christmas every day'. Stransky, thus unceremoniously stripped of his composure, was sent spinning to the sidelines by the high-kicking fillies, where, bewildered, he teed up another shot at goal. The heightened din in the stadium now seemed to press heavily upon him, the beautiful things happening on the halfway line appeared to distract his unshakeable attention and he pulled his kick hopelessly wide of the uprights. He took up his kicking tee and walked back into the tunnel, bemused and indignant at the interruption of his preparations.

A couple of routines later, the flashing smiles and glittering pompoms removed themselves from the halfway line to the mouth of the tunnel, where they celebrated the arrival of the two teams. In another compromise of player preparation, the Saracen players, having run on to the pitch, were then obliged to kick rugby balls into the crowd for the half-time kicking competition. It was presumably felt that the Saracens Crown Jewels were less adept than the players at administering rugby balls to far-flung corners of the auditorium. But the Saracen players, in turn, proved less adept than the Crown Jewels at accompanying their ball distribution with dazzling smiles, what with 15 snarling Tigers awaiting them the other side of the whistle. There were soon plenty of smiles, however, from those in the crowd. Paul Wallace, struggling to temper his pre-match aggression with the required diplomacy for this PR exercise, sent his ball thundering over the North Stand. One hoped, for the balance of the half-time kicking competition, that it was not one of the two marked balls.

The game was then set under way by a more delicate example of the kick. Delicacy, however, was harder to come by thereafter, as the two sides tore into each other with all the pent-up frustration that a Christmas of abstinence must have cultivated. A number of niggling brawls culminated in a spectacular punch-up in the south-west corner of the field, from which Danny Grewcock, Saracens' new lock forward, and Martin Johnson, Leicester's victorious Lions skipper, picked up a yellow card each. Two more Lions were to follow into referee Morrison's book shortly after, when opposing props Graham Rowntree and Paul Wallace were unable to agree at yet another disrupted scrummage, before the game was allowed to settle a little, a couple of penalties apiece from Stransky and Lynagh mediating between the factions. Lynagh then dropped a goal to give Saracens a 9–6 half-time lead.

Down in the changing-room during the interval, Diprose and Evans were urgent in their concern to remedy the lazy rucks that had so far stymied Saracens' progress in attack. After they had delivered technical instructions to that effect, Pienaar rose to his feet and spoke in an intimidatingly matter-of-fact manner. 'Guys, I've just got one thing to say. I've played in a lot of games of rugby, and I want to know: is this a team of men? Or are we going to fold against a good side that's playing aggressively?' Pienaar paused to let his words sink in. 'Are we a team of men?'

The question was tossed out to the assembled throng and hung in the air as Pienaar stalked the room, interrogating the company with his stare. The silence that replied was received without judgement and only broken as the players rose to propel each other towards the second half.

A Stransky penalty shortly after the break levelled matters once again, before a threatening breach of the Leicester defence suggested that the half-time silence had been one of steely resolve. Then followed the suggestion that the half-time silence may have been one of uncertainty when Leicester finally broke the try-scoring deadlock. A scuttling half-break from Stransky allowed Leicester's latest South African signing, Fritz

Van Heerden, to burst through to the line. Stransky's conversion gave Leicester a 16–9 lead. Mark Evans twitched in his seat. 'Now this is a test,' he warned.

Although it took another 13 minutes to arrive, the initial response to the test was precise. In the space of three minutes, Saracens twice located that elusive passage through Leicester's defence. From a scrum on half-way, Diprose picked up and played a dummy scissors with Ravenscroft before feeding Bracken, who launched a coiled back division. Ryan Constable, at outside centre, was released through a half-gap. With the pace that made him the fastest Saracen over 30 metres, he scorched towards the right-hand corner and managed to get there momentarily before the covering Austin Healey for the try. Lynagh converted from a fiendish angle on the touchline to bring the scores level again and spur the home team on to take the lead with only nine minutes remaining.

Leicester's young wing Leon Lloyd was given a run at the Saracens midfield, which stopped him and duly stripped him of the ball. Bracken pounced, dashed blind and found Alex Bennett, the young flanker and Saracens' outstanding forward on the day, who fed Richie Wallace in space. Wallace senior in space was enough in itself to send Vicarage Road into paroxysms of excitement, but when he skipped nonchalantly past Waisale Serevi (Leicester's celebrated Fijian with a copyright on non-chalant skipping) the place went wild. When Wallace finally completed his cameo by reaching out of Healey's cover tackle to score the try, the stadium somehow attained a yet higher level of feral euphoria. It did, however, register a token groan of disappointment as Lynagh pulled the relatively straightforward conversion across the face of the uprights, but Saracens had surely now completed the test and been passed as the men that Pienaar had hoped them to be.

A Stransky penalty five minutes later conjured a small furrow in the brow, bringing Leicester to within two points with four minutes remaining, but it was not until the dying minutes that the furrow became a fully fledged frown. Wound up by their recently triumphant Lions skipper, the Tigers pack exerted sustained pressure upon the home defence and only Lynagh's hand prevented Stransky from reliving past glories in the 1995 World Cup final as the South African's attempted drop-goal fell narrowly short. Matt Singer's subsequent touch-finder provided only temporary relief.

As the teams moved towards the line-out, every last soul in the stadium knew what to expect. After a standard catch and drive from the

Leicester forwards had secured the ball and a series of rucks had brought them in-field, Stransky wound up for the kick. A second later, the ball completed its prescribed course between the posts. 22–21. Leicester were back in front. The Saracens Crown Jewels had been silenced. Stransky could walk tall again.

The final whistle blew shortly afterwards and Leicester arms were thrown into the air with delight, the left arm of Joel Stransky proving particularly virile. The tannoy burst into a sympathetic rendition of 'Always Look on the Bright Side of Life', to which the gloating Leicester fans sang along. Saracen heads were hung in disappointment as the players trudged back into the comforting warmth of the dressing-room, the defiantly posed question surrounding their manhood still un-answered.

Evidence could be garnered, however, to support their claims to that fabled mantle. Apart from their response to going a try behind to the notoriously frugal Tigers, the manner in which they handled the defeat was impressive. The changing-room mood after the match was not appreciably different from that after the Bath match. It was measured, it was calm and it was rational. Whether having inflicted an unprecedented thrashing upon the biggest rugby name in the country or having lost agonisingly to the second biggest, level-headedness was retained. In the same festive season, they had met with triumph and disaster and treated both those impostors the same, fulfilling at least Rudyard Kipling's criterion for manhood. But they had lost. And the realisation was to bite hard.

Mark Evans addressed the huddle that forms after every match: 'When we lose, we take it and we learn from it, but we *never* accept it.' Pienaar, clearly exhausted, managed to squeeze out a few of his thoughts between the spasms of hiccups that convulsed his body. Then, a few minutes later, he somehow handled the post-match press conference as immaculately as a seasoned diplomat, albeit still bearing his rugby kit and the scars of battle. He was good nature itself, careful to pay handsome tribute to Leicester's efforts as a team. Bob Dwyer, Leicester's coach, was equally magnanimous after the game, highly relieved that his team were now only four points behind Saracens rather than the eight points that had seemed likely at one stage. 'Never in doubt' was his tongue-in-cheek assessment of the game. He went on to reveal, 'A guy from Australia was here today on holiday. He's a teacher and a rugby coach back home, and he said to me after the game, "That was Super-12 stuff." I said, "I don't think it's quite top-level Super-12, but it's certainly bottom-level." The intensity's there, the standard of play's there and the crowd is there.'

Ah, the holy grail on the horizon at last! Had English rugby's quest come so far? Surely this was not another spurious comparison boasted of by a little Englander? Here was one of the southern hemisphere's own likening our humble clubs to those mythical knights of the Super-12 table – a fairytale indeed.

The events at Vicarage Road over the Christmas season of 1997 would certainly have constituted the stuff of dreams for the Saracens of Christmas past. Despite the acute disappointment of losing by a point to Leicester, the club had now firmly established itself in the vanguard of the game's new order. But, as Christmas gave way to the hangover of a New Year, the club needed to rouse itself for fresh challenges. The fray of the Tetley's Bitter Cup had still to be entered, and a team whose name conjured appropriate images of a recently built fortress stood proudly between the marauding Saracens and their crusade for the top of the table.

Newcastle had yet to fall.

6

Lynagh, Sella and the Coming of Twenty Thousand

They were welcomed to English rugby in the claustrophobic confines of saturated press conferences and left to the airy overtures of delirious thousands.

Michael Lynagh and Philippe Sella took their leave of rugby in circumstances of fitting pomp bathed in an incongruous burst of sunshine in early May 1998. That window in the clouds was to remain closed for most of the dreary summer that followed, but it opened for a brief period as the 1997–98 season drew to a close and admitted the streaming rays that seemed to bless two of the great rugby careers just as they passed.

Their arrival had been greeted with scepticism by many. Both in the autumn of their terms on the field, Lynagh and Sella were trumpeted into the English game by the obnoxious *nouveaux riches* that many perceived Saracens to be in early 1996. Allusions to mercenaries and cosmetic luxuries were prevalent in the press and down the pub.

But Saracens had done their homework. The spectacular achievements of Lynagh and Sella clothed men of impeccable character and integrity. Beneath the glamour lay the evidence. Sella had been born and raised in the obscure French village of Clairac and had gone from there to play his entire first-class career at Agen, where he was fêted as a hero. Lynagh, meanwhile, had only ever played for Queensland University and Queensland itself, before demonstrating his appetite for adventure by playing in Italy for five years during the Australian summers.

Lynagh was enjoying his fifth season in Treviso, having retired from international rugby in the wake of Australia's quarter-final defeat against England in the World Cup a few months earlier, when he received a letter in October 1995 from Angus Stewart advising him of Saracens' proposals. When the motion of the club's incorporation as a plc was accepted by the membership soon after, Lynagh flew over to England with his Italian fiancée, Isobella, to meet Nigel Wray. Both were immediately impressed by Wray and his vision, and they quickly decided that London would constitute a perfect place to begin their married life. Lynagh was soon delighted to hear of Saracens' attempts to attract Sella, his old adversary from countless international playing fields across the globe.

Sella, meanwhile, was an institution in Agen, the captain and talisman of their proud rugby team. There was no need whatsoever for him to come to London other than to accept the thrill of one last challenge. Not even the standard accusation of financial motivation is applicable here. Sella was not actually paid a particularly large salary. Like any other international's, it was handsome, but it was nowhere near the levels that one might have expected. Had Sella wanted to boost his pension significantly, he could certainly have secured himself a better deal. Indeed, Richmond are said to have offered him more. And even Lynagh's salary, although larger, was well short of some of the packages that one hears bandied about.

The news of their recruitment was announced to the wider world at the start of 1996. On Monday, 8 January, after he had secretly watched Wasps send Saracens one step closer to relegation, the upstairs room in Café Flo, opposite Wray's office in the West End, was packed to welcome Lynagh, the first international superstar, to the English game. Seven weeks later, on Tuesday, 20 February, the Rugby Club of St James extended a similar West End greeting to a bowler-hatted Philippe Sella, with Saracens having moved a couple more steps closer to relegation.

When their flirtation with relegation was finally consummated at the end of the season, English rugby did not know whether to laugh or cry at the prospect of Lynagh and Sella playing second-division rugby the following season. One of the more opportunist parties acted swiftly. Harlequins, realising the absurdity of the concept, offered Lynagh an escape route to the first division by inviting him to join them. Lynagh's contract with Wray had been a verbal one and nothing had yet been signed, but Lynagh politely declined Quins' tempting offer. Along with Sella, he would ride out a season of second-division rugby rather than break his word. But Lynagh had been closely informed by Mike Smith of developments behind the scenes and remained pretty confident that the relegation would be reversed. When it was, he came over to join the club in August, two weeks before the first match against Leicester.

He was extended a spartan reception. When he arrived at Bramley

Road's rickety pavilion, he found an old-school atmosphere thick with the precursors to initiation. A record 911 international points or not, the club was older than Lynagh and his new team-mates had been there longer. They were not about to bow graciously to the glamorous new boy.

Almost immediately, a primitive drill was set up that saw players line up and face each other across the twenty-two. One by one, each attacking player would have to beat his defensive opponent. As mentioned earlier, Lynagh's first task was to tackle Charlie Olney, the pugnacious and powerful hooker. It was clear what tactic Olney would be adopting to beat his man and, true to form, when it was his turn the ball of fire hurtled straight at Lynagh. With a top-flight career that stretched back 14 years, Lynagh both recognised this genre of drill as a rather unsophisticated throwback to another era and understood it as a necessary hurdle for him to clear if he was to win any kind of acceptance in the short term. He knew life would be hard if he did not meet the man head on and put him down. With the rest of the squad watching, Lynagh put his shoulder down and satisfied the first requirement for acceptance, earning a round of applause for his pains.

When Lynagh and Sella made their debut in the August sunshine two weeks later before a crowd of 6,000 at Enfield, it was a happy occasion, with Saracens beating traditional giants Leicester 25–23 on the opening day of the season and Lynagh kicking 20 points' worth of goals. But the next league game at arch-rivals Wasps' new home, the impressive 19,000-seat Loftus Road, was to prove as black for Saracens and Lynagh as the shirts of their marauding hosts. Going down 36–21, Saracens lost Lynagh with a shoulder injury in the first half. It was the first of several injuries that were to plague him for the rest of the season.

From that first game against Leicester, Lynagh was never to find his form again until he put together a couple of injury-free games at the end of the season, particularly in the impressive defeat of Bath. That victory over the other traditional giants of English rugby rounded off Saracens' Enfield season in some style and hinted at the form that was to come in the next. Between the two ends of the season, Lynagh found life very difficult. A relatively quiet and introspective man by nature, he came across as distant and aloof. And while the injuries continued to keep him down and reduce his form on the field to the unconvincing, his popularity waned, and that in turn reacted back upon him in the unsympathetic attitude adopted by the coaches towards him.

The nadir came in the away defeat at Northampton in February.

Saracens had developed a game plan in which they would keep attacking the same side from successive phases. If they were going right from a set-piece, for example, they would continue going right after the first phase, then right again from successive rucks and mauls, until they ran out of field. Then they would move back the other way across the field. It was a simple game plan designed so that players of all standards could keep up. It was a game plan for which Lynagh, along with the newly arrived François Pienaar, had considerable contempt.

During the game at Northampton, Saracens won a line-out and play broke down in-field. Lynagh, receiving possession from the breakdown, looked up and saw just the two Northampton props standing in 20 yards of blind-side space. Most of Lynagh's team-mates were lined up open, with only Pienaar standing blind. Lynagh took matters into his own hands and broke down the blind side against the game plan, taking out the Northampton props and feeding Pienaar. They made about 40 yards and might have scored had there been another player to hand. There wasn't another player to hand, however, and Lynagh was hauled in by the coaches, who asked him to explain his transgression of the game plan.

Matters came to a head. Lynagh asked if they seriously expected him to ignore an opportunity when it arose, even if it went against the game plan. He was aghast to hear that they did. It was all very well for him, but other players could not spot opportunities in the same way, so the game plan had to be structured to account for them. 'You're basically asking me to play with my eyes closed!' retorted Lynagh, who had never before had to answer to the kind of rigid game plan that had been famed as inimitably English throughout the rugby world. 'What am I here for? You don't need me to play that kind of game. You could get anyone to play fly-half with a game plan like that.'

Lynagh went home that night and said to Isobella, 'Right, we're going.' It was a petulant threat. Lynagh is nothing if not a balanced man and he was soon back on a sufficiently even keel to review that particular piece of decision-making. It was the decision-making being denied him elsewhere that really exasperated him. He had never been the fastest or the biggest player and had secured his pre-eminent status in the game through the deftness and precision of his ability to spot and take opportunities. By effectively asking him not to exercise that ability, the coaches were, he felt, turning him into a bad player. Nigel Wray was paying him a lot of money for his experience and expertise, yet the coaches were giving him no kind of licence to influence proceedings at the club. And the press, not to mention his team-mates, were beginning to notice that the fabled Michael Lynagh was looking a merely mediocre mortal on the field.

Lynagh had never been a militant and was reluctant to force his views openly on the club. It all contributed to the impression that he was uncommitted and an expensive luxury, which further antagonised relationships with the authorities and caused the vicious circle to spiral ever downwards. But Lynagh had been developing a close alliance with another powerful figure at the club. Quite apart from Nigel Wray, who was becoming a close friend as well as an employer, François Pienaar, from a similar southern-hemisphere school of World Cup winners to Lynagh, was struggling to come to terms with what he perceived to be archaic training conditions and ideas. On Lynagh's recommendation, Pienaar had bought a house in Hampstead, a stone's throw from Lynagh, and the two quickly became soul mates.

Lynagh began to emerge from his purgatory when Pienaar was installed as player-manager. And in the season that followed, Lynagh, now afforded greater licence, began to exert an influence worthy of his stature. He revelled in the improved conditions at Bramley Road and the immaculate turf at Vicarage Road. He quickly re-established himself as the revered and universally popular figure who had graced teams in Australia and Italy and who was to be euphorically swept to retirement come the end of that season.

Other than the unparalleled extent of his achievements in rugby, perhaps Lynagh's most striking quality, particularly in view of those achievements, is his charming deference. Put in crude terms, he is just very polite. But it is not a meek politeness. It is not possible to achieve the things he has without the most iron of wills, and if he felt something had to be said, he would quietly say it in no uncertain terms to the relevant people. His is simply a politeness that admits little of his staggering stature and, as far as is possible, with the world and his cousin wanting a piece of Michael Lynagh, he tries to extend the simple graces to all and sundry.

My first meeting with him was eye-opening, if only for its banality. It was January 1998 and Matt Singer had recently suggested to me that we write this book. To that end, he recommended that I come down to Bath on a Tuesday afternoon to witness one of the less glamorous aspects of professional rugby. Saracens' midweek team were playing their equivalents from Bath, a month after the 50-point thrashing that the show team had administered to the West Countrymen at Vicarage Road. The game was being played at Kingswood School, whose playing fields were perched vulnerably atop a windswept hill above Bath. I had travelled down for the game and stood exposed in the swirling weather as people arrived in dribs and drabs to watch a match that was clearly about to be played in tortuous conditions. Lynagh was standing nearby and suddenly turned to offer me his hand. He might have recognised me; he had probably seen my face around in the previous month or so that I had been researching the book. But I was immediately taken aback that he should have bothered to approach me.

'Hello,' he said. 'Michael Lynagh.'

'Oh, so *that's* who you are!' the more sarcastic side of me thought as I shook his hand. 'I knew I recognised the face.'

Thankfully it did not say it. Instead, the more star-struck side of me mumbled something about being called Michael Aylwin.

It was generally a rather surreal afternoon in Bath. By the time kick-off had arrived, there was a small crowd huddled along the length of the pitch which included about 25 international rugby players. The pitch itself was appalling. It might kindly be described as a cow field were it not for the length of grass that betrayed a lack of grazing cattle. In fact, the groundsman seemed to have been at pains to mow everywhere but the playing surface. The lines of the pitch had been meticulously mown (I suppose he had to mow them in order to paint them), but otherwise the state of the field was enough to provoke unbridled mirth among the present Bath and Saracen players who were not obliged to play upon it.

It was an unspoken requirement of the rest of the Saracen squad to travel to support the midweek team. That, along with the presence of the rest of the Bath squad, who also turned up, accounted for the strange sight of this blasted school pitch lined with luminaries. With the game about to start, the international spectators looked behind them from the top of the hill out to the north-west, where a vast black cloud was being whipped their way by the already-uncomfortable wind. A mild hysteria descended: laughter at this further elemental discomfort with which their colleagues were about to contend, and terror at the thought of having to endure it themselves with precious few umbrellas in sight.

While there was a huge aggregate collection of international caps on the touchline, there were almost as many on the pitch, because Philippe Sella was making his comeback from injury in that Saracen midweek team. In the 19–15 victory that followed, Sella threw himself into the grizzly proceedings alongside his young team-mates, not seeming to remember the august occasions to which his career had taken him to date. The irony, however, was not lost on those watching. Tony Diprose, holding court among those touchline philosophers who had not by now retreated to watch from the shelter of their cars, found the whole thing most amusing.

'A total of 111 Tests and crowds of 70,000. Now look at him!' laughed Diprose, as the absurd conditions in the third quarter of the match made doing that very difficult indeed.

'Show a bit of respect, Dippy!' Kyran Bracken retorted above the howling elements.

'He's done pretty well, I suppose,' opined Diprose. 'Another 107 caps – I wouldn't mind that!'

Philippe Sella is a different animal from Lynagh. Sella is an inveterate extrovert. On one thing everyone at Saracens seems to be agreed: Sella was priceless from start to finish. Able to speak about four words of English when he arrived, he could still reduce his Saracen colleagues to tears of laughter, and not just because of his linguistic shortcomings.

If Lynagh's is more of a subtle charisma, Sella's is instant and explosive. It is impossible to exaggerate the esteem in which he is held. It is an esteem that is not solely attributable to his 111 caps but derives also from the energy and *bonhomie* that he brings to a cause. When he arrived at Saracens his stature in the game and his boyish enthusiasm did not seem to sit properly together. Lynagh's name, of course, was also huge, but as the more retiring character his first season at the club saw him retreat into his friendship with Pienaar. Sella's extravagant charm, however, insisted that he be one of the boys. There were a lot of new faces that year and Sella, with his indiscriminate socialising, became a recognisable point of reference to which people could turn.

Saracens embarked upon a pre-season tour to Scotland before the 1996–97 season and Sella immediately launched himself into the fray. At the first hotel in Newcastle, each of the several new foreign signings had to sing their national anthem, and 'La Marseillaise' rang loud and unbridled throughout the foyer of the peaceful hotel. At the end of the tour in Stirling, the players' court session required the foreigners to perform yet more humiliating acts, each having to wear a pair of thick spectacles purchased from a joke shop. In addition, Sella was given the mandatory beret for his head and had onions placed around his neck. A map of Aberdeen was thrust in his hands. Throughout the evening, on the given call, he had to approach one of the locals and in his best Scottish accent ask them to direct him home on the alien map. His team-mates loved it, but it seemed that Sella loved it even more. While others drifted off for curries as the evening wore on, Sella could still be found in the night-club, asking the Stirling clientele if they could show him the way home. On his map of Aberdeen.

Like Lynagh, Sella was an example for his team-mates to follow in the professional era. His attitude was impeccable. Playing 111 times for your country requires more than just exceptional ability. Sella brought a peculiar will for self-advancement to Saracens that had kept him at the cutting edge of world rugby for a decade and a half. In the week building up to the Tetley's Bitter Cup final, having begun to look like a man of 36 in recent performances, Sella sat down on his own for 80 minutes a day and took himself through a real-time visualisation of the game in his mind. He visualised every tackle, every run, every scenario. The sort of thing to which captains everywhere pay lip-service in pre-match warm-ups Sella meticulously and repeatedly carried out in preparation for his last great hurrah. The subsequent final was to witness Sella's finest per-formance in a Saracen shirt.

That sort of ferocious mental discipline had a profound effect on those around him, as did the aura of the man. Players felt safe with Sella on their side, not necessarily because of the way he was playing (well before he arrived at Saracens his prowess on the field had begun to wane from its glittering peak) but because of who he was and the achievements he represented. It might also be argued that his aura affected those who played against him. The awe in which he is held in rugby circles seemed often to compromise the performance of opposition centres who were no doubt acutely aware of just who was treading the same field.

In the light of such a reputation, his gregarious and all-embracing nature was almost disconcerting. To see the world's most-capped player running around the club with the same innocent enthusiasm as his young son Joffrey constituted the most delightful anomaly. That and his unshakeable reliability in going out with the boys. When the players would go for a few drinks, Sella would often tell them that he would be along later after he had been with his family. Initially, the players tended to take that as a gentle decline on his part, but they soon learnt better. Without fail, Sella would arrive at the pub at about nine o'clock, sometimes with his wife, and carouse with them into the night.

As his English steadily improved (with sufficient speed to hint at yet another example of his tireless efforts to make the most of himself and his environment), so did his contribution to the club. The only drawback was that it was becoming increasingly difficult to stop him talking. With Lynagh finding his feet too, the pair of them formed an enormous presence in Saracens' midfield in the first year at Watford. Saracens' drive for honours that season was built upon their experience and guile. It culminated in Twickenham's glorious sunshine, with Lynagh and Sella the outstanding players on the pitch as Saracens won the Tetley's Bitter Cup, but it also kept them in the hunt for the league until the bitter end.

Since the Boxing Day defeat to Leicester, Saracens had trailed Newcastle by one extra defeat, but they were given renewed hope by Newcastle's defeat at Richmond on a mid-March Saturday. The following day, Saracens trotted out on the notoriously hostile turf at Kingsholm to face mid-table Gloucester. Despite looking comfortable with a half-time lead, Saracens faced a torrential onslaught in the second half from the Gloucester pack, who bulldozed them into a 38–15 defeat in front of the baying Shed. Their chance to cancel out that extra defeat had been missed.

All the more significance was placed on the clash between Newcastle and Saracens at Kingston Park on the night of Wednesday, 25 March. In one of the most riveting games of the season, Newcastle triumphed 30–25 to surpass Saracens on points difference at the top of the table with two games in hand. Easter weekend was to prove the next crunch of the season with both title-chasers journeying to the West Country. On Good Friday Saracens registered a victory over Bath to become the first club to record the double against the erstwhile champions of everything in English rugby. The following day Newcastle took on Gloucester in an epic contest. The Shed were simply salivating for the blood of Sir John Hall's men and the breathless climax to the game did nothing to calm them down. Gloucester ran Newcastle ragged in a wonderful display of running rugby but Newcastle took their chances with ruthless precision. Gloucester fly-half Mark Mapletoft's drop-goal attempt in the last minute of the game floated agonisingly wide and left Newcastle with a 29–27 victory. Watching the game on Sky at Bramley Road, the Saracens squad were distraught, as was Michael Lynagh, who watched it bouncing around in front of the television on his hotel bed in Bath.

If Lynagh, who had stayed in Bath with Isobella for Easter, had felt acute frustration in his hotel room during that Gloucester game, he was to make the most of his and Saracens' last chance to keep their dream of a league and cup double alive. The following weekend, Newcastle came to Vicarage Road. Club rugby in England had never seen a day quite like the one that followed.

It had been apparent for some weeks that this would be a peculiar afternoon, but the news that Saracens' home game against Newcastle was a 20,000 sell-out had lent the occasion extra significance days before it arrived. These were exciting times for English rugby, but for months 19 April 1998 had been pencilled in as the defining date on which the potential for the club game might be judged. The early announcement of the sell-out confirmed it as both a tumultuous climax in the domestic season and a sign of the enthusiasm that club rugby could generate.

Because Saracens sell tickets without seat numbers on them, the police would only allow them to sell a maximum of 20,000 tickets, 2,000 short of the stadium's maximum. Nevertheless, with a crowd bigger than those of some of that weekend's Premiership football fixtures, Saracens' extraordinary growth in popularity had already reached its current capacity. And everywhere one turned there were smaller indications of the dizzy heights that Saracens had scaled in so short a space of time.

A father led his young son through the throng outside the stadium as the hordes jostled for position to gain entry. The boy had a Saracen crescent and star shaved into the back of his head. Such a display of loyalty would have been inconceivable even a year ago, but now one half-expected him to turn around and reveal the words 'I love Saracens' tattooed across his forehead.

It had become a cliché to marvel at the surreal events that were taking place in the new age of professional rugby, but to be at Vicarage Road on this April Sunday was to experience something fundamentally bizarre. An hour before the game, the queue in the Saracen merchandise shop spilled out into the street, merging into the swarm of black shirts that buzzed about the ground.

And then there were the fez hats. Everywhere. What had started as the trademark of a small band of hardcore Saracen fans, the Fez Boys, had escalated into a central pillar of the Saracen marketing campaign and a new craze in the Watford and Southgate communities – not a bad metaphor for the club itself, in fact. The Fez Boys themselves, however, had long since taken position in their stronghold in the heart of the West Stand. There was an intense concentration of beer and crescendo of song in this little enclave of the ground, and the focal point of the Saracen support was set.

Meanwhile, Mark Evans, Mike Scott and the injured Richard Hill stood on the touchline by the mouth of the tunnel, surveying the scene. Having survived the transition from the club's humble roots to the august atmosphere and surroundings of the present, any looks between the three were knowing ones. 'Well, it's good, but it's not Bramley Road,' suggested Evans with a mischievous glint in his eye as the four walls of support were steadily built around them until the 19,764th building block was in place.

With an unprecedented roar greeting their arrival, Saracens then took to the field with a spring in their step and immediately translated that into a vibrant opening attack. The game was all Saracens' in the opening quarter. But in the 16th minute a high and late tackle on the audience's darling, Kyran Bracken, from the pantomime villain, Dean Ryan, had the England scrum-half struggling. Lynagh missed the resultant penalty and looked worryingly off-key as he went on to miss two more before making sure with his fourth attempt a few minutes later.

On the half-hour, however, Saracens were dealt a vicious blow. In making a smother tackle, Pienaar tore his hamstring and immediately signalled to the bench that he would have to retire. Blind-side flanker Alex Bennett was sent on, leaving Saracens without a recognised open-side as Pienaar limped down the tunnel. The first half ticked down to its conclusion with Saracens leading 6–3 and Mark Evans observing that Bracken was practically playing on one leg.

At half-time, the atmosphere in the Saracen changing-room was seething as Diprose and Evans issued instructions. But the door leading into the physio room was ominously shut as Bracken received attention behind it. When the door finally opened, an ashen-faced Bracken hobbled into the room followed by team physio, Barney Kenney, shaking his head.

Pienaar whipped up the team morale and Marcus Olsen, Bracken's replacement, removed his tracksuit to prepare for the fray. Players were now on their feet, the room ringing with the agitated chatter of studs on the stone floor interspersed with cries of '40 minutes' and '20,000'. Bracken, though, sat forlornly on the edge of proceedings with an ice pack pressed against his groin, his game over. And when the team were safely on their way to the pitch, Pienaar's inspirational air suddenly dissolved too into one of frustrated dejection as he spoke with Evans about his injury.

Thus stripped of two crucial members of the side, Saracens were facing a critical test. The crowd seemed to sense it as well, their animated chants subsiding into a murmur early in the second half, prompting the announcer to call for greater support. 'Ladies and Gentlemen!' he chastised them with disc-jockey brashness. 'Outside of Twickenham, you're the biggest crowd ever seen in the history of English club rugby! I can barely hear you!'

The decibel level was to rise, however, as Saracens started to develop a sustained siege upon the Newcastle line. Diprose was stopped inches short after he had been released by a clever variation at the front of a line-out with Gary Armstrong clinging to his right foot. But another Lynagh penalty was all that Saracens could take away from nearly 20 minutes' pressure, and that proved the signal for Newcastle to begin flexing their muscles. The worst fears of 20,000 people were realised as the visitors pulled the Saracen defence across to the east of the pitch before spinning the ball west and releasing the rampaging Samoan Pat Lam on an arcing run to the try-line. Andrew's conversion gave Newcastle a 10–9 lead with ten minutes remaining.

The silence was deafening. It seemed then that the league was over. To emphasise the point, the now-insatiable Newcastle pack came again straight from the kick-off. Winning a line-out deep in Saracens' twenty-two, they drove remorselessly and only desperate Saracen defending managed to hold Lam up over the try-line.

An enormous weight bore down on Vicarage Road as 20,000 people sat heavy and motionless in their seats. But, undeterred, the Saracens Crown Jewels skipped around the stadium gaily, attempting to rouse the sickened thousands from their depression. Their pleas went largely unnoticed by the simple rugby folk who were suddenly less inspired by the more glitzy trappings of new-age rugby. It was Michael Lynagh's right boot, however, that was to have a rather more decisive effect upon their flagging morale.

At the end of normal time, with the ball finally back in Saracens' possession, Lynagh sent out a pass to Sella on a pre-planned move with which they were hoping to open the Newcastle defence. But Sella did not take it well and juggled with the impudent ball before having to abort the move and take the ball to ground. The resultant ruck formed about

15 yards inside Newcastle's half, left of the middle of the field. As the ball was recycled, Lynagh started to move left for a dart down the blind side but then, seeing nothing on, moved right again. Olsen found Lynagh with his pass and Lynagh quickly realised that, in terms of options, he was suddenly on his own. With the unyielding Newcastle defence ranged before him, it was clear that a try was a long way off. Because of his distance from the posts, however, neither had a drop-goal seemed a particularly realistic proposition. But something had to come soon, and after a split second's thought Lynagh decided that there was no time like the present. This was it.

Twenty thousand spectators and 29 players (well, probably 30 players) held their breath as he made his intentions clear, steadying himself, dropping the ball, keeping his head down and swinging his right boot. The South Stand were the first to react. The turning ball soared on its 40-yard arc towards their goal. As anxious eyes in the other three stands followed its path, a volcanic upheaval ripped through the murmuring backdrop behind the goal. The sweet purity of the strike was obvious but the South Stand were able to appreciate the triumphant destiny of its outcome most quickly and they reacted accordingly. Immediately, a wave of noise swept wildly throughout the stadium as the referee's arm confirmed the success of the kick. On all sides, fists were clenched furiously and faces distorted maniacally as people leapt about in a Saracen celebration of unprecedented intensity and volume.

Amid the furore, Lynagh strolled back into position, head bowed in the heavy drizzle, images of his opposite number, Rob Andrew, dropping his goal for England against Australia in Cape Town in 1995 no doubt flashing through his mind. But the apocalyptic roar consuming the stadium tested even Lynagh's sanguinity and after a few seconds, with head still bowed, he finally allowed himself to punch both fists in the air triumphantly.

Predictably, Vicarage Road soon reverberated with the symphony of whistles with which the crowd tried to inspire the referee to end the game, while a series of Saracen scrums consumed the remaining minutes of injury time. With five of those minutes gone, Lynagh sent another Saracen penalty high and safe into the East Stand, and finally the only legitimate whistle in the stadium sounded.

Lynagh and Andrew immediately sought each other. They had first played against each other 15 years before, with Lynagh in the colours of Queensland University and Andrew in those of Cambridge University.

Countless contests across the globe later, this was their last showdown and the two old foes exchanged a few words before Lynagh was collared for an interview with Sky television. His team-mates, meanwhile, had embarked upon a lap of honour acknowledging the record-breaking crowd that screamed their delight. After a quick interview, Lynagh, itching to join the rest of the team, politely excused himself from the cameras and trotted over to the celebrations.

Lynagh, however, was not to extricate himself from the press so easily. Once in the changing-room, he was urgently informed that the newspapers and radio wanted him immediately, but he had to explain to them firmly that he was to spend the next few minutes inside with his team-mates. The squad had gathered in a huge circle, blazered non-playing members linking arms with sodden players. Spontaneously they sang 'Happy Birthday' for Mike Scott before anything was said.

A beaming Pienaar had greeted them all in the changing-room and now he alerted them to a message that he had written on the whiteboard. The circle broke to reveal the words 'Thanks, guys' scrawled in red ink. A giggle of appreciation broke from the ranks, which grew into laughter as Lynagh drily observed, 'You've spelt it right!'

The joyous sense of relief within the ring was tangible. Relief that the team had kept its head in the most testing of circumstances, relief that they possessed a world-class fly-half, relief that the league was still alive. Pienaar voiced the room's feelings when, having praised the team performance, he turned to thank Lynagh, saying, 'That's why you're a world star.'

After Stransky's late drop-goal at Vicarage Road on Boxing Day had forced Saracens to start playing catch-up with Newcastle, Lynagh's *coup de grâce* had now helped them to catch up one vital step. But they had still not quite caught up. 'I don't care what Newcastle do now: it's out of our hands,' said Diprose. 'We've just got to win our last four league games. That's our only aim.' The focus for the season had been set. The broader picture was for others to determine.

When Lynagh was finally whisked away to the pressroom, he fielded the inevitable comparisons with that climactic day in Cape Town when Rob Andrew's late drop-goal for England had eliminated Lynagh's Australia from the World Cup. 'It was nice to get him back for that,' joked Lynagh. 'It's been a bit of baggage to carry around. I don't know if I would have preferred this one or the other game: if you asked me now, I'd probably prefer this one!'

As Andrew himself entered the pressroom a few minutes later, his path crossed with the departing Mark Evans. The two clasped each other's arms. 'I hope you lose [to Leicester] on Saturday!' cried Andrew with mock aggression, before adopting a similarly jocular manner throughout the subsequent inquisition. 'I think he [Lynagh] owed me that one. Extraordinary. I don't know where the script's coming from. Just extraordinary. I said this morning that I thought today would be a watershed in the club game and I think that everything that happened out there has proved it beyond a doubt. It's a privilege to be part of it and I'm just bloody delighted that Michael Lynagh won't be here next season.'

But, having played against him now for 15 years, didn't he think it would be nice for Lynagh to finish off with the double?

'I've already said they can have the cup. I'm being very fair about the whole thing. We can share it around. But we'd like the league.'

They certainly would. Newcastle's Ireland prop Nick Popplewell stood in the corridor outside the visitors' changing-room, meditating with his fellow prop Paul Van-Zandvliet and injured centre Inga Tuigamala. 'I thought we'd won that,' Popplewell ruefully reflected. 'We would have been home and dry.'

The big Irishman, it ought to be added, was delivering his ruminations as he casually leant against the wall wearing nothing more than his jockstrap and smoking a fag. The tradition of almost-naked prop forwards frantically pulling on cigarettes the minute they are off the field is as old as the game itself. It was pleasing to see that even at the highest level, amid all the conditioning and hype, the ancient custom was still surviving.

If, however, the sight of the scantily clad Mr Popplewell was of questionable aesthetic value, the young man who next emerged from the Saracen changing-room was an indisputable hit. It had reached that time of day again when the Kyran Bracken groupies (young females particularly prominent) gather at the mouth of the tunnel and remorselessly chant their idol's name. They tend to start shortly after the game has finished and they do not stop until he has showered and changed and emerged from the players' corridor to greet them. This takes about half an hour to an hour. It can get quite oppressive.

This time, Bracken hovered in the doorway between the players' corridor and the tunnel. The hordes remained behind the gate at the mouth of the tunnel that had been shut to keep them back. He was immediately spotted and the clamour for his attention suddenly reached a yet more feverish pitch. Bracken was engaged in conversation, however, and had not yet summoned the energy to tackle the braying gaggle. Had he looked more closely, though, he might have noticed the perilous danger he was in. There were no stewards manning the gate. The door was effectively ajar . . .

Such temptation was never likely to be denied. One plucky girl pulled back the bolt of the gate and the dam burst. The England scrum-half was immediately submerged under a tidal wave of programmes, pens and pleas, and he was forced to write off the next few minutes of his life. Relief was soon to arrive with the emergence of Pienaar into the tunnel, which diverted much of the attention. Meanwhile, anxious-looking Saracen officials had arrived at the scene like flabbergasted schoolteachers asking where the stewards were.

But it was too late; the tunnel was irretrievably swamped. Having accounted for the league leaders, though, the Saracen players could look after themselves among the admiring throng. Nobody was too bothered by the chaos. Newcastle had been beaten, the double dream was still alive, and the evidence for Saracens' extraordinary transformation as a club bubbled all around in the Vicarage Road tunnel.

Saracens were now level on points with Newcastle, who had a comfortably superior points difference and one game in hand. The following Wednesday evening, Newcastle took their weary bodies across London to Wasps, whose title they were trying to win, and lost by a point, again using up their game in hand. But because of their points difference, Saracens still needed Newcastle to lose once more if they were to stand a chance of overhauling them. That Saturday, missing Lynagh, Bracken, Hill and Pienaar from their middle five, Saracens travelled to Leicester, where they had never won in their history, and came away with a 10–10 draw. The dropped point was immaterial; they still needed Newcastle to lose one more.

Andy Lee deputised for Lynagh in the Leicester game and the league games against Harlequins and London Irish that followed. Lynagh's performance in the Vicarage Road epic against Newcastle had been even more heroic than it had looked at first glance. The Tuesday before the game, Lynagh had visited the doctor about a lump that he had noticed in his groin. The doctor diagnosed it as cancerous but benign. There was, however, the tiniest element of doubt and he was keen to remove it as soon as possible to be 100 per cent safe.

Naturally, this was of some concern to Lynagh, who sat down the next day and informed the management that there was a problem. They arrived at a compromise. He would play in the Newcastle game that weekend. If they lost he would have it out; if they won he would have to make the decision himself. They won and Lynagh decided that there were more important things in life than rugby and went ahead with the operation. It put him out of action for three weeks, but Saracens secured all the points they needed in the league with Lee at the helm. Lynagh was not to play again until the cup final.

The final game of the season and the final game in the careers of Lynagh and Sella came on the Thursday evening following the cup final. It was against Northampton at Vicarage Road. With Newcastle having won all three of their games since the defeat at Wasps, Saracens had to win and hope that the Falcons lost that weekend at Harlequins. After the flag-waving at the cup final, a carnival atmosphere pervaded at Vicarage Road on the evening of 14 May 1998 on a suitably balmy night. There was a lightness in the air, yet a strong undercurrent of emotion. It was goodbye to two of the greats of international rugby, an occasion of celebration and of sadness.

The two teams came on to the pitch and formed a guard of honour before the kick-off, while Lynagh and Sella were held back in the tunnel. With a raucous announcement from the compère, the two old warriors walked on to the field of play for the last time. Vicarage Road rose to its feet to acclaim the pair of them as the Northampton and Saracen players stood side by side and applauded their esteemed colleagues. The Saracen players themselves felt choked. Several had to look twice but swear they saw tears in the eyes of both men as they walked to the centre of the field, where Nigel Wray embraced them and presented them with gifts.

After the highs of the preceding weeks, the game itself was inevitably an anti-climax. Saracens trotted out winners, 43–20, but the action on the field was destined to play second fiddle that night. After the game, dazzling flashes of light exploded off the Tetley's Bitter Cup as the team were photographed parading the trophy in front of their home fans. Lynagh and Sella held the cup aloft together and gratefully received the acclaim as both the announcer and a banner in the crowd thanked them for the memories.

The serenity with which both men took their bows that night suggested that they were ready to call it a day. Sella had acknowledged when he arrived two years earlier that his sojourn in north London was to represent one last knees-up before he gracefully retired. 'There are three aspects of rugby,' he had observed back in February 1996. 'The preparation, the game and the party. I have had three clubs: little Clairac, where I prepared, Agen, where I played, and now Saracens. Playing for Saracens will be the party.'

To the very last, he had been true to his word.

Lynagh, meanwhile, took his leave with characteristic humility. One felt particularly with Lynagh that he had had enough. The roller-coaster ride of the previous month, which had incorporated his match-winning performance against Newcastle, a diagnosis of cancer, his match-winning performance in a cup final at Twickenham and the nostalgia of his last appearance in first-class rugby, had reminded him of the sheer exhilaration that the game could incite. It was both supremely invigorating and spiritually exhausting. After 16 years in first-class rugby, he was now ready to step off that roller-coaster.

Some people love the crack of performing on the big stage; others just love playing the game and perform on the big stage only because it represents the pinnacle in their field. Lynagh, it seems, fell into the latter category. He was always appreciative of mass acclaim but he never looked completely comfortable in its raucous glare. When Australia won the 1991 World Cup at Twickenham, his most vivid memory of fulfilment was sitting next to Nick Farr-Jones at the front of the team coach on his way from the stadium with the heavy gold trophy resting on his lap. The quiet contentment that he felt then sticks more poignantly in his mind than the fevered emotions in the immediate aftermath of victory, which he remembers as being predominantly of relief that they had not failed. Similarly, his final hour of glory in the same stadium, nearly eight years later, recedes into haziness. He remembers as clear as day, however, waking up the next morning in the beautiful Hampstead sunshine, walking to the local shop to buy the papers, reading them on his patio with breakfast and then sipping champagne with his wife, parents and in-laws, looking out over the little square on which he lives.

Newcastle went on to beat Harlequins the following Sunday in the last game of the season to clinch the title, but Lynagh and Sella were already content with their final curtain call. After the cup final, Sella had remembered how he had started his first-class career in 1980 by winning the French Championship with Agen. He had now finished it by winning the English Cup with Saracens. For Lynagh, the end had incorporated victory in the same Twickenham venue that had hosted his greatest hour with Australia. As the unbroken sunshine withdrew its endorsement for the rest of the grey summer that followed, having apparently chosen to shine for just two weeks at the start of May, the Twickenham victory lent a final neatness and symmetry to the iconic playing careers of Michael Lynagh and Philippe Sella.

It could have been no other way.

7

Twickenham Cruise

I do not mind admitting that I hate Hollywood.

By that I mean, among other things, the ridiculous all-American-hero, feet-stomping, multi-million-dollar-generating storylines that the movie moguls churn out relentlessly. Apart from the mindless imbecility of it all, and the shameless profiteering, and, while I think of it, the ceaseless repetition of the same formulaic plot and, in fact, any number of other things, I hate them because life never happens like that.

Tom Cruise, the maverick hero, after lengthy downtime because of the death of his co-pilot and best friend, takes to the sky once more to save his fellow countrymen, and probably the rest of the known world, from the nasty critters of some indefinable Eastern race. In the process, he purges himself of the fall-out from his friend's death, lives up to the legend of his hero-father and moves his bitter rival and enemy to note, with a manly hug amid the whoops and cheers of their honest compatriots and the soaring strains of a nearby soft-rock outfit, how he could be his wingman any time. A niggling incompleteness remains, however, and with that in mind Cruise returns to the bar where he enjoyed such happy times with his beautiful but sadly estranged lover. He sits on a stool, staring into his beer. On cue she arrives and puts their favourite song on the jukebox. They kiss and no doubt proceed to make wild and unmessy love happily ever after, him in his fetching Navy SEALS uniform, her in some mildly kinky flight-instructor get-up.

I hate *Top Gun* and all the myriad films in its genre. I could happily take you through the film and highlight every excruciating moment as and when it occurs, but basically the problem is one of reality. *Top Gun* is ludicrous. In real life, at least one of those wonderfully perfect set-pieces would foul up. Tom Cruise would probably be shot down, or trip as he leaves his cockpit. Upon his triumphant return, his compatriots would probably just get on with their daily chores, his bitter rival probably begrudge him his success, the soft-rock outfit probably not be heard. And the thing with the girl would surely not materialise. As one who has researched the matter thoroughly, I can assure you that sitting alone and forlorn on bar stools rarely wins you the girl of your dreams.

If I had one complaint about 9 May 1998 and the build-up to it, it is that it severely examined and totally discredited my above *Top Gun* theory. While my reluctance/inability to leave the bar stool in Eros that evening proved as fruitless a tactic as ever, I otherwise found myself in the middle of a true real-life Hollywood extravaganza. In fact, even the desolate bar stool seemed to prove a happy hunting ground for the likes of Kyran Bracken and Ryan Constable that night (that it should work for them and not me is one of the crueller, if more readily explicable, injustices). I have not seen the screenplay that Angus Stewart developed in the mid-1990s, inspired by Saracens' early foray into the professional era, but I warrant it could not have reached a more perfect climax than the real-life version that was to unfold.

The margins between corny melodrama and emancipatory euphoria are slight and might be said to boil down to the difference between fantasy and reality. Had Tom Cruise experienced those final scenes of *Top Gun* in real life, I should imagine it would have been a pretty special time for the boy. As it is, it constitutes no more than cringe-inducing gibberish. Invested with the credibility of actual fact, however, the events of Saracens' cup triumph were profoundly euphoric and moving. For the playing squad, management and support team at Saracens, the 1998 Tetley's Bitter Cup final was a real-life experience and will forever remain a pretty special time. For them, and even for this outsider looking in, that day reclines in a peculiar seat of the memory, as if it were slightly out of time, a swirling dream. And it cannot be attributed entirely to the effects of alcohol.

Wherever one chooses to begin the story, it contains all the right ingredients and plays to the same mounting rhythms, all tending towards one enormous crescendo on a sun-kissed May afternoon. One could start with F.W. Dunn in 1876, or the pre-war seasons wandering north London in search of a suitable home, or the years of noble defiance on the fringes of the top flight, or the professional revolution, or the arrival of Lynagh, Sella and Pienaar, or the rise of the Fez Boys, or the start of a treacherous cup run in January 1998. The story remains neat.

The cup run could hardly have been more gruelling and was not a little symbolic. Saracens spent most of it on the road, laying to rest successive demons from their past. The first stop was an away trip to Blackheath in the fifth round. Blackheath are the oldest first-class rugby club in the world and, indeed, their noble history is such that their nickname is 'the club'. For decades, like the aristocrats at Harlequins, Blackheath would not afford humble Saracens the honour of a fixture. It was with some satisfaction, therefore, that the old guard of Saracens watched as the new wave, without their Five Nations internationals, inflicted a record 59-point victory upon Blackheath in their own back yard. For those long-time Saracen committee members, the process of emancipation from the dark old days of the underdog had well and truly begun, albeit against a traditional giant that had slipped a little from its throne. It was also a match that saw the emergence of one of Saracens' homegrown talents, Ben Sturnham. That evening in the mud at Blackheath he began a journey, under the guidance of François Pienaar, that was to end in an England cap five months later.

When each round of the cup was drawn, the players developed the habit of crowding around the radio in facility manager Mike Hampson's small office at Bramley Road to hear the details of their next assignment. Their reward for beating Blackheath was the only home draw they were to enjoy on their trek to Twickenham. The disadvantage was that it was to be against Leicester, the team that only a month earlier had beaten them by a point at Vicarage Road. A point was once more to prove the margin of victory in the ensuing cup-tie. Again, Leicester were to score the first try and take a 13–3 lead. Again, Saracens were to play their way back into the match, a sparkling Bracken-inspired try from Constable redressing the balance. Again, the match-winner was to prove a nerveless kick late in the game, this time a penalty from Michael Lynagh. It earned Saracens a 14–13 win that neatly avenged the Boxing Day defeat. This had been an equally nail-biting game culminating in another pressure-cooker moment for Lynagh, with Vicarage Road's hopes resting once more on his shoulders as he prepared for his kick. 'I knew it was a pretty tense moment,' said Lynagh after the game. 'When I lined up the kick, all I could hear was the engine of the airship whirring overhead.'

The quarter-final assignment was then a mission into south-west London to another old rival, Richmond. The added drama here was the imminent arrival of a baby Pienaar. Tony Rocques, Saracens' young flanker, travelled with the squad in case Pienaar suddenly had to be called away. At half-time, Saracens returned to the cramped changing-rooms at the Athletic Ground trailing 14–9, but a burst of 27 points in

28 minutes in the second half gave them sufficient breathing space to allow Pienaar to race off the field to get changed. By the time he had returned to pitchside, less than ten minutes later, two injury-time tries had suddenly dragged Richmond back to within six points. But, with the 36–30 scoreline safely registered, Pienaar sped off to hospital, where he waited until dawn for Nerine to give birth to a son, Jean. Meanwhile, most of his charges, who had sped off to central London after the game on a mission themselves, also saw in the dawn but for rather different reasons: they were in the semi-final.

Saracens next drew Northampton at Franklin's Gardens. In the previous round Newcastle had found that particular combination too much and had been swept out of the cup by the imperious Saints. As the tie approached, most observers anticipated a similar fate awaiting Saracens. Their league form since the quarter-final had been fitful. They had scraped past Wasps at Vicarage Road and lost badly to Gloucester at Kingsholm. The Five Nations was well under way, and over half the team were involved in the various international squads. Then the news came through that their vital league game at Newcastle, which had been postponed from before Christmas, was to be squeezed into the overcrowded fixture list on the Wednesday night before the semi-final. The players, particularly those Englishmen and Irishmen playing in full or A internationals the preceding weekend, gritted their teeth.

After Ireland had lost to Wales in Dublin on the Saturday and England had beaten Scotland in Edinburgh on the Sunday, the Saracen squad travelled up to Newcastle on the Tuesday (with the English having travelled down to London in the interim). That Wednesday night, Newcastle triumphed 30–25 in one of the great club matches of the season, before Saracens retreated to a hotel in the East Midlands to be wrapped in cotton wool for Saturday's semi-final. This place was so secluded that mobile phones did not work. The players unwound with a diet of golf, snooker, board games and cards. Aggression was channelled purposefully in the card school, where Gregg Botterman ruled with a reign of terror. One of the real bonuses of professional rugby for Botterman, a wizened card sharp, was the arrival at his club of a myriad of international sportsmen with incomes to match. Botterman, who over the years has relieved countless Saracen players of their hard-earned cash, now had some genuinely juicy wallets to sink his teeth into. The next time players saw those teeth tended to be when he thanked them for the game.

When Saturday came around the nerves began to tighten, but in front of 3,000 fez hats Saracens produced one of their finest performances of the season. In view of the exhausting circumstances, it might even have been the very finest.

Paul Wallace, that most lovable and genial of Irishmen, once again demonstrated his extraordinary appetite for the fray. This was the third time in eight days that he was forming the cornerstone of a first-class scrummage. His opponent this time was the fearsome South African Garry Pagel. The Saracen scrum, however, was in its most ruthless mood and splintered the home pack repeatedly. That gave Bracken, himself nursing a popped shoulder from the first half, the licence to run riot and the finishing of Constable and Singer, the latter coming off the bench to score two tries, completed a supremely invigorating afternoon that seemed to capture the imagination of the press and the public.

Nothing did more to inspire the assembled scribes than the lap of honour upon which Saracens embarked after the game to acknowledge the travelling support. Again, dry comments abounded: Saracens had never before had supporters in front of whom to lap – they could have lapped the entire borough of Southgate and not met anyone they knew. But here in Northampton, 3,000 fans celebrated the clinching of their first appearance in a cup final. One genuinely began to feel that rugby might be getting somewhere.

The semi-final constituted a remarkable climax in itself. One might have imagined it to be the happy ending already. But our film still had another hour to run. At this point, I would have been in the cinema rubbing my hands in glee, anticipating a spectacularly tragic ending as our heroes fell from grace.

As the international players left to prepare for the following weekend's games in the Five Nations, the news came through that made the day complete and set up our film for a final scene of true Hollywood symmetry. Wasps had beaten Sale in the other semi-final. It was perfect. Saracens would be pitched against Wasps, their neighbours and oldest rivals, in the first all-London final. For years Saracens had lived in the shadow of their more illustrious north London cousins. Twickenham in May would be the perfect setting in which to step out, once and for all, into the sunlight.

Following the semi-final victory, there was a lifting of tension in the Saracen camp. It had not gone unnoticed that the vagaries of the shambolic and overcrowded domestic fixture list had required them to play two fixtures that would make or break their season in the space of four days. And all of that amid the fury of the Five Nations. Having lost the first to hand Newcastle a distinct advantage in the league, to lose the second would more or less have ended their season and required Lynagh and Sella to play out their last days on the rugby field in a string of meaningless formalities.

That was an intolerable scenario, hence the remarkable display of team spirit against Northampton that had pulled so many through in such trying circumstances, and hence the dissipation of the tension that had coiled up within the squad over the preceding weeks. As the realisation had begun to dawn that there was a genuine possibility of securing the double, so the sleep-disturbing fear had crept in that the season could yet end with nothing. Now, for the time being, they could rest assured that, if all else failed, they could look forward to the security of the final at Twickenham. It suddenly lent definition to all their efforts over the season and guaranteed Lynagh and Sella a fitting stage on which to bid farewell.

The league was still alive, however, and the subsequent victories against Bath and Newcastle further resuscitated it. Yet the signs of fatigue were beginning to set in and, having come so close in the league, the squad looked increasingly in danger of losing their direction after the Newcastle game as key personnel became distracted through injury and/or other issues. After the Newcastle game, Lynagh and Pienaar were not to play again until the final.

Lynagh's cancer scare removed him from competition and shook up the squad, not to mention the man himself. Pienaar had also had to withdraw with the hamstring injury that he had suffered against Newcastle, and he then left the country altogether after the news of the death of Kitch Christie, his coach, mentor and close friend in South Africa. Christie died on the Wednesday night following the Newcastle game, after a long 19-year battle against lymph cancer. In 1995, he had steered Pienaar's South African team to their famous World Cup triumph. Pienaar would describe him as a father figure and was devastated by the loss. He had spoken to Christie a few days before his death. 'I was rambling away about Saracens and the cup final to Kitch on the phone last week,' Pienaar told the press after Christie's death. 'I'm not sure he understood. But he listened and listened. Then he simply said, "Cappy, when we get to a final, we don't lose, do we?"'

Pienaar is a man who feels things very intensely. The images of the 1995 World Cup were writ large across his mind with the sweeping grandeur that makes such memories seem almost surreal. Christie's words now lent those images an added emotional spin and, in an already emotional time, heightened Pienaar's passion to do them justice at Twickenham and to honour Christie's memory. First, however, he flew out to Johannesburg straight after Saracens' next game at Leicester for Christie's funeral, where he was to give an address.

The Leicester game ended in a 10–10 draw. But if Saracens were unlucky not to win that game, they got away with murder in the next two league outings. A flu bug was now also beginning to work its way throughout the squad to stretch their endurance levels further. Victories were snatched from the jaws of defeat against Harlequins and London Irish.

The engine was spluttering, but sheer bloody-mindedness was keeping them in the hunt for the league. Pienaar, who had returned from South Africa only the previous day, watched the London Irish game from the stand and afterwards, in the time-honoured fashion, insisted that Wasps must now be the favourites at Twickenham.

That was not a difficult logic to follow. Wasps were coming into form at just the right time as the multitude of injuries that had reduced the defence of their league title to a near-disastrous flirt with relegation began to clear up. They had beaten Newcastle, Northampton and Leicester in recent weeks and clearly fancied the tonic of a cup triumph to ease the sores left from their abject league campaign.

Saracens, meanwhile, took themselves away from the hurly-burly of the league programme and cocooned themselves together as they prepared for the only game that really mattered to them now. Newcastle had dominated the league that season and Saracens could only win it if Newcastle lost it. Of the two trophies, the cup was the one they could win on their own terms. Again, the thrill of that prospect was mingled with the gut-wrenching fear of falling at the last.

Endless promotional stunts were negotiated by the players as the new world of commercial rugby exacted its pound of flesh. But these were enjoyable. The dominant theme was that of the Men in Black as the photogenic brigade of Bracken, Constable, Wallace (Richie, that is), Hill and Diprose donned their black suits and black shades for a photo shoot in front of a galactic backdrop, *à la* Will Smith and Tommy Lee Jones in *Men in Black*. Sky got in on the act too, engineering any number of moody set-pieces for the players to ham up. Press conferences and Tetley's Bitter promotions also had to be attended. Judge Tony Copsey took it upon himself to confiscate the bountiful quantities of Tetley's Bitter cans that were being bandied about by the cup sponsors, manfully protecting his more impressionable team-mates from the notorious thrall that beer can wield. Nothing was being left to chance. The handsome new Tetley's Bitter Cup was introduced to both teams in the Tuesday press conference, but that was where the fun stopped. Nobody in the Saracen squad dared touch it.

As the week wound on, Saracens set off for the country retreat that would host their final preparation for the big occasion. On the Thursday, they left for the Oatland Park Hotel in Weybridge, Surrey, but first stopped off at the studios of Disney Channel-UK in Kensington. Etienne de Villies, a friend of Pienaar from South Africa, was the president of the company and had entertained the team in the build-up to the Richmond game. This time he had a real treat in store for them. They were ushered into the private 50-seater cinema, where they were initially inspired by the aesthetic qualities of the actresses in Wild Thing. Then de Villies played a special short film that left the players transfixed.

His engineers had put together a five-minute show-reel that flashed a dazzling sequence of action clips from the season set to the spine-tingling majesty of a Carmina Burana-type soundtrack. In the state-of-the-art studio with its big screen and surround-sound facility, the effect was truly startling as the short film exploded to its shuddering climax. Every last hair on the back of each player's neck was charged to attention while the fury of the film's apogee crashed into the seething silence that greeted its end. For a few moments, nobody moved.

Suddenly, the silence was shattered and the whirring emotions further fanned as news from the outside world broke mercilessly into the players' cave. Mark Evans came in to announce that Brendon Daniel's father had just died in New Zealand and that Daniel would be flying home straight after the cup final to be with his family. Already paralysed by the stirring emotion that the film had incited, the players were rocked again by the news. Something had clearly been afoot during the showing of Wild Thing, when Daniel had been summoned from the studio, but the players had had no more than an inkling of any serious problem. With their humour already disorientated by the short film, this further development now set the room swirling.

Daniel was a popular member of the squad. He had arrived in

Saracens

www.saracens.com

Fan Focus Centre **01923 496200**

Kyran Bracken · Danny Grewcock · Rob Thirlby · Jeremy Thomson · Alan Penaud · Paddy Johns · Ryan Constable · Francois Pienaar · Paul Wallace · George Chuter · Roberto Grau · Gavin Johnson · Tony Diprose · Brendon Daniel · Roland Hill

ABOVE: bond of ages: Tony Diprose and Richard Hill
BELOW: the Trinity complete: François Pienaar joins Michael
Lynagh and Philippe Sella at the Trocadero (Action Images)

Two worlds collide: Bramley Road and professional rugby (Action Images)

It did happen: 20,000 watch Saracens (Action Images)

The man who made it
happen: Peter Deakin
(Action Images)

The management: Mark Evans, Mike Scott, Mike Smith,
Tim Wright and Bruce Millar at Twickenham (Formula 1)

Danny Grewcock scores the decisive try at Twickenham (Action Images)

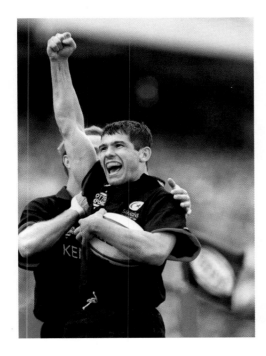

Steve Ravenscroft enjoys
life at new Saracens
(Action Images)

ABOVE: iron and velvet: Pienaar and Lynagh lift the cup
in front of a delighted James Wyness (Action Images)
BELOW: Michael Lynagh is paraded before the fans at Twickenham

Michael Lynagh and Philippe Sella take to the field for the last time . . .

. . . and take their final bow amid dazzling flashbulbs (Action Images)

Celebrating in the dressing-room (Formula 1)

Nigel Wray enjoys his other
passion (Action Images)

The wedding of Matt and
Allison Singer, May 1998

Tony Coker looks on as François Pienaar addresses the squad (Action Images)

Mark Evans holds court
(Action Images)

The Hands: Tony Diprose
(Action Images)

Festive cheer: Kris Chesney during Christmas training (Action Images)

Less cheerful: defeat against London Scottish (Action Images)

ABOVE AND BELOW: the agony and the ecstasy: Alain
Penaud disputes his sin-binning against Northampton before
celebrating victory in the same game with David Flatman (Action Images)

Va'aiga Tuigamala sends Saracens out of the cup (Action Images)

Tim Wright administers video treatment to Gavin Johnson (Action Images)

'Here come the Men in Black': the team run out at Vicarage Road
(Action Images)

Cashback ceremony: the half-time ritual of bestowing money
upon the community with Bracken and Grewcock (Action Images)

Brendon Daniel receives his Player of the
Year award at the end of a long season (Action Images)

The Fez Boys get in the mood for the visit of Tonga (Formula 1)

Kyran Bracken touches down (Action Images)

Matt Singer contributed a great
deal to the Saracens cause
(Action Images)

Gavin Johnson kicking his
way to another conversion
(Action Images)

England during the previous summer as a 19-year-old recently married to his wife Kylee, who was expecting their first baby. It was a frightening time for the young winger. He had never really left home, but when he found himself with a pregnant wife and outside the 125 players that were offered full-time professional contracts by the New Zealand Rugby Union he was in a critical position: unemployed, married and with a baby due very soon. A sevens specialist, he had been spotted by Saracens playing in the Middlesex Sevens at the end of the previous season. The move to the other side of the world constituted a massive upheaval for Daniel, however, and upon arrival in England he quickly gained a reputation as a loose cannon.

One can often learn a lot about players as people by watching them on the field. Daniel was a classic example. When he first arrived, he was a pure distillation of danger. On the field he was spectacular to watch. He would follow none of the rules, not because he wanted to defy them but because he simply could not assimilate them. Technically, he was limited, but the raw, energising talent that he boasted could not be ignored. He played with his heart on his sleeve, in much the same way as he lived. A self-taught guitarist off the field, on it he followed the wild and unorthodox tune that played in his head and defied the rest to keep up. Sometimes it wreaked havoc in the opposition defence, sometimes it threw his own team's pattern into disarray.

Two incidents defined his early period at Saracens, one on the field, the other off it. The first came in the league game against champions Wasps in October at Loftus Road. Wasps were looking in fine form at that stage, but the subsequent defeat to Saracens was to initiate the slipping away of their championship crown. Twenty minutes into the tight match, Daniel seized upon a loose ball on his own try-line and raced 95 yards, outstripping the Wasps cover. As he approached the try-line to score an already spectacular try, he decided to make it even more spectacular by diving for the line. Unfortunately, he chose the wrong line over which to dive. With perfect acrobatics, he launched himself over the five-metre line in what he imagined to be a moment of great triumph. In mid flight, he noticed, just out of reach ahead of him, another line, which he recognised to be the crucial one. While landing, he desperately attempted to remedy his misjudgement and the ball spilled from his grasp. Wasps gratefully accepted the resultant scrum.

Fortunately for Daniel, Saracens scored the only try of the match moments later through the more phlegmatic of the two wingers, Ryan

Constable. This time showing his more constructive side, Daniel was also heavily involved in the build-up. Afterwards, Pienaar was questioned by the press about Daniel's incredible miss in a game that had hung in the balance to the very end. 'He watches too much television,' was Pienaar's darkly dry response.

Pienaar and Evans both came down hard on Daniel during his early months, recognising him as an errant schoolboy who needed close attention. But the talent was also recognised and time was often taken in training to iron out the imperfections in his game. A more serious example of his wayward nature, however, was to strike a few weeks later.

After another victory at Northampton in November that further indicated Saracens' rising stock, the players held their Christmas party at Bramley Road, which was a fancy-dress affair. Daniel attended the party in a Hawaiian grass skirt. After the party, however, he drove himself home and wrote his company car off on the way. With only a provisional licence and over the limit, he was in serious trouble and was taken to spend the night in prison, still in his Pacific Island dress. With the subsequent court case and accompanying fine and ban, it was a desperately low time for Daniel. The management despaired of him and they let him know it.

Since the low of that dark period, Daniel had matured rapidly both on and off the field. Without diluting any of his wild, untameable adventure with ball in hand, his extraordinary athleticism gradually became informed by a steady improvement in his technique and defence. It was sometimes easy to forget how young he was.

Never was that new maturity better demonstrated than in the immediate aftermath of his father's death. In this he was helped by the imminent cup final, which enabled him to focus on something else. When the news broke, nobody knew what to say. Daniel's father had fought a battle against cancer and had seemed to have recovered from it well. His death was the result of a sudden stroke. Although he had been ill, it was unexpected. Brendan Reidy, who had quickly established himself as something of a father figure to the young New Zealander, immediately took Daniel away. They walked through Kensington together and had a prayer. The squad then left for Weybridge and Daniel and Reidy roomed together in the hotel.

Reidy, who had joined the club the previous season, had himself suffered a bitter blow earlier in the week. In scoring his match-winning try against Harlequins just over a week before, the Samoan international prop had torn his calf muscle. He failed his fitness test on Wednesday and was thus prevented from assuming his place on the bench. Pienaar nevertheless invited him to be with the squad during the entire affair and, finding the option of staying at home intolerable, Reidy gratefully accepted the less frustrating ordeal of travelling as a non-playing member of the party. His presence, however, proved invaluable, as he was able to concentrate on helping Daniel through his bereavement while the rest of the squad prepared for the big game.

Despite the mounting air of the peculiar that was gathering around the players, the squad retained a blissful sense of calm. The glorious sunshine secured its purchase on the south-east the day before the cup final and the players relaxed at their lavish hotel. The setting was idyllic as they stood and chatted on the balcony in their shirt sleeves after supper. Only Botterman's interventions at the card table did anything to jolt the players out of their easy composure.

On the day itself, however, the mood had become more charged. Nobody quite knew what to do. Lynagh, for example, that most seasoned of veterans who had stayed at the same hotel with the Australian squad when they won the World Cup at Twickenham in 1991, was desperately nervous. Taking his newspapers into the foyer, he tried to keep his mind occupied in the morning without betraying his deep-seated nerves to the others, who inevitably looked to him for a measure of guidance.

Faxes of support were circulated, including one from Sir Elton John, whose Watford football team had formed such a productive relationship with Saracens at Vicarage Road. Sir Elton was in Atlanta, but told them that his mother and step-father would be there supporting them, even though he could not.

The players, meanwhile, began to change into the designer suits that had been made for the occasion. Peter Deakin had recommended a friend of his called Jonny Hamburger as a good man to see about getting some suits made. The players had looked sideways at each other, none too convinced that they should place their credibility on the big day in the hands of a man called Mr Hamburger. Nevertheless, Bracken put his lucrative sideline in looking beautiful to good use by visiting Hamburger with the muscle of Diprose and Copsey and the lady's touch of his girlfriend Nina. They picked out some handsome materials and Mr Hamburger did the rest. The results were immaculate.

At the final team meeting, the short film from the Disney studio was played again. The emotions were now running high. Sella and

Ravenscroft were in tears as the players made their way to the coach. The hotel staff gathered to cheer them off and the coach wended its way through the leafy Surrey countryside to the spartan highway that led to Twickenham.

An audio tape of the players' requested tunes had been prepared for the journey. Brendon Daniel's favourite, 'Here Comes the Hot-Stepper', had been the first to be included and as the journey unwound so the pitch in the coach cranked up. When they reached south-west London and stood still in the traffic around the ground, the players looked out at the number of fans in the street wearing Saracen colours. For the old guard in particular, the sight of such a flourish of support stirred the emotions. There were a few more tears in the eyes as the coach pulled into the West Car Park and made its way through a corridor of cheering fans.

Having pulled in under the imperious gate that opens the way to the players' entrance in the West Stand, the new breed of Saracen stepped down from the bus to complete a remarkable two-year journey from Bramley Road and muddy kit to Twickenham and designer suit and shades. Once their bags had been transferred to the Twickenham changing-rooms, they trod the sweltering pitch in their elegant outfits, prompting many a gag from Wasps players enquiring after the where-abouts of the wedding. Players stood about in clusters eyeing the august scenery of the stadium. Lynagh and Sella, however, remained slightly detached, both deliberately pacing to and fro under the north goalposts locked in thought. The final scene was approaching.

Having retreated to the cool changing-room, the players prepared in earnest. Normally laid-back individuals were changed and charged uncharacteristically early. The likes of Diprose and Sturnham were itching to get into the fray. Once changed, however, photo shoots had to be negotiated on the field by both teams as the noise from the growing crowd in the stadium continued to build.

In the final formality before kick-off, Peter Brook, the president of the RFU, Chris Wright, the owner of Wasps, and Nigel Wray were intro-duced to the players one by one. It is never a comfortable moment for either party concerned. Wray felt acutely awkward marching along the line shaking hands with the players, while for them the proximity of the kick-off had stretched their patience to the limit. They wanted only one thing now.

Their wish was granted as the dignitaries retired to the royal box with the exception of Wray, who joined his family amid a Saracen contingent in the West Stand. The morning's agonising wait was now over. From now on, of course, time would flash by.

Almost immediately Lynagh and Sella took control. With magisterial aplomb, Lynagh sent one of the rolling kicks in which he specialises scudding into the north-west corner. Wasps could only clear the danger partially. After Grewcock claimed the ball at the resultant line-out, it was driven to the edge of the Wasps twenty-two. Lynagh sent a miss-pass to Gavin Johnson, who made a smart mini-break before feeding the ball inside to a rampaging Sella. With five minutes gone, the Frenchman charged and pirouetted through four tackles to register the afternoon's first try, which Lynagh converted.

Wasps struck back with a Gareth Rees penalty, before Lynagh replied immediately with a drop-goal. Within the first ten minutes, the two old-timers had neatly shared Saracens' first ten points. Ryan Constable quickly got in on the act five minutes later, showing a ludicrous turn of pace to round his man and score Saracens' second try. He got to his feet and mimed an extravagant baseball strike on his return from the try-line. Saracens were on their way.

Soon, however, the perfect script went awry. Lynagh directed another subtle kick towards Wasps' try-line, which Daniel chased with urgency. In so doing, he felt a tug in one of his hamstrings as the slight injury that he had picked up against London Irish the previous weekend informed him of its continued presence. Wasps, meanwhile, began to develop threatening momentum with the game now demanding that they take swift action. In view of the scoreline's fledgling status, Wasps were at their most threatening in the following period and the Saracen mood at its most anxious. That trend reached its peak on the half-hour, when a furious Wasps drive into Saracen territory whipped up the volume in the crowd and required the Saracen bench to burst into action.

Pienaar, who had himself passed a fitness test on his hamstring a couple of days earlier, was forced off to have a cut over his ear stitched and Mike Scott rushed down to pitchside to preside over the necessary activity as Alex Bennett filled Pienaar's position. Moments later, the script completed its cruel twist when Daniel finally resigned himself to the injury and came off the field to sympathetic hugs. Richie Wallace trotted out to replace him. Once the changes were complete, Rees kicked another penalty to bring the score to 15–6. Mark Evans shook his head. 'We've lost control of this,' he said with ominous gravity.

Control, however, was quickly re-established. Johnson burst through to score after Diprose had been worked into the Wasps midfield and then, two minutes before the interval, Danny Grewcock accepted a pass from his housemate, Kyran Bracken, to surge under the posts after a bullocking run from Ben Sturnham off the base of a scrum. That was 29–6. The stadium roared. There was a perceptible release of tension with that try. The other tries had been greeted with unsurprising enthusiasm, but there was an added edge to the celebration of the fourth. The air surrounding the Saracen coaching staff was punched with peculiar aggression. Grewcock, still on the ground, shook the ball over his head with both hands and then, having risen to his feet, flung it in the air and screamed. Pienaar approached his young charge and seized him by the scruff of the neck with both fists. Their faces inches apart, Pienaar fixed Grewcock with a furious smile. Grewcock looked back into Pienaar's eyes and screamed again. No one admitted it, of course, but, at 29–6, it was difficult not to feel the game was won.

In the changing-room at half-time, the players were more relaxed than usual. They were immediately told to remove their sweaty shirts and drink copious amounts of fluids, while Diprose, Evans and Pienaar, in their various ways, guarded the players against the obvious temptation to think the game was over. Diprose expounded the virtues of concentration in defence, and then, with what looked like the faintest of smiles on his face, he gave way to Evans, who was particularly animated in his address. 'Don't play the scoreboard!' he implored them, 'Do NOT play the scoreboard! Play the patterns, play the game, let's make this a magical day.'

Pienaar then took the floor to motivate the side in the way that only he can. This time his words were lent added credibility by the exposure of his ferocious physique. The changing-room was rapidly taking on the qualities of a sauna, but if anyone had thought they might wind down and relax in the humidity, Pienaar's glistening torso suggested they do otherwise. 'You will never get an opportunity to do this again!' he cried. 'The chance to take a team apart in a cup final – I'm telling you, it will never come again in your lives! I want 70,000 people to leave today as Saracens fans.'

An ambitious marketing campaign, indeed, but Saracens gave it a good shot. They were to score a total of seven tries in the match and equal Bath's cup-final record of 48 points. Perhaps not even Hollywood, however, could have countenanced a happy ending of 50 points against

Wasps, and referee Chris White blew his final whistle with Saracens still in the hunt.

Sella, who had just been substituted, held his arms out wide, as the PA system, in a noticeable break with Twickenham tradition, immediately burst into a rendition of 'Men in Black'. The Saracen players collapsed into a series of embraces. Sella, having shown off his extraordinary talent on the field just like in the old days, next demonstrated his extraordinary talent for partying. He bounced about joyously with his comparatively mature six-year-old son, insistently hugging his team-mates and leading them in countless renditions of his favourite French ditty, which goes, 'Laa, la, la, la, laa; laa, la, la, la, laa; laa, laa, la, laa; laa, laa, la, laa; laa, la, la, la, laa' (repeat to fade).

After a few minutes of bonding, Saracens climbed the steps to the royal box, where Tony Diprose was presented with the first piece of major silverware in Saracens' 122-year history. Former Saracen players from years back had by this time spilled on to the pitch and welcomed Diprose, Ravenscroft et al. when they descended from their lofty perch to parade the silverware on a triumphant lap of honour.

The euphoria was unbridled, with black shirts and red fez hats bouncing around the Twickenham auditorium. The relentless chant of 'Sarries, Sarries' echoed around the stadium as even the Sky Sports analysts became carried away. 'This amazing journey,' commentator Miles Harrison enthused, 'which began just over two years ago, from park pitch to Twickenham, is now complete. This long, hard season now has silverware for Saracens and the perfect ending for Sella and Lynagh – an amazing story.'

Stuart Barnes, the former England and Bath fly-half, picked up the baton: 'I remember those games at Saracens, just outside Cockfosters, where the dogs walk with their owners. You never felt this would happen so quickly. Wray had a vision. He's bought wisely: Lynagh, Sella, Pienaar. He's merged it with the likes of Diprose and Hill, Bracken's come in – what a team!'

The phrases 'four and a half million' and 'Nigel Wray' were never far away as the man himself watched with pride from his vantage point in the West Stand. Meanwhile, the Sky cameras panned throughout the cheering ranks of red and black into which Wray had melted anony-mously for the game's duration.

'They're developing into the community,' Dewi Morris, the former England scrum-half, observed. 'The Fez Boys have got it together. The marketing behind this whole thing is phenomenal. It's a good day out: there's music, there's no trouble. If this is professional rugby, it's the best thing that ever happened and it's the way forward.'

Things were getting dangerously close to the sickly sweet as images of Tom Cruise, whooping Americans and soaring soft-rock bands threatened to materialise. So the show continued down in the cramped Twickenham interview room, where Graham Simmons chatted with a stream of players. A somehow serene-looking Pienaar kicked off. 'It's been a fantastic day. The club has come on so much in a year and a half. There's been a terrific family atmosphere. It's great to see the guys win a trophy for once, guys like Stevie [he then put his arm around Ravenscroft, who was standing next to him] who have been at the club so long. To score a try as well – it's a terrific day for him.'

It was difficult to tell, with all the sweat from the heat, whether players were in tears or not, but Pienaar's cheeks looked particularly moist as he went on to dedicate the victory to Kitch Christie.

Ravenscroft, ecstatic at the unfamiliar feel of the triumphant spotlight, immediately deferred to the careers of Lynagh and Sella, before describing how great it was to see so many friends from the old days enjoying the occasion. Lynagh himself next described how nervous he had been and gratefully received the magnum of champagne that was his reward for being man of the match.

Then everything stopped for the Philippe Sella show. Little did Simmons know that his next interviewee would seriously test his time-keeping skills. 'How did that feel, Philippe?' he asked innocently.

Sella looked at him before replying deadpan, 'I feel very tired.' The room burst into laughter as Sella, with his imperfect English, then built up his momentum. 'But is great, is great, a great game for Saracens. At Twickenham, we saw today one great rugby. We tried to play the best rugby that we played all the year, but in one game. It's always very difficult, because we were a little bit tense, we tried to stay relaxed, but the emotion was inside and we tried to focus on the game. But after the kick-off, it was great. Is a fantastic day!'

Any second thoughts about retiring?

'I will retire after the next two games – we have one league game this week and afterwards I play in the Sanyo Cup. And after that Bermuda, the seniors tours [universal laughter again], so a lot of games, but differently!'

The camera went to move on to Ryan Constable, next in line, but, enjoying his English, Sella continued.

'But I will come here back to watch the Saracens games, because I spent two years – marvellous. Because the team spirit is a family spirit. [Simmons's microphone hand began to waver as the camera gave up and zoomed back in on Sella.] Saracens of London is a great team and have a great team spirit. Like the international-class rugby players, like the Saracens rugby players, Andy Lee, Steve Ravenscroft, Gregg Botterman. All of them were very kind with me when I arrived, because now is a little bit better, but when I arrived just I spoke with my fingers!'

The laughter rang out once more, before the camera finally moved on to Constable and then Gavin Johnson, but not before Simmons had asked Constable if they could ever get a word in edgeways with Mr Sella around. 'No,' replied Constable with a respectful smile, 'we just listen to what he has to say.'

Meanwhile, in the changing-room, Copsey had relented and brought out the cans of Tetley's for the players to enjoy. The thought remained at the back of the mind that there was a big game against Northampton on Thursday and a couple even casually mentioned the fact. But abstinence was never seriously entertained as a realistic policy for the evening. The thought was more or less erased altogether when Lynagh returned from the interview room and soaked the players with his magnum of champagne.

Thereafter the changing-room reverberated to choruses of Sella-led 'la's. Sella, like so many others, did take time out of the celebrations to tend to Daniel, who was inevitably more subdued than the others. As Sella began to undress for the showers, he removed the black armband that he, along with the rest of the squad, had been wearing to honour Daniel's father. He turned to Daniel and, holding the band in his hand before putting it in his kit bag, said, 'I will keep this.' Daniel, sitting on the bench leaning back against the wall, nodded gratefully.

Nigel Wray soon entered the steaming changing-room and expressed his affection for them all as people as well as players. Pienaar, on behalf of the squad, replied in kind, telling Wray that it was his cup. All that remained was to ensure that those constituted the last memories of the day. There was never any danger of that particular tradition being neglected. After a brief meal at the Rose Room, the squad left for Watford, stopping off in Richmond for another few crates of beer.

One more stop had to be negotiated, however, and that was at Heathrow. Brendon Daniel bade farewell to his team-mates as the coach dropped him off at the airport for his flight home to New Zealand. The celebrations stopped dead in their tracks. Daniel said goodbye to each person individually, then collected his bag and suitcase from the hold, slung one over his shoulder, held the other in his hand and walked off into the terminal.

Until then his bereavement had not had an opportunity to sink in. The strange dream world of the previous three days had buffered him against the iniquities outside it. But now, settling down for the 24-hour plane journey that awaited, he sat alone. The long journey was eased by the provision of Jack Daniels, but when he reached New Zealand and was met by Kylee (who had returned a month before) and his brother, the process of mourning began.

The players had also found the farewell difficult, especially as Daniel with his guitar was their chief song leader. Nevertheless, the momentum of celebration quickly picked up again. Once the team was back at Watford, one of the gates at Vicarage Road was scaled to gain speedier access to the bar, which was already populated with numerous fez hats flying joyously through the air at the team's arrival. Thereafter, the party moved on to Eros, where bar stools and memory blanks awaited. World Cup-winning captain drank with part-time squad member until the management at Eros decided to call it a day at some as yet unidentified hour of the morning.

Unable to get enough of each other's company, the entire squad and their families then gathered the next day for a barbecue at Bramley Road, returning to the humble shed where the story had begun. The cup stood on a table in the middle of the party. Glinting proudly in the spring sunshine, it constituted a glamorous emblem with which the old ground was most unfamiliar. Meanwhile, a Sunday afternoon cricket match was being played on the adjacent park. Kids were giving their parents the runaround. Paddy Johns' delightfully cheeky son Christopher entertained all and sundry. Johns had recently been announced as captain of the Ireland team for their forthcoming tour of South Africa.

'Christopher, Christopher, who's the captain of Ireland?' the questioning would go.

'My daddy!' the reply would be yelled as he demonstrated his own flair for tackling against any number of colossal thighs.

It was a scene that both exposed rugby's relative poverty as an industry and illustrated its enduring appeal. One could never have imagined the Arsenal team that won football's equivalent trophy the following weekend enjoying a similar gathering at nearby London

Colney, where they trained. And not just because the clamour of press and public would render it unfeasible. There were names as big in rugby as any in the world relaxing with their families in the security-free charm of Bramley Road that beautiful spring afternoon. Nobody batted an eyelid. It may be that rugby fans are more respectful than football fans. It may be that nobody knew about the party. It may be that rugby players, albeit now famous and professional, still enjoy the honest pleasures of each other's company. Yet the realist insists that it is because rugby was still small-time. In order to survive, rugby would have to become genuinely big-time, and one feared it was to be at the price of its simple soul.

Hollywood might not have included that cosy scene in its movie, but even Tom Cruise probably went home to see his mother some time after he had enjoyed the fruits of his bar stool. Rather, the movie moguls might have ended with the scenes at Twickenham or those the following weekend when Saracens paraded the cup on an open-top bus tour of Watford. Yet even that PR exercise had to be conducted in the wake of their Vicarage Road co-tenants. Watford Town FC were showing off their spoils from winning the Nationwide second division and the Saracen bus followed behind, the players waving at the 15,000-odd Watford fans (and the 2,000-odd Saracen fans) who lined the streets and warmly extended their applause to rugby's cup-winners. Donning their film-star suits and shades again, in more divine weather, the Saracen players thrilled at this further departure from rugby's conservative norms. It nevertheless underlined the fact that Watford was still a football town and England still overwhelmingly a football country. A few miles across north London, meanwhile, Arsenal paraded the FA Cup and the Premiership trophy in front of 100,000 ticker-tape-hurling fanatics.

Yet, if it had been the symmetry and romance of the story that Hollywood was after, they could not have improved upon the tale of Saracens that culminated in those glorious few days in May 1998. The dream of a small-town club had grown into a flag-waving reality that touched the lives of thousands. Rugby was changing and Saracens were in the vanguard. The challenge for Saracens, as for rugby, would be to maintain it.

8

Wray

When I was a boy, I had a mild obsession. Who was the richest man in the world? How much did he own? What was it like to be so rich? Was it at all feasible that I might fill the role if no one else wanted it?

My parents could not answer all of the above questions. Nevertheless, they would sit me down and tell me stories of oil and gold and mysterious men in the Middle East. The Sultan of Brunei was it, they said. And he grew to become a figure of mythical power and mystique in my psyche.

It seems quite ludicrous that, if Angus Stewart and Mike Smith had had their outrageous way, a little patch of parkland in north London, and the collection of 'athletes' that gambolled thereon, might have benefited from the power of this fiscal Titan. I might even have met him by now. I might have discussed with him the future of London Scottish or the merits of a British league. Ludicrous.

The Sultan must remain to me, I fear for ever, a figure of impossible allure and inaccessibility. The screen of wealth is one from which I do not expect him to emerge. But he and his buddies behind that veil in the multi-millionaire club still, I regret, wield a certain thrall. It is with a degree of wonder, therefore, that I annually flick through the pages of the 'richest' list in *The Sunday Times*, gawping at the accounts of unimaginable wealth recorded therein. Those pages constitute a dreamy warp into which I sink for a couple of hours.

It never ceases to amaze me to see the name Nigel Wray in the records. I have met Wray. He is a delightful man to stumble across in a bar. He is charming and courteous in a refined sort of way, and generally has a word for everyone. He is very familiar and approachable. Yet there he is, on £100 million, rubbing shoulders with David Bowie (now he really was an iconic figure in my formative years). Ludicrous.

Wray's very presence in those pages, however, and his willingness and ability to have invested, at the time of writing, £5.5 million in the Saracen venture more than hint at the extraordinary. It is, indeed, difficult to equate the multi-millionaire property magnate with the affable gentleman who smiles his way around Vicarage Road on match-days and anonymously melts into the Twickenham euphoria on cup-final day. The real triumph of Sky television's coverage of the Tetley's Bitter Cup final was to locate Nigel Wray amid a sea of fans and home in on him rejoicing with them after Kyran Bracken's try. It was a still greater triumph on the part of the commentators then to convince us that this was in fact the cold-eyed businessman whose money had facilitated the imperious display that we were witnessing. Wray likes to be one of the people, and his mother, wife, daughter and son are never far from his side. He is adamant that Vicarage Road and Saracens should be an experience for the family and, with some success, he leads from the front. None of this, though, sits easily with the one-dimensional stereo-type of the ruthless tycoon.

The possession of charm, however, and the accumulation of wealth are not mutually exclusive. And neither, of course, should love for the family and affinity with the community be deemed beyond the compass of a successful man. Nevertheless, one does not build a multi-million-pound empire without a certain cutting edge and ruthless driving energy.

It is more or less impossible to find anyone at Saracens who does not speak highly of Wray – and with good reason, a cynic might argue. It would, however, be excessively cynical to attribute his popularity solely to the payment of lucrative wages to his staff. To a man, as far as I can tell, the players have a genuinely warm affection for him. Even when I have spoken to players after their Saracen adventure had gone belly-up or their enthusiasm for the place had drained away, the respect and admiration for Wray as a person seems to remain as strong as ever. Those on the next level up in the business structure at Saracens, who have more than just social contact with the man, will also pay handsome tribute to him. On one thing everyone at Saracens is agreed: of all the tycoons that swept into rugby when the game turned professional, they got the best one.

It is also possible to garner from some of those who have had more than just social contact with him an impression of deeper, more turbulent waters within. A great man, they will say, but he is not as he seems. One can, if one looks hard enough, detect the slightest hint of combustibility beneath the effortless charisma that cascades from his person. Wray has a tall, thin figure that, one feels, may have been shaped by a life of high and fraught energies. He has stubby fingernails, at odds with long, slender fingers, that may have been shaped by a life of anxious chewing. And his eyes are set deep within a fiercely eyebrowed pair of sockets. One lid droops a little lower than the other to produce a slightly disorientating effect. In everyday interaction, the quality of his eyes passes unnoticed because of the warmth and charm that he conveys. But when frozen in a photograph, the eyes can be unnerving. One senses that, despite the easygoing public-school charisma, Wray is not a man to cross.

Worry, I suspect, has been the chief architect of his life. He has even admitted as much to me in his mellifluous Received Pronunciation accent. His speech is eloquence and smoothness personified, but the subject matter races by at breakneck speed, spurred on by a roaring train of thought. Keeping him to the subject in hand is like trying to contain a rhinoceros with an olive branch. Yet it is worry and a racing mind that have kept him ahead of the pack.

'I am one of life's natural worriers,' he confesses. 'Every now and then, you wake up in a cold sweat at night, even if you think you've calculated every single thing that can conceivably go wrong and make you bankrupt by the end of the year. And anyone who is involved in business to a reasonable level will empathise with this. I can construct scenarios under which the whole economic world, or certainly my little economic world, collapses. To take a simple one, suppose the government introduces the confiscation of property. I mean, I'm taking an absurd situation, but nobody should be so arrogant that they think they've got it taped.

'Worrying is part of the ability to survive. You've got to be able to worry about what could happen. If you think, "Nothing can happen, I've got nothing to worry about, I'm brilliant," well, then it's only a matter of time.'

There is a nice story about Wray's worrying and the way to handle it. Mike Smith, in the early stages of his role as chief executive, was beginning to be bothered by phone calls from him at anti-social hours. Nick Leslau, a long-standing partner of Wray, is said to have given Smith some advice. He, too, used to get phone calls from a concerned Wray at unorthodox hours. One time, Leslau rang him back at 2 a.m. 'Nigel,' he chirped, 'I've been thinking about what you said when you rang at 11 o'clock. I've got a few ideas. Have you got a minute?'

After that, Wray is supposed never to have rung Leslau at an unreasonable hour again.

Wray is described in the richest list as Britain's answer to Warren Buffett, the American investment genius. Investing is what has made Wray's fortune. The subtitle in the annual report of Burford, his property company, reads, 'Anticipating future demand, spotting hidden opportunities and creatively exploiting new angles when the time is right.' With net assets approaching the £500 million mark, they seem as good as their word.

Another cynic might guffaw, then, in the light of Wray's involvement with Saracens, that he seems to be losing his touch: a projected £9.5 million invested by 2002 (in February 1999 he was to estimate a further £5 million investment required in the following three years) and an operating loss of roughly £5 million to date. On the surface, it is not good business in anyone's language. But this is where the human touch, rather than the businessman's audit, comes into play. Wray simply loves his rugby. And he loves his sport. When one has climbed through several floors of functional offices at his headquarters in the West End, one finally comes out into an elegant shrine to sport. This is his lair. Amid the impressive array of cricket paintings in the foyer, his secretary remarks with affection, 'It's sport everywhere you turn up here.'

A door deeper, his lair opens up into a spacious sitting-room-cum-study that is festooned with more paintings and sporting memorabilia. There is a handsome oak (I think) sculpture of two rugby players in action and a painting of an England line-out against Ireland *circa* 1995, but the overwhelming majority of paintings are of cricket. ('It's not that I prefer cricket, but cricket is more conducive to art.') He does, however, draw attention to a painting of an early rugby scene from the nineteenth century, still featuring a round ball, before proudly professing that he has an older one at home.

One of the reasons his employees at Saracens seem to trust him is that Wray is a rugby man through and through. He played for the Old Millhillians and for Hampshire as a centre in the '70s. In those days, Old Millhillians played Saracens every year, so Wray knows well the homely tradition from which the club derives. There is no question that his involvement with Saracens is a labour of love. It is also a crusade to make the new age of professional rugby viable. He has no illusions of rugby as a corporate monster in the future, but he believes passionately that it can be self-sustaining. He knows, however, it will be at some cost.

'Sport is very, very expensive. People say "all rugby clubs are losing money", well, so are all football clubs. Manchester United are fine, Aston Villa, maybe Arsenal and Leeds, but then you're scratching around. Virtually every football club in the land is losing money and they survive by transferring players. Football is not a solvent industry by and large.

'That is one of the conundrums in sport, which is why, with rugby, you must invest in the brand. There are only going to be a few at the top that are economically viable. You must invest in the brand for the long term.

'There's a constant battle at Saracens between keeping costs down in the short term and investing in the brand. Oddly enough, I don't think the same applies to other clubs because I don't think they've got the same brand potential. The Saracens brand has enormous potential, but we've got to pay the bills today in order to get there. We could cut our losses down enormously if we didn't bother to invest in the brand, if we didn't have community officers, if we chopped the marketing budget. But we wouldn't be building anything. And I think a lot of clubs aren't building anything.

'The value of what we're doing will come through in the brand, not in the profit-and-loss account. At the end of the day, the venture has to stand on its own two feet. If people quite plainly aren't interested, then it becomes a thing of self-indulgence on my part. But I think Saracens means a lot to a lot of people. But it's not enough; we need 20,000 to every game. Then that encourages sponsors and maybe it even begins to generate some cash which can be reinvested. This is never going to be a business that gives you a huge cheque every year.'

Wray clearly has a keen eye for investment potential. He notices things like the fashion of club colours. Standing elegantly in the Vicarage Road tunnel, a black Saracen scarf around his neck with its shades of red tastefully woven into it, he muses that one can in fact wear Saracen colours in everyday life without making a brash statement. Leicester were the visitors that day.

He is also excited by the neutral name. 'Saracens' owes no allegiance to any locale. Anyone can identify with the name, which itself conjures appropriate images of glamorous mystique and adventure. And the Vicarage Road stadium at which they finally arrived is perfectly situated in a constituency of great potential. In the corner of the M25 that opens up to the rest of the country, it is minutes from the M1, a few miles from the M4, within easy reach of London and convenient for fans in any of the Home Counties. There are many local rugby clubs but no major rugby team in the area, and playing on a Sunday taps into the energies of the local Saturday-afternoon rugby player.

But Wray's certainty in Saracens' potential has grown largely from the enormous strides made in the 1997–98 season. It has not always been so focused. In the second half of 1997, with money seeping out of the organisation and the Deakin revolution in attendances not yet wrought, Wray looked about him to share some of the cost. He suggested to Ashley Levett, his counterpart at Richmond, that Richmond and Saracens merge. Levett was also losing a fortune. Richmond had a high-profile, and correspondingly expensive, squad and shared the modest Athletic Ground with London Scottish. The Athletic Ground, stymied by the council's intransigence over development, would clearly never generate the relevant funds to finance the organisation. To the despair of Mike Smith, the merger became ever more likely. Amalgamated squads were drawn up on the back of envelopes, laying off players from both camps. Despite intense lobbying to the contrary from Smith, and then James Wyness, the merger would have happened. That it did not was due to Levett's dislike of Vicarage Road. Saracens would not be moving and Richmond would have to come to Watford. In view of Richmond's subsequent move to Reading and their collapse into administration after Levett's withdrawal, perhaps Levett now regrets his decision. There is little remorse, however, in the Saracen camp. The vexed issue of the fusion of the brands was close to their hearts: what would the new club be called? Would the Saracen brand be compromised?

The issue rose again in the build-up to Christmas 1997, when Wray next courted Frank Warren and Bedford. Saracens thought the new team would be called 'Saracens Blues' or 'Saracens Bedford'; Warren fancied 'Bedford Saracens'. Warren also fancied the deal. He was due to begin a long, financially damaging court case with fellow boxing promoter Don King and was manifestly keen to share his financial burden at Bedford. By then, however, the crowds at Vicarage Road had started to pick up and Wray had grown excited about the future of a pure Saracens. His enthusiasm for the merger drifted away.

Wray's role in the Saracen venture has become increasingly hands-on. The gesture of extending 51 per cent of the veto to the club members when he first arrived has since been replaced by a voting power that reflects his level of investment. There is now, however, substantial financial input from elsewhere in the club with a rights issue to the public over the summer of 1998 that raised £1.2 million. Over the previous winter, Saracens also converted from a public limited company to a private limited company (i.e. from Saracens plc to Saracens Ltd), which I understand (not very well) is more appropriate for a company whose assets are regularly outstripped by their liabilities.

Wray has since effectively become Saracens' chief executive. He was to part company with Mike Smith in September 1998. 'Mike was the person who, in many ways, did more for the club in the changeover to professionalism than anyone else. He loved the Saracens. They meant a lot to him.'

Was he businesslike enough?

'Well, I suppose the answer is he's not chief executive now. He was terrific for Saracens in the early days, but I think his job was becoming increasingly redundant: Mark Evans was director of rugby; Peter Deakin had taken over the marketing and commercial side and given us a direction and philosophy which no rugby club had ever had, including us. We now know what we're trying to do for years ahead, hopefully.

'Mike went off to pursue other interests and I think he made the right decision. Hopefully he'll be very happy with the settlement.'

Wray has become Saracens' representative on the English First Division Rugby board (the umbrella organisation of the country's top clubs), a job that Smith had filled with some controversy. It is a position that, along with the rest of his business with Saracens, has grown to occupy more of his time than anything else. The damaging squabbling that has characterised so much of EFDR's dealings with the RFU, the European Rugby Cup, other unions and even each other is something of which Wray despairs. It is impossible to build the brand of Saracens when the industry of rugby within which it is set is being compromised, and possibly even shrunk, by the adverse publicity of in-fighting. Wray will get more than a little earnest on this subject, yet one can rest assured that he is fighting with the best of them to preserve the interests of Saracens.

When one has invested several million pounds in a concern, it would be reasonable to feel quite intensely interested in its operation. One of the great imponderables is Wray's hands-on control of the day-to-day running of the club. To what extent are playing and recruitment issues shaped by his input? Wray, Pienaar and Evans would meet once a fortnight at Wray's offices. Wray plays down his involvement in such matters, probably with some honesty, yet one suspects his influence inadvertently wields devastating force.

'I don't know that I have the qualifications to interfere, nonetheless I do have some qualifications. But I think, by and large, you have to leave it up to the relevant people. In any business there's no point in having a chief executive and then trying to run it for him, and likewise if you've got a coach then playing matters are up to him. I am told what the team is, not the other way round. I might speak every now and then to some of the players, but all I'm going to say is, "Look, you've got a wonderful chance here, I think you can be a better player." I hope I will always be positive. But ultimately I think François Pienaar is better at doing it than I am.

'On recruitment, I want François and Mark to tell me who they want. But I'm a great believer that you need some high-profile players, because they market the club and lift the brand. So I am regularly coming up with ideas for players from a marketing perspective. "What about so-and-so?" I ask. "Well, he's been retired for about four years" is usually the answer.

'But, if there are any major decisions going on, I do want to know beforehand, obviously. It would just be staggeringly discourteous if they didn't tell me that they were going to drop X, Y or Z, or wanted to bring in so-and-so.'

When an institution relies as overwhelmingly on one man as Saracens do on Wray, such smooth organisation of responsibilities can inevitably become blurred when things go wrong. The big man will wonder where his money is going and, more importantly perhaps, the men working for him, if they are as honourable as Pienaar and Evans, for example, will worry that they are not repaying the faith (and money) that has been invested in them. This can lead to a corruption of behaviour. When playing matters started to go awry in the following season and Pienaar's jaw tightened ever more severely, the playing and coaching staff sensed he might be feeling considerable pressure from Wray. And that, in turn, rubbed off on the players.

Sport is, of course, a cruel mistress and it is always tempting to wonder why men with so much money should wish to risk so much of it in an industry that yields so little in the way of tangible return bar the odd trophy. The love, of the sport, the team, the community or all three, has to be passionate and all-consuming.

People liken the ownership of a sports team to the ownership of a train set. It tends to be both a derogatory put-down and a bitter criticism of men like Wray who buy, and then set about building, their own special rugby club. The analogy is a valid one, as there are undeniable parallels, but it is unfairly invoked as a malign comparison. People who collect train sets love them intensely and they look after them with meticulous care, insistent that they be the best. There is no doubt that the kudos involved in owning a rugby club is substantial and, assuming Wray is human, it must have been an enormous mitigating factor in his decision to invest in Saracens. Wray is a huge fan of rugby and openly confesses to feeling unalloyed boyish excitement when heroes like Michael Lynagh and François Pienaar come to play for him. The venture has turned him into a national figure, and to have the likes of Lynagh and Pienaar whirring around your train set would captivate the imaginations of most people. Yet, once the initial thrill of possession has passed, the more mature business of the train set's maintenance becomes the priority. This is when the owner shows his true colours. Wray's relationship with Lynagh and Pienaar has now matured into that of close friends. Saracens have now grown to consume the energy of a man who is said to be worth £100 million. This is not the idle fantasy of a fickle egotist.

One danger of the train-set phenomenon is that the owner indiscriminately collects all his favourite pieces. This is a very real problem, but such mistakes as there are on this front are honest ones. Wray's track record here is ambiguous. One can only garner hints as to the extent of his interference. But he had, for example, always been adamant that Pienaar captain his side, and he had always been a great admirer of Paul Turner, the Welsh maestro. It is conceivable, as well as debatable, that both these fascinations served to compromise Saracens' campaign in the following season.

Another unfavourable interpretation of the train-set phenomenon is that train sets are inconsequential things of whimsy. Wray's train set, however, has provided thousands with an unforgettable day out at Twickenham and every day brings joy and excitement to yet more thousands within a hundred-mile radius of Watford.

It is small-minded to begrudge Wray his train set and misguided to consider his possession of it a thing of self-indulgence. The argument is whether rugby should have admitted train-set owners in the first place. Most are agreed now that it was inevitable and necessary. There are too many train sets in rugby, and some train-set owners, if they have not done so already, will no doubt consign their sets to the skip in the coming years. But, should it ever come down to it, Wray would probably be one of the last.

9

Fuming

Matt Singer's first season as a full-time professional rugby player was, like those of his colleagues, pretty eventful. Not only was he to enjoy the status of cup winner at Twickenham and share in the glory of Saracens' lofty position in the league, but he was to flirt with international honours and become engaged to and then marry his long-term girlfriend Allison. Yet the trappings of nuptial bliss and cup glory notwithstanding, the 1997–98 season proved a less-than-smooth initiation for Singer into the brave new world of professional rugby.

Having frantically completed his teacher-training course at Cambridge University, he quickly launched himself into the arduous pre-season programme now required by Saracens' new hyper-professional Pienaar-constructed regime. Gathering in July 1997, the streamlined squad, nearly all full-time professionals, were put through the most horrendous two-week fitness schedule in which they did not set eyes on a ball. The squad consisted of players from all over the world and all were agreed that they had never worked so hard, or run so far, in their lives. Pienaar was intent on putting down an early marker. Under the jolly, but sadistic, supervision of Mike Yates, the programme was actually designed to foster togetherness in the squad as well as fitness. The idea was that players would have to pull together in order to survive such unremitting purgatory.

The training crashed on into August and two warm-up games, the first at Bedford and the second a christening of Vicarage Road against Wasps. On a sunny afternoon, Saracens entertained the reigning champions and the newly proactive marketing department threw open the doors to the public, who were invited to the pre-season friendly for free. Only 3,500 of them turned up.

Wasps won and Singer played full-back, his favoured position. But his confidence was low. He was the first-choice full-back but he had not played in the position regularly since his near-disastrous first Varsity match, and rumours were rife that a big signing was on the way. Singer was haunted by the uncomfortable feeling that he was merely keeping the seat warm.

Mark Evans, however, pulled him aside and gave him a thorough confidence chat, pointing to the fact that Singer was fitter now than he had ever been and that the position was his. The desired effect was achieved. The opening game of the season saw Saracens return to the scene of the previous season's nadir at Sale. This time, however, Saracens triumphed with relative ease and Singer dominated the game from the back, winning the man-of-the-match award.

He was deprived of the opportunity to build on his burgeoning confidence the following weekend when Saracens' scheduled game against Richmond was postponed because of the death of Diana, Princess of Wales. And his confidence was to take a severe knock later that week.

The marketing department had just alighted upon the idea of playing the song 'Men in Black' when the team ran out on to the pitch at Vicarage Road. In order to develop the idea, they circulated a list of the players' names throughout the squad and asked them each to write beside their name a signature tune that could be played whenever they scored. Singer cast his eye down the list in amusement. 'Deeply Dippy' had been written by Tony Diprose's name, 'Pineapple Head' by that of Brendan Reidy, the ponytailed Samoan. Suddenly his eye alighted on a new name in the list: Gavin Johnson.

His heart sank. It was not the ideal way to discover the news of Johnson's imminent arrival. Johnson was a points-scoring machine from South Africa. He held the South African record for the most points scored in a Test match. He had sat on the bench for the Springboks in the World Cup final in 1995 and had won countless honours as full-back for Pienaar's Transvaal outfit. He would not be coming over to play second fiddle.

Singer continued to play full-back in a largely successful campaign in the European Conference that incorporated just one defeat, in France to Castres. A few days later, in early October, Johnson arrived in England. Singer had always tried to foster good relationships with his immediate rivals over the years and it proved extremely easy to get on with Johnson. The tall, slender South African had the driest sense of humour, the wickedest grin and an affinity for life with the boys. Singer and Johnson immediately hit it off.

Johnson made his debut as a substitute in the rearranged game against Richmond and Singer, who had started the game at full-back, moved to the wing. From there, however, Singer, having played with composure at full-back, upped his game a gear and on one particular occasion ripped the Richmond defence apart with a scything run from deep in his own half. The watching Wales coach, Kevin Bowring, was impressed.

Johnson, supremely disorientated by the cold and heavy conditions in England, was soon to pick up an injury to his hamstring, earning Singer a stay of execution at full-back. After a victory against Wasps at Loftus Road, Singer then received a call from the Welsh selectors inviting him to train with the Welsh squad for the forthcoming fixtures against Tonga and New Zealand.

Singer was naturally delighted with the recognition. With cries from his Saracen team-mates of 'posh Taff' and 'Dai' ringing in his ears, he packed his kit bag and set off down the M4 for a midweek training session in Wales. Upon arrival, he immediately felt at home, catching up with several acquaintances from his days at Neath. He was, however, required to pose in a Welsh shirt for the pen-portrait photographs, something that made him feel mildly uncomfortable.

It is said that we never shrug off the formative effects of our upbringing and much of Singer's had constituted the perennial reaffirmation of his Englishness during his early life in Wales. The banter had always run high as he crossed swords with his Welsh schoolmates in the playground. Pulling on the Welsh shirt suddenly felt strange. He had the relevant qualifications. His grandfather was Welsh and his parents still lived in the same house near Porthcawl to which they had moved when he was two years old. Moreover, he had played for Neath for three years. Yet, in the context of his English identity, many of these qualifications seemed only to heighten his misgivings.

The issue came to a head in the first week of November when Singer was selected on the wing for Wales A for the midweek fixture against the All Blacks at Sardis Road. It was time for a decision.

Looking around at the time, the chances of playing full-back for England seemed as great as those of playing for Wales. Full-back was still one of England's problem positions, while the Welsh had a few quicksilver youngsters coming through. Equally, Wales were not picking from full strength; he may just have been a stopgap. Once he had played for Wales A, he would be excluding himself from the reckoning with

England for the foreseeable future. If he were to do so and the appearance turned out to be a one-off, he would have ruined what chances he had with England.

His profile, however, would improve with an A-team cap, although Singer felt that would be a mercenary motive. Although he was a fully paid professional now, he could not yet see rugby in terms of a career ladder. Rugby was still an emotive adventure and he had always wanted to play for England. He was also playing in England. Had the call come when he was at Neath, he might have felt more comfortable with Wales, but, at the moment, he felt entirely English.

Nevertheless, the A-team cap would look good on his CV and, although there was no provision for it in his contract, he knew that players with equivalent international honours commanded basic salaries up to twice his current earnings. He would be in a stronger bargaining position with a Wales A cap. He also knew that breaking into an international squad was the hard part. Staying in was a lot easier. Even if one were filling a gap, one tended to be retained in international squads for the short term. Unless he had a complete disaster (not inconceivable against the likes of Jonah Lomu, the prospective opposition), he would probably remain in contention for the immediate future.

Singer sought advice from many quarters. Several of his team-mates at Saracens felt that he must surely be in the running soon with England A and advised him to stick with the mother country, as did most of his other sources of advice. Yet, much to his frustration, the Saracen management had nothing to say on the matter. They clearly did not think he would make an England player and they were clearly not furthering his cause with the England management. More importantly, perhaps, there was no word from the England management themselves.

Singer was extremely close to agreeing, but he eventually rang Kevin Bowring and had a long chat with him in which he declined the offer. Bowring was understanding and, with less than a week to go, was forced to rejig the Wales A team. Singer's mind, meanwhile, was turning to yet more important issues.

He had by now moved with Allison into a smart semi-detached house in Shenley, near Watford. They had been together for five years, since falling into one of those inimitable drunken snogs in which it is traditional to indulge in your first few weeks at university. Few, however, have such lengthy sentences attached to them. Nevertheless, having watched the flighty and immature dalliances of so many of their fickle friends, here they were, five years later, still together, both in employment, both living in the same house and both paying the same mortgage. I need not elucidate, I am sure, upon the next logical step in the progression.

The pair had discussed the issue of marriage and Singer decided that the talking had to stop. Saracens won their final league game before the November break in Northampton, further establishing their position at the top of the league. The following Tuesday, the squad celebrated the wedding of Brendan Reidy to his girlfriend Paula, while the Wales A team lost by 50 points to the All Blacks. Now with a two-week break for the pre-Christmas England internationals, and suitably inspired by Mr and Mrs Reidy, Singer prepared for a weekend away with Allison in Oxfordshire.

Proposing to a girl requires the purchase of a ring, but, not professing to be an expert in that department, Singer took the opportunity to exercise his formidable sense of humour. Allison worked in personnel for Argos and had often joked about the tacky Elizabeth Duke range peddled by the store. Singer duly obliged by investing twenty pounds in an example of said range. Then, on the evening of Friday, 14 November, armed with his jewellery, he drove the unknowing Allison up to the country manor hotel that was to host their weekend away.

Up in their hotel room, Singer was extremely nervous. Blissfully unaware of this, Allison was taking an age watching television and doing her hair before they went down for drinks before dinner. Singer, however, was mentally rehearsing his imminent proposal and, before he knew it, he found himself standing inside one of the walk-in wardrobes, gently banging his head against the wall in subconscious anxiety. Allison came out of the bathroom at that point.

'What's the matter, Matt?' was her understandable reaction to the sight of her boyfriend headbutting the inside of the wardrobe.

Singer was seized by an uncharacteristic bout of decision. He snapped out of his head-rocking seizure and took Allison by the hand. Sitting her down on the four-poster bed, he got down on his knee, whipped out the Elizabeth Duke and asked her to marry him.

He had not really considered the possibility of her saying no. Fortunately, that did not become an issue. Now it was Allison who looked like she needed something against which to bang her head. Finding nothing to hand, however, her subsequent reply consigned her to a future that would doubtless know that feeling again.

The couple went downstairs for dinner. Singer had to eat most of Allison's share of food that night, but no such assistance was required when it came to her share of champagne and wine. The following day, they journeyed into Oxford to buy a proper engagement ring. It was just as well that Singer had not tried to do that on his own. He would have been several hundred pounds short. On the Sunday, they travelled down to Gloucestershire to tell Allison's parents the news, before returning to Shenley that night.

With another week's break, life was good for Singer. He was engaged to be married, he was playing well and he had been courted at an international level. The episode with Wales and his decision to stay with England had received significant publicity and Singer was confident that, if he continued in his current form, recognition from England would soon follow. At the end of November, he played full-back in a dazzling 80-point hiding administered by a heavily depleted Saracen team over the touring Tongans. It was to be seen as Saracens' best performance of the season.

Yet there were blots on Singer's horizon which were drawing ever closer. The precociously talented 19-year-old David Thompson had come on as a replacement full-back in the home game against Gloucester at the end of October and turned the game with his brilliance. Saracens had high hopes for Thompson, clearly more than they had for Singer, and he was given a couple of starts in November, forcing Singer on to the wing. The youngster was not to play so well in either and he had poor games in two further starts in January, but Saracens were eyeing him for the future, although his following year and a half was to be plagued by injury.

Meanwhile, Johnson was coming back into full fitness and Singer knew full well that Saracens were not paying the South African his substantial salary just to sit on the bench. And Pienaar had not gone to great lengths to persuade his old friend from Transvaal to move to England to act as back-up for an uncapped utility player in his first season of professional rugby. The inevitable came to pass in a squad meeting in the second week of December, in which Johnson was read out as full-back for the forthcoming game against Bath at Vicarage Road. With Richie Wallace also returning on the wing, it was the first league game that Singer had not started that season.

Pienaar pulled Singer in to discuss the situation. They wanted to give Johnson a run-out so that he might put forward his case for the full-back spot that Singer had done much to make his own. But the omens were there.

'What do you think is your best position, Matty?' asked Pienaar.

'Full-back,' replied Singer.

Pienaar looked at him from behind his desk.

'We'll talk about it,' he said. 'We'll go for a meal or for a drink and decide what your best position is and we'll give you all the support to develop in it.'

'Well, I've played full-back, wing and centre to a high level and I think full-back is my best position and I'll go furthest in it.'

'I think it probably is. Let's go for a drink and we'll talk about it.'

Singer was not too perturbed by his exclusion. There was logic behind the decision. He was still riding high and had proven himself. It was now incumbent upon an unfit and unsettled Johnson to do the same.

Saracens played some inspired rugby against Bath, scoring 50 points against them, and Johnson scored two tries. Yet he had not looked entirely sure in defence, and he looked distinctly unsteady in the following league defeat against Leicester. His troublesome hamstring injury flared up again in January and Johnson, supremely disillusioned with the wintry conditions in England and the weary condition of his 31-year-old body, thanked Nigel Wray for his support but advised him that he would be retiring at the end of the season.

Johnson, like Pienaar when he had first arrived, was shocked by the effects of the English winter. The soft ground had done for his hamstring and the mud and rain had done for his confidence with ball in hand, something around which he had built his reputation on the high veldt. If apologists for the traditionally conservative rugby of the English want any ammunition, they would do well to consult Johnson on the implications of life in an English winter. As far as he was concerned, players in the southern hemisphere had no idea just how severely the conditions in Britain could compromise and alter the style of play. Skills that he would not think twice about performing in the Transvaal became operations that required the utmost concentration and care on the heavy playing fields of Britain.

Johnson's injury gave Singer another run at full-back and another run in the favour of the management. Singer, however, was beginning to grow sensitive to a new perception that was forming within his psyche. Whenever Johnson was injured, Singer seemed to be the golden boy, yet whenever Johnson was coming back to fitness, he seemed to get singled out for criticism. When Johnson was playing, he felt simply ignored. But he always had the thought at the back of his mind that Johnson would be retiring at the end of the season. After his latest run at full-back, Singer's performance was scrutinised in the video analysis of a Valentine's Day victory at Bristol and Johnson took his place at full-back for the next game against Sale.

Singer was becoming increasingly disillusioned. Every other Monday he was waiting for a call from the England management, hoping that he might have earned a place in the A squad. It never came. His team-mates at Saracens spoke to him about it regularly, expressing their surprise that he was still being overlooked, but there was no word from the Saracen management. Singer was starting to feel that they held his ability in little esteem.

Johnson himself, nothing if not gracious, expressed his mild embarrassment at being picked ahead of Singer in view of his own current form and his problems with injury. In the cold world of objectivity, however, it was inevitable. No matter who the form player was, Johnson was costing Saracens a significant amount of money and, in the new age of professionalism, that had to have a bearing on selection. Singer, meanwhile, was a utility back with a relatively modest salary who had obviously been marked down as a squad player. And he did not have the pedigree of a glittering international career upon which to call. Realistically, Singer would have to be forcing his way into international reckoning if he was to stand a chance of overturning those sorts of odds. Johnson was clearly going to be given more opportunities to prove himself. Nevertheless, in the height of his frustration, Singer could not help feeling seething resentment towards Pienaar, whom he saw as favouring his old friend from the glory days in South Africa.

Singer, however, was given one more chance at full-back. Midway through March, Saracens lost a crucial league match in Gloucester. Johnson had played poorly again, while Singer had been absolved from blame on the wing. With their championship challenge hanging in the balance, Saracens travelled to Newcastle for a top-of-the-table clash on a Wednesday night. Johnson was dropped and Singer played full-back. It was a riveting match, but Newcastle triumphed 30–25. Singer was wrong-footed by Stuart Legg for one of Newcastle's tries, but it was his decision to pass at one point that incurred most of Pienaar's attention. Singer, with the Newcastle cover coming across, passed the ball to his winger. Pienaar argued that a player with vision would have sold a dummy and been in under the posts, or at least found his open-side in support with one man to beat. Singer felt the criticism incongruous and over the top: he was not the only person who had made a mistake in the game. Pienaar himself had made them.

The team left Newcastle and spent two days in Northamptonshire, preparing for their cup semi-final at Northampton. Mark Evans informed Singer before the team meeting that he had not been picked for the semi-final and that Johnson was back in. Singer was devastated and furious, as much because he knew it would happen as anything else. He was brought on in the subsequent semi-final, however, as a winger and scored two scintillating Bracken-inspired tries to take Saracens to Twickenham. It was a performance that put him firmly in the hearts of many of the fans, who saw him as the man who had taken them to Twickenham. Singer's status as a Fez Boy favourite was secured. But, as well as he took the tries, they were both scored on the back of a magnificent team performance. It would not be enough to reverse selection policy.

Singer was interviewed on television after the game, with Pienaar standing alongside him. The interviewer alluded to his last appearance at Twickenham in the 1996 Varsity match, in which he had also scored two tries. Singer played along with the parallels.

'Yes, I wouldn't mind scoring two tries in the final!'

When he and Pienaar walked away from the interview, Pienaar turned to him with a glint in his eye.

'You're very confident you're going to play at Twickenham, Matt!'

It was said in jest, but Singer knew what they said about true words.

Pienaar and Singer finally had their chat about his best position the following week when Singer approached Pienaar at Bramley Road. Pienaar told Singer that he did not think full-back was his best position. He told him that he did not think he had the vision to play there, before attempting to cushion the blow by observing that he did not think himself to have vision either. Being put in the same bracket as Pienaar, in this instance, Singer considered little consolation. Pienaar did, however, reveal that he had actually wanted Johnson to play against Newcastle. The rest of the selection committee, though, had gone for Singer.

Singer was to start one more game that season, on the wing, as Johnson's form started to kick in. He was awarded a sleek hi-fi system from sponsors Kenwood (a none-too-shabby perk of professionalism) as achiever of the month for his two-try display against Northampton, but on the field, where it matters to a player, he was relegated to a role as bit-part player. He came on as a substitute for the last couple of minutes of the cup final and was as sucked up as anyone in the Saracen momentum that built up to that season's climax. But, despite the invigorating excitement of the experience, he suffered from the unavoidable emptiness of not being in the XV.

The most devastating blow, however, was to come. The one thing that had kept him going was the thought that there would be a clean slate next season with Johnson retiring. Singer was never naïve enough to believe that he would become Saracens' first choice. But even if they got someone else in, it would be a fresh challenge for him and he was confident that, over the course of the season, he would get his fair share of chances.

On the Monday after the cup final, Singer received a phone call from a friend who told him that he had read in the paper that Johnson had been talked out of retirement and was staying for another year. Singer was knocked for six.

Johnson had started to find his form as the pitches firmed up and he had revelled in the buzz of the cup final that seemed to bring back the good times for him. For the top players, there is nothing like the thrill of a big final to capture the imagination and keep the edge sharp. It had all constituted a new lease of life for the South African, who would also get the opportunity to kick Saracens' goals next season with Lynagh retiring. For Singer, though, the news was a sickening blow. Suddenly, a long season of the same impasse was stretching out before him. He knew he would now be taking a step backwards as a player, having progressed so much in his first year as a professional.

Singer suddenly lost all his enthusiasm for the team ethic. He could not wait to get away and, as preparations for his impending wedding approached, he readily immersed himself in non-rugby matters. The last game of the season was played at Vicarage Road the following Thursday. Afterwards, Singer immediately left for Wales. A party of his close friends gathered there to celebrate his stag weekend with a golf day at Royal Porthcawl, his local club, followed by a dinner and subsequent excursion to one of Porthcawl's night-spots (or, rather, Porthcawl's one night-spot). It was an establishment of dubious repute, whose clientele displayed a curious, if mildly threatening, fascination for people in blazer and tie.

Singer married Allison at the chapel of Wycliffe College, his old school in Gloucestershire, on the penultimate day of May in glowing sunshine which defied all meteorological predictions. There was a minor hiatus in the ceremony as Singer had to grease his enormous knuckle with Vaseline in order to slip the ring over it, but otherwise the day was perfect. The newlyweds took off for a honeymoon in Scotland and, upon his return, Singer launched himself into another project.

At the beginning of the season, he had approached me with the idea for the book that you are currently reading, but, for various reasons, it was not going to be ready for the end of that season. Nevertheless, we decided to produce a celebratory magazine to mark Saracens' successful season. *Year of the Fez* was the result, a fascinating insider account of the Men in Black's cup-winning season, retailing at a very reasonable, I am sure you will agree, five pounds (we still have a warehouse full of copies, if anyone is interested). We needed substantial funding to get the project going and Singer, inspired by the sceptical words of the Saracen marketing department, who seemed to doubt its feasibility, identified another avenue through which to prove Saracens wrong about him. His was undoubtedly a persecution complex, but he set about ravenously contacting Saracen sponsors to try to raise sufficient advertising revenue. By August he had raised over £14,000 and *Year of the Fez* was duly published for the start of the next season, to much backslapping from various sectors of the Saracen organisation.

It was that time of year again that Singer found so liberating. During pre-season there were no preconceptions, there was no pecking order, and everyone seemed to be competing on a level playing field. Training favoured the athletic and skilful players. He was playing for himself. *Year of the Fez* had diverted his attention from the team ethic and had enthused him with some good old-fashioned backs-to-the-wall self-validation. Now he was transferring that kind of energy to the freshness of pre-season training. And he was on fire.

10

The Missionaries

Deep in the Sir Stanley Rous Stand at Vicarage Road, platinum discs were hanging on the walls of the Sir Elton John suite and the air was redolent with terms like 'incentivise' and 'community development'. Outside, the stadium's new state-of-the-art pitch was in its first flush of youth as the August sun immaculately nursed the virgin turf to perfection. A new season was fast approaching and there was a strong sense of genesis.

The sun streamed in through the French windows that afforded Sir Elton's hospitality box its view of the high-tech Watford pitch. Its light skidded across the long, lacquered table around which sat about 25 representatives from the marketing departments of the Premiership's rugby clubs. Finding their focus, the bouncing rays finally converged upon a white-board at the end of the table and the neat figure of Tim Lawler, Saracens' community development officer, who stood beside it with marker pen in hand. His soft Geordie accent and boyish good looks conveyed to the assembled guests the importance of an extensive and energetic community programme. It was the cornerstone of the revolutionary marketing strategy that had so spectacularly transformed Saracens in the previous season.

Lawler stood aside for Hannah Godwin to take the assembly through the 'Chalk and Talk' project that would be one of the pillars of year two of the three-year 'Rugby in the Community' programme. She handed over to Simon Hoskins, who explained the famous Cashback scheme that had attracted so much attention the previous season, before Peter Deakin filled the room with his dazzling enthusiasm that momentarily seemed to eclipse every last shaft of solar light.

Deakin was a big man, both physically and ideologically. His sharp suits somehow managed to embrace his enormous shoulders and on match-days at Vicarage Road their material would flap as he strolled around the ground surveying the buzzing fruits of his labour, his walkie-talkie never far from his ear. Deakin would greet you like his long-lost brother. The burst of enthusiasm when you asked him for a quick word could make you feel very good about yourself. His mountainous charisma rendered him a pinnacle in the marketing world. He probably could have attracted 20,000 to Bramley Road.

Deakin was the eldest of seven children from a family in Oldham. A child of rugby league, he used to play in the second row for Oldham St Anne's before signing professional forms with the Oldham club proper. He had spent five years in sports marketing in the United States, mainly as general manager of a soccer franchise in Milwaukee, before he brought his prodigious talents to Bradford Northern rugby league club. He assisted in their name change to the Bradford Bulls and transformed the match-day experience with the introduction of pre-match entertainment that included dancing girls and signature tunes for the players. He fostered relationships between the club and the community. In his two-and-a-half-year stay, the average attendance at Bradford's games rose from 5,000 to 15,000 and the commercial yield increased by 500 per cent. In May 1997, Nigel Wray travelled to a Bradford Bulls game and liked what he saw. Two months later, Deakin had been lured to Watford.

His most famous innovation at Saracens was the Cashback scheme, an idea he had picked up from his days in America. It was ingenious. Commonly misconstrued as a discount scheme, it actively motivated institutions to sell tickets for Saracen matches by giving a proportion of cash back to each institution in line with the number of tickets that it had sold. 'Cashbackers' (as they were known), be they schools, rugby clubs, prisons or chip shops, applied for match tickets, and Saracens presented each institution with a cheque for half the face value of the tickets sold. In other words, for every £12 ticket sold by an institution, that institution received £5.10, after VAT had been deducted, back from Saracens. People who had not even heard of Saracens therefore bought tickets to the games so that they might earn their institution five pounds. The hope was then that the people might enjoy a great day out and feel inclined to repeat the experience. It seemed that, by and large, they had done.

Hoskins explained to the attendant marketing representatives some of the achievements of the Cashback scheme. There were 141 Cashback organisations under Saracens' jurisdiction, stretching from Leeds in the north to Dover in the south and from Newton Abbot in the west to Ipswich in the east. By the end of the following season, that number would grow to 295. A total of £70,000 had been put back into the community by the end of the first season in Watford. By the end of the second season, the grand total would rise to nigh on £200,000. Local rugby club Fullerians, for example, would earn themselves £9,000 over the course of the scheme's first two years.

The upshot of it all was new and invariably young blood for rugby in its professional era and a life-giving buzz in the local community. Combined with the community programme, the Cashback scheme sent myriad roots spreading into the surrounding areas that soon secured an unshakeable purchase. Mike Smith had always been proud of the first Saracen player contracts, which he described as the best of their type, securing the services of the players off the field as well as on it. The players were the company's principal assets and Deakin urged the assembled audience at the seminar to use their players as much as possible. Saracens' players were each issued with detailed rotas explaining where they were going, when and why in any given week. In little squadrons, they would visit schools and rugby clubs to coach and lecture the kids. They would even help instruct the teachers in how best to communicate the gospel of rugby to the children. They would visit hospitals, shopping precincts and community centres, signing autographs and shaking hands. Charming to a man, the players rapidly became darlings of the public. People would often adopt a favourite and would attend matches to look out for them. Socialising with players after a game could be a long and drawn-out process as wave upon wave of children (and adults) scurried up to them with pens and earnest requests, all of which would be unfailingly honoured with patience and grace. The interaction between the players and the fans was extensive and contributed to a warm atmosphere on match-days that was best captured in the bar after the game, where players and public alike would mingle.

The atmosphere in the stadium before and during games buzzed with an uplifting energy that represented as radical and sudden a break with the traditional image of rugby, let alone of Saracens, as it was possible to conceive. As Deakin pointed out to his guests, with average Saracen gates a year earlier at a meagre 3,000, the concept of 20,000 people watching the team in a league game (not to mention the average gate rising to 9,500) would have constituted the patently absurd. As would the scenes that greeted match-days at Vicarage Road: loud rock music, immaculately choreographed troupes of dancing girls (the shapely Saracens Crown Jewels would be replaced for the following season by the dangerously young but no less supple Saracens Starlites), fluttering programmes, signature-hunting kids, fez hats, enormous pointing hands and a rather excited master of ceremonies. All of this in a 20,000-seat stadium that was usually at least half full. This was a very new world for rugby.

Many quarters in the sport loathed the Americanisation of their beloved game. When London Irish came to visit Saracens before Christmas the following season, the master of ceremonies bawled the announcement of a new feature at Saracens' home games: 'WENDEEEZZZ FIIIIVE MINUTE MAAAYYHEMMM!' The idea was that, if Saracens scored in the next five minutes, spectators could claim a free medium portion of chips from Wendy's takeaway upon production of their match ticket. It was, of course, an exclusive arrangement with Watford's noble eatery, so everyone in the stadium was instructed to scream to the team his or her very urgent desire for a bag of chips. Amid the subsequent orgy, the guests from the London Irish committee looked at each other, shaking their heads. 'What's happening to this game?' they asked.

It was an attitude that attracted both sympathy and scorn depending upon whether you fell into the traditional or the revolutionary camp. One of the difficulties, however, was the uncomfortable position in which rugby found itself, hamstrung between these two stools. Whereas the more tribal character of football crowds tends to generate its own atmospheric momentum, the family character of rugby crowds was not so conducive to the transmission of unbroken noise and energy. On several occasions, the atmosphere at Vicarage Road seemed self-sustaining. But it was sometimes incumbent upon the master of ceremonies to remind the crowd of their rousing responsibilities, occasionally with awkward results.

It was hard work. No one, however, worked harder than the team of missionaries that had been recruited and commissioned since the move to Watford. Over the course of the next season, it would grow in number to 18. Their achievements had been spectacular: the absurdity, in the context of the club's history, of 20,000 watching Saracens cannot be overstated.

The more traditional parties in rugby had necessarily been cried down. The crippling new economics of the game demanded that something extraordinary happen to transform the face of rugby. Saracens, with Deakin at the helm, had been the first to break from the pack and show the 'bums-on-seats' achievements that were possible. The quality of experience was ultimately an irrelevance now; it was the quantity of the audience that was the only standard. It was to this end that Saracens had been inundated with calls from marketing departments at the other Premiership clubs seeking advice. Deakin had arranged the seminar to bring them all together and offer advice on strategies. There was a strong feeling of unity. If professional rugby was to work, every club needed to show progress on this front. Saracens needed other marketing departments to be as successful as they had been. And it was not just rugby clubs that sought Saracens' advice. Nottingham Forest, for a while Wray's other sports interest (although football never held his heart), Sunderland and the English Cricket Board were among those other sporting institutions to tap Deakin's brains.

Whether or not one decried some of the garish elements of the match-day experience, there was no arguing with the impact that Saracens had in the community. Their 'Rugby in the Community' pro-gramme won the national community sports award for 1997–98 in the face of over 200 competing organisations across 40 different sports. The evening before Deakin's seminar, the members' bar below Sir Elton's suite was heaving with hundreds of excited Cashbackers who, along with Clare Ward, MP for Watford, attended the second Cashback open evening of the summer (through which Saracens launched their new Kitback scheme) with palpable excitement for the coming season.

Saracens were criticised for masquerading as a benevolent social service when, of course, they were a rugby club first and foremost trying to attract a fanbase and the money that would come with it. Yet this was one area in which the objectives of Saracens Ltd and Saracens, friend of the community, could dovetail neatly. Not only was it financially beneficial to get out into the surrounding area, it was also socially honourable. The twin goals of revenue maximisation and social contri-bution were mutually reinforcing. A grand total of 50,000 children were touched by the players' visits into the community over the course of the following season. Rugby clubs would put on festivals that benefited from the support and attendance of Saracens and as many as 20,000 people would enjoy a family day out totally free from the sort of intimidation that can be found at football matches. The Junior Fan Club was also to start up in the new season, run by Jess Smallwood (whose charms were surely wasted on the little nippers), and nearly a thousand excited children had joined up by the end of the year.

All of this, however, costs a considerable amount of money. Most clubs simply do not have enough to spend on such resources. Neither would Saracens, were we to remove the input of Nigel Wray, in which case the whole venture would fold anyway. After the first year of professionalism, Saracens made a loss of £2.2 million, which fell to £1.1 million in the second year. The projected loss for the third year was back up towards £2 million again, with the loss of European competition, along with a fractured fixture list, costing the club an estimated £1 million. The journey towards viability was proving long and arduous, but Wray remained adamant that he intended to build for the long term. He did not appear to be joking: in the coming season, he was to pledge another £5 million for the following three years.

The following season, however, was to see the departure of Deakin after his beloved rugby league came calling for him once again. In January 1999, Warrington Wolves offered him the post of chief executive, an opportunity the big man could not resist. He remained part-time at Saracens until the following March. Thereafter, he was on the end of a phone for them, where he would stay for the foreseeable future on an advisory basis. Tim Lawler was promoted to managing director and Simon Hoskins to marketing director. The momentum that Deakin had set in motion continued more or less unchecked. All the various statistics relating to membership, season-ticket holders, Cash-backers and institutions incorporated into the community programme would constitute yet new highs, come the end of the 1998–99 season. And the average attendance figure had edged up to just shy of 10,000 for the season, despite the faltering form that would plague the team on the field.

Saracens, through Deakin and then Lawler and Hoskins, had nurtured a new philosophy among rugby clubs that was designed to ride the fickle fortunes of sporting achievement. Whether the team were winning or not had to become as much a side issue as possible. It clearly became harder when they were not winning to generate the relevant enthusiasm, but the continued high profile of the players and the club nevertheless wielded enormous magnetism in the community, whatever the form on the field. The only constants that the marketing department craved were a settled fixture list (the following season they were to host two home games in February, one of which was a Cheltenham-and-Gloucester irrelevance, one home game in March and one in April), a more peaceful political environment within which to operate and, of course, the continued support of Wray.

As the representatives from the other clubs filed away from Sir Elton's sunlit suite that August afternoon, they mulled over the lessons of Deakin's seminar and considered the evidence. Saracens had hinted at what the future might hold for English rugby off the field. It was impressively spectacular.

But it cost an awful lot of money.

11

Smith

In the summer of 1996, my family and I were enjoying our customary holiday on the south coast of Devon at the charming little time-share complex that we have visited annually since the early '80s.

The great thing about time-shares is that they can engender the most close-knit atmosphere among the shareholders. For the same two weeks every year, we come together with the same old friends and indulge in the same antics in the same cosy enclave of stone cottages. It is all very idyllic, all very middle class. Golf, tennis, Pimms, drinks parties, labradors – we retreat into our introverted little haven and escape for two weeks. None of us would change it for the world.

Usually, when someone can be bothered to organise it, there is a tennis tournament between the residents held during the week. All age groups and playing standards are represented and those who do not play are usually watching with a drink in their hand. There is only one court, so at any one time there are plenty of people sitting on the bank that overlooks the tennis court, drinking and bantering with each other.

In the 1996 version of the event, a new figure participated. The whispers immediately permeated throughout the posse on the bank as a mysterious, heavily built man walked on to the court to play his opening-round tie, drawn to partner one of the young daughters of our gang in a match against one of the young sons and one of the mothers. Apparently he was staying in number eight, the whispers informed us, just down for the week, never been before. He looked a nice enough man, with an unassuming smile and thick, curly hair.

It was not until he started playing, or, more specifically, serving, that the whispers took on a more disapproving tone. He tossed the ball high and with his six-foot-four-inch frame sent the missile whizzing past the ear of the defenceless mother before dispatching another stinger at the hapless boy. Thirty love.

This did not go down well. The high-spirited banter on the bank suddenly subsided into a mildly stunned silence as the ruthless terminator administered successive rockets past his frail opponents. Our blissful utopia of gentility and camaraderie seemed shattered by this outsider with no sensitivity to our refined principles. You just *don't* serve hard at the ladies. Or the children. Who *was* this man?

My father ended up talking to him afterwards. It turned out his name was Mike Smith, an official of some kind at Saracens, knew my mate Matt Singer. I had heard of him. He had just been instrumental in securing Saracens' continued status in the top flight of English rugby the following season, having sweet-talked the RFU and clubs into flying in the face of convention to reverse the previous season's relegation. He was clearly a man who did not stand on ceremony.

I do not think Mike Smith served hard in our little tournament because he was contemptuous of the conventions of recreational tennis. It is more that he has no conception of conventions at all. Those comfortable norms that govern and sometimes compromise the lifestyle of the tried and trusted are shackles from which he is blissfully free. It is a freedom that rendered him somewhat unpopular during the mid-'90s with those rugby people still ensconced in the game's amateur values. Which were most of them.

Perhaps what most prejudiced opinion against Smith was his inveterate addiction to wheeler-dealing. One sensed that he could not resist the crack of hammering out deals even if the deal did not particularly need to be hammered out. Whispered stories abound of Smith going back over deals that had seemingly been agreed, only to return before pen was finally put to paper with yet more revisions to them. The deal was never struck until the signature was rendered. Yet, for all the knowing tales of Smith's unpopularity, it nevertheless remains difficult to get anyone to elucidate in clear terms just why no one was supposed to like him. The phrase most often associated with him is 'he ruffled feathers'. Most people agree that he was unpopular, citing said phrase, yet it is far harder to find anyone who will put their hand up and say exactly why. It is also quite difficult to find, out of those who know him well, anyone who will readily confess to falling into the 'I hate Mike Smith' camp.

Smith was just the sort of figure that the traditional face of English rugby feared and loathed most: entrepreneurial, *nouveau riche*, a wide boy who had no respect for the game's noble heraldry. Despite not being the financial power behind Saracens (although he was not short of a penny himself), Smith was the Saracen representative who continually clashed with the RFU and offended the defenders of rugby's realm. He filled the role for Saracens that Sir John Hall filled for Newcastle, persistently challenging the RFU's authority. Any adverse publicity that arose inevitably grew from Smith's mouth and was incorporated into Smith's persona. In the meantime, Nigel Wray's refined image could remain impeccable.

It is easy to see why Smith has an unpopular image and equally easy to see why so many admire him and credit him as much as anybody with the transformation wrought in Saracens since 1995. He will make things happen and he will never bow to authority or convention, but at the same time he will, on the surface at least, take care not to give those authorities any tangible cause for complaint, just a persistent sense of disquiet. In our little tennis tournament he did not break any of the rules of the game, but it was the manner in which he took over our comfortable recreation that upset people. Needless to say, he won.

Yet, despite the gung-ho bravado, it is quite clear that Smith wants to be liked. He might be quite embarrassed, maybe even upset, to think that he offended some people over the Devon tennis affair, bearing in mind that on this occasion there was little in the way of achievement to compensate for it. And he openly admits that for a time he was very keen to get in with the players at Saracens and tried to be one of the lads, before realising that in his position it could not be done. His reaction, inadvertent or not, was then to go to the other extreme and become distant and unfriendly.

Shortly after he left Saracens he asked me, with what seemed the genuinely resigned air of one who was weary of the perpetual conflict and confrontation, whether he was going to get a hard time in the book I was writing. While the overriding energy of his life has always been the thrill of the chase and the urge to succeed, occasionally the noise gives way to reveal the odd glimpse of soul. Age and the love of a good woman now appear to have brought out the gentler side of him more permanently.

I went to see Smith at home in the wake of his departure from Saracens, his contract as chief executive having been terminated. He had always been very keen on talking, but this time the soulful side of him was in the ascendancy and we sat for about four and a half hours in his study.

In earlier conversations he had spoken the cocky patter of Del Boy, which one senses is his default manner. Of the many stories that he likes to tell, he took great pleasure in describing how he had been a perpetual thorn in the side of his captain as a young lock forward in the Saracen first XV (he also played for England Colts). He relates with the glint in his eye that informs much of his conversation how he was not a great team man and found his social life far more appealing than his rugby, to the extent that he retired from the game at the age of 21. Repeated wounds to the head, however, culminating in his being taken out by Welsh internationals Ian Jones and Mike Roberts during a cup-tie against London Welsh, may also have contributed to his retirement.

'I took a few weeks off after that with concussion, and then my social life took over and became more important than my rugby,' remembered Smith. 'In fact, it was more important than my rugby while I was still playing.

'A stand-in skipper for Saracens was a chap called Ian Player, who was very keen on his rugby. He was giving the half-time team-talk during one game and he suddenly said to me, "What are you doing? What are you doing? You're not paying attention!"

'"No, no, no!" I said. "I'm just looking at that bit of crumpet in the stand."

'"Why?"

'"I think I'll give her one later!"

'"You can bugger off!"

'So I started walking away.

'"Where the bloody hell do you think you're going?"

'"Well, you said I could go!"

'"Get back here!"

'I mean, I was the ideal team man. Hair down to my shoulders, beard – like a child of the '70s. I was a real team man.'

Smith is not a team man. One of his favourite expressions is that he does not believe in committees, only committees of one. As a young man, he wanted only one thing: to be the richest man in the world. That London Welsh game, in January 1972, was his last game for Saracens, as he devoted more and more of his time to this overriding aim. While still at school, he had worked for his father, a builder, and he had soon started up his own trade before finally diversifying into property. He was addicted to his work. The settlement for his first divorce detailed how he had taken only 15 days' holiday in 13 years. He and the boys would work on Christmas Day because they enjoyed it and the money was coming in.

At one stage Smith had 656 people working under him in the building trade before he decided it was becoming more trouble than it was worth. 'It's a huge pay roll, and you're fighting all the time, having arguments – you end up getting paranoid. I used to go round the sites checking on them. I used to sit there with a calculator, working out how much money I was wasting on idle time with 70 people on a site, going to the canteen, coming back five minutes late, going to the loo. I realised that 10 per cent of my money was going on nothing. I also realised that it was time to wind up. What was the point? You're wearing yourself out. So I moved into the property game.'

He made the money to go into property from his building days. Property seems to have sat more easily with his sensitive side, allowing him to indulge his interest in the more refined aspects of life. He owned Jacobean mansions and, for a time in the '80s, owned a small village in Oxfordshire.

'I like interesting things. If there's a property I want developing, I could tell you what it's going to be like. I couldn't draw it, but I could tell you what I wanted. It's nice to look up and say, "I did that," or drive round London and say, "I built that, and I built that, and I own that." It's my thing.'

But any cultural side to him has always had to operate within the more spartan circumstances into which his hard-nosed side brought him. In his youth he knew the likes of the Krays and saw people nailed to tenement poles and wired up on the corner of sites. On the building sites, there was a regular diet of accidental deaths that Smith witnessed first hand, and he encountered a near-death experience of his own in a car crash in 1975. Having been taken to casualty and left momentarily, he remembers standing up and seeing that one of his eyes was out on a stalk, his nose was sliced off and his legs were broken and cut open, as were his ribs. He came round five days later. For the rest of our chat, I could not help noticing the scar that runs around the bridge of his nose.

'It made me a lot harder, thinking that, at the end of the day, it's only you. You're in charge of your own destiny. Dying's not the problem, it's the people you leave behind.'

One of the people he would have left behind was his first wife, who he says never came to visit him in hospital. They divorced soon afterwards in a settlement that cost Smith everything bar a pair of white stereo speakers. His second separation cost him a seven-figure sum, and a run-in with the taxman cost him nearly seven figures again. Each time, Smith had to start from scratch. He also sold up at the age of 33 and retired for a couple of years, then sold up again in 1991. The wheeler-dealer and the gentler soul within were continually struggling with each other. But gradually his appetite for wealth began to wane.

'Once upon a time, I wanted to be the richest man in the world, but what's the point? You can only ever wear one shirt. And when I retired young, there weren't many playmates around. I would want to play tennis – I play a lot of tennis and I play a lot of golf – and I got bored, basically. It's occupying the brain. You've got to occupy the brain.'

Having sold his village in Oxfordshire, Smith moved to Hertford and started hanging around his old club Saracens at the start of the '90s. However much one may want to interpret it as a return to comforting roots, Smith will never admit to harbouring an affection for the place. When the then president George Sherriff suggested to him that he might like to get involved and put a bit back into the club for all the enjoyment he had got out of it, Smith was reticent. He claimed never to have extracted much enjoyment from the place – he remembered getting a lot of stitches from it, but not much enjoyment.

He seems ferociously proud of his hard-man image. It would be anathema to Smith to concede that he felt an emotional attachment to Saracens. He says he never cheered or clapped when the players scored because they were merely completing the duties they were paid to perform. If he is to be believed, Smith sees Saracens as no more than another one of his business projects and he views his separation from it as philosophically as he does the termination of any other business deal. Those who know him well, however, will tell you that if you shovel enough beer down his throat, he will quietly confess his feelings for the place.

Smith keeps his cards close to his chest and hides behind the beguiling smile with which he regularly decorates his face. For a hard man he smiles a lot. And it is not the sharp grin that you might expect of the wheeler-dealer, but a gentle, easygoing smile. The mouth would seem to protest innocence and shyness, but the animation in his eyes tells you that there is another more feisty force at work inside him.

Smith is always at his most enthusiastic when discussing his ducking and diving at Saracens. Approaching the Sultan of Brunei with Angus Stewart for funding, securing the backing of Nigel Wray, negotiating with the players, getting the relegation decision reversed, setting up the Saracen brand, displaying contempt for the blazered establishment of the club from whom he was so keen to distance himself: they are all tales that inspire the Smith sparkle. They also tend to be the areas from which his unpopularity arose.

With Bruce Millar he would negotiate with prospective players and their agents and provisional deals would be struck, very often by Millar. Smith would then come back with revisions to the original agreements, continually trying to chip away at them. Millar was often embarrassed by it, not to mention feeling undermined, and the players affected would become distrustful of the regime. But Smith could not resist the bartering and ultimately, of course, had the prime directive as chief executive of keeping costs down.

It had been Nigel Wray who placed Smith in the role of chief executive. Smith received a call on his mobile phone from the man with whom he had recently done such productive business. Smith and Stewart had just secured Wray's investment in the club and the task then had been to find a chief executive. Wray called Smith and told him that he reckoned he had found one.

'Do I know him?' asked Smith.

'Oh, yes, very well,' replied Wray with the sort of light playfulness that characterises so many relationships in their early stages. 'It's you.'

By the end, however, nearly three years later, the relationship had turned sour and in late September 1998 the pair parted company. Smith had recently been quoted in the press belittling Scottish and Irish rugby and suggesting that there was no place in the domestic game for a British league, which at the time was the favoured vision of the establishment. He and Sir John Hall at Newcastle were keen on a European competition incorporating only Welsh, English and French clubs before extending the competition towards sides from South Africa. It was the sort of radical and provocative view for which Smith had become famous. It was an embarrassment to Saracens. The staff were told that Smith was going away for a week and he never returned. They were later told that he had left the club having expressed views that were contrary to the official line of Saracens.

Marilyn, his childhood sweetheart and girlfriend of the last 11 years, found it very difficult to handle Smith's departure from Saracens having been around from the start, but Smith claims to have taken it in his stride. He remembers on one occasion, in the week following his departure from the club, falling about laughing with her for several minutes in their living-room. He speaks of a great weight lifting with his departure, but it clearly rankles – and it was not because of the comments in the paper.

'We [Smith and Wray] hadn't got on for some time. I was trying to run a business, and he wanted to get more and more involved. When I took the job, it was my company for me to run and do what I liked with. I told him when I started that I had never worked for anybody, that I had always worked for myself, and he said "Great".'

Smith became increasingly exasperated at what he saw as extravagance on the part of Wray. He maintains that it was the conflict between the business and the hobby. He felt that Wray, like more or less all of the rich men in rugby, treated the project like a hobby, attracting publicity through the lavish sums that they invested in the game. 'Someone used the analogy,' reflects Smith, 'that in the old days it was lion skins on the wall that were status symbols, then it was the Ferrari and the Porsche, now it's famous sportsmen. And it's common in other sports; the chairman has to have his favourite player.

'I think Nigel had this thing about the publicity of spending money. Wasps were advertising in the financial pages of *The Times* – why weren't we? And it was the same with the other owners looking at us. They don't run a business. I'm sure it's a hobby with them. A very expensive hobby. Whereas I was trying to break even. I was trying to be the most success-ful rugby club. Only one team can win a trophy. It's not the be-all and end-all to me if we win, but we can be a successful business. We can all do well out of it. But the owners – and it's not just Nigel, be it Chris Wright or Sir John Hall – they must win. But only one team can.'

Smith felt that he had to keep what he saw as Wray's occasionally flighty tendencies in check. His concerns reached a peak during the period when Wray started flirting with the idea of merging with Rich-mond. Smith, although he had always been keen on the idea of clubs joining forces as a prerequisite for the professional game's advancement, despaired at the idea of Saracens doing it.

'I have been for the idea of *other* clubs merging,' explains Smith, giving a flash of his two-tone smile, 'but not Saracens. I never wanted to dilute the name. I did this in 1995 with the intellectual rights and the licensing rights. Sort the logo out, get the name right. It's Saracens. Yeah, it's a great idea to merge and everything else, but not us.

'Nigel was losing a lot of money and we would have merged with

Richmond except Levett didn't like Watford. There were inevitable problems with the club's new name, which was my main argument with Nigel. He'd spent all this money building up a brand. You can't then dilute it by taking on Richmond. There's no synergy there at all. I just kept on and on at him. And I got James Wyness to lobby him as well.

'Then he jumped into bed with Bedford. Because of the situation Frank [Warren, Bedford's owner] had, there were a lot of liabilities there. That was going to be compromised as well. The name was going to be the Saracens Blues. Again, it took plenty of lobbying to convince Nigel. He was losing a lot of money and had felt hard done by. But he saw the light and we started winning a few games. I kept on saying to him that he had invested so much in the brand and built it up. Then he probably listened to his road sweeper and the milkman and the last person he spoke to, and felt perhaps there was a future in Saracens after all. We started talking about the rights issue and the gates picked up a bit. Saracens started to do well, and he felt a bit more positive about it. Frank would have been on for the deal. Bedford had no future in Bedford.'

When Smith discusses his adventure with Saracens in the '90s, he generally speaks with a cold detachment. Excitement does occasionally seep into his voice, but not in the sort of places we might expect of someone who was at the cutting edge for much of the club's spectacular journey. He will get heated at discussion of the economics involved in the game's administration and particularly the lack of adequate provision in the domestic game for the 1999 World Cup, over which he claims to have been crusading since 1996. In terms of his own personal gratification, in terms of reward that he felt on a personal, not just a business, level, he points to three highlights that brought him genuine pleasure in his time at Saracens.

'Getting the relegation reversed in 1997 is the best deal I have done in rugby and one of the best deals I've done full stop. And I've done a few. I wined and dined and lobbied, and pushed and pushed and pushed, and never let go. I might say, for example, that, going into the professional era, it was not morally right that we should get relegated in the first year. Anything you could think of that made sense I'd come out with. First I had to convince the clubs, then the RFU, and that took some time. I had to make a presentation to 54 of the committee at the Hilton. I think selling Saracens was fairly easy [cue Smith's two-speed smile], but it would have meant West Hartlepool staying up as well! Phillip Yuill, West's chairman, thought I was a god in those days.

'Then I was pleased on the day of the cup final. They'd lifted themselves and it was a really good team performance. It took me back to what I'd said to them at the beginning of the season: "It's a memory for your kids." They could all turn around and say, "It was a record win, we thrashed the Wasps, we had a good turnout." No one's ever going to take that away from them, that they were there. The best thing for me was going around on the lap of honour afterwards, looking at the crowd. To me, there were 20,000 people who had colours on. Again, I was thinking of the business: people are supporting the Saracens.

'The previous time to that would have been Boxing Day against Leicester. Boxing Day was not my favourite time for having a match. We had a new James Bond film at the cinema, there was a £20,000 jackpot at the bingo hall around the corner, it was a big horse-racing day throughout the country, a family day – and we got 14,000 people there. And I thought, "We're starting to crack this."'

The retiring smile that wreathed his face at that point was once again betrayed by the animation in his eyes that suggested there was more to it than that. If they were the only three moments of fulfilment that he experienced during his spell with the club, one can safely assume they were highlights that registered profoundly with him.

But that particular chapter is now closed for Smith. To an outsider, it is tempting to draw parallels between Smith's work at Saracens and his work with any number of other properties, being instrumental in transforming a ramshackle little concern. If Smith likes to drive around London, look up and say 'I built that' as he passes examples of his work, he will probably feel moved to say a similar thing on future meanders through Watford. But ultimately Saracens never belonged to him and that, combined with his desire to shape it as if it did, formed the root of his conflict with Wray. He had started to feel that he was becoming increasingly superfluous to the Saracen cause. As had others. Peter Deakin had started to transform the club's profile in the community and its attendance figures, while Wray was growing more involved with EFDR.

'I'd known for some time that it was pointless carrying on. It's business. There are no arguments. If you're not wanted, so what? I don't have to work. I've got other things to do. I'd given it a lot, I'd done fairly well, but it was no great wrench.

'The properties I own now were all developed by me and they're still mine. And I've got the choice. But when you're working for someone else

. . . [Smith pauses, then starts again] I never worked for Nigel Wray, which he never liked. One of the directors said the reason was that I was the only person who stood in the way of his total control.

'When you're digging the hole and you put the concrete in and you're building the walls and putting the roof on and it starts finishing and gets money, you think, "I'm part of this." And with Saracens, having got through the relegation thing, got through the Richmond thing, the Bedford thing, winning the cup, we were looking fairly good, hence the rights issue. And if we'd had Europe, we'd have probably broken even this season. And that's the success, taking Saracens from Bramley Road with tuppence turnover to turning over £5 million plus and being successful. But when it's taken away, you think, well, what's the point, why fight it? Other things to do, life's too short now.

'It's business. A deal's a deal. I've taken the severance payment. I never got as much as I wanted, they paid me a lot more than they wanted. So that's done. I had a good run at it, I did a fairly good job – they're better off now than when I took over. But, at the end of the day, it wasn't mine.'

There's the rub. The incongruous references in his conversation to working for Wray and not working for Wray reflect the intolerable situation in which Smith found himself at Saracens. Most are agreed that it was a situation with which Wray became increasingly uncomfortable as well. Smith had always been prepared to devote his time to the club, but he never wanted to invest his money. Wray did – and, of course, had enough to give Saracens a realistic chance. If one of them had to go, it was obvious which one it was to be. Yet, notwithstanding the odd barbed comment that slips into his conversation, the hard businessman that Smith likes to be will not let him bear any grudges against Wray. And it will not admit to any mourning for the passing of the Saracen chapter in his life. He will still occasionally visit Vicarage Road, invited by some of the shareholders, but otherwise he has moved on. 'It doesn't feel the same back there any more,' he says, echoing the sentiments of any number of former players, officials and characters from the club. 'It's just one of those things.'

With that, he eases his heavy frame back into his chair, stretches his long legs to their full extent and breaks into another one of his smiles. This time, however, I am sure I notice just the slightest softening in his eyes.

12

The October Crash

Blood was seeping from the wounds in British rugby's credibility. The English had been thrashed by 76 points in Australia and in their two Tests in New Zealand had conceded 64 and 40 points respectively. The Welsh had lost 96–11 to South Africa and the Irish had also lost to the Springboks in a bad-tempered series. The heady days of the 1997 Lions tour seemed a long way away.

Saracens had been well represented on that Lions tour the year before, and the Saracen training camp in Biarritz that preceded the 1998–99 season was also stocked with returning internationals. But this year's crop were on less of a high.

The rest of the squad, however, were on great form. The crack of last season had been retained and a spicy sprinkling of new faces had blended into the general enthusiasm.

Over the summer, Lynagh, Sella and Sturnham had departed. The first two were inevitable, but the third was very definitely not. Sturnham was another of Saracens' homegrown gems. He was a wild and reckless talent in his youth, but Saracens had hewn from his phenomenal physique and athletic prowess a back-row forward who played for England on that summer tour. In the previous season, Sturnham had risen from squad player to first-team regular, benefiting from the injury to Richard Hill that allowed him to play in the cup final and make the England tour. François Pienaar had taken him under his wing and had personally nurtured his unfettered talent. His stock had risen immeasurably: he provided cover for the second row and back row and he was only 24.

He also wanted to stay. He had his eye on a flat in St Albans, his home town, and was after a pay rise, which in view of his rising status was not unreasonable. His negotiations with Saracens had been conducted around the £25,000 region in early 1998, but he and Mark Evans had

146

been unable to arrive at a suitable agreement. By the end of the season, Bath had come in with an offer that roughly tripled that. Sturnham would have stayed at Saracens for less, but the handsome new deal that Evans put before him was still well short of Bath's extravagant offer. Evans, less convinced of the player's worth, was not prepared to go any higher and Sturnham went. Running out of time to find a replacement as the summer wore on, Evans eventually alighted upon Troy Coker, an experienced Australian international offering the same cover across the second and back rows. Coker was 35 years old and in the end cost Saracens more than Sturnham had cost Bath. It made little commercial sense and a few of the Saracen staff, past and present, who had helped nurture Sturnham since his wilder days as a player were up in arms. Pienaar himself felt hugely frustrated, having spent a year working on the player.

Nevertheless, Pienaar endorsed the recruitment of Coker. It was a stance that Coker found surprising, not professing to be a great mate of Pienaar. The two had been agents for Kerry Packer's proposed World Rugby Circus that in 1995 was on the verge of revolutionising the amateur game and forced the International Rugby Board to throw rugby open. When Pienaar and the South African squad, however, went with the offer of the South African Rugby Football Union, Packer's circus was effectively dead in the water. Coker had seen Pienaar as batting for both sides throughout the episode, playing Packer and SARFU off against each other. Coker's feelings towards Pienaar were correspondingly frosty, and it was thus with some surprise that he received the offer from Saracens over the summer. But it was an offer to which he would not say no.

Another southern-hemisphere signing arrived at Saracens in Jeremy Thomson, a 31-year-old centre from Natal who a couple of years earlier had been one of the leading centres in South African rugby. He had been a South African tourist in 1996 but was never capped.

The crucial signing, however, had been that of Alain Penaud, the sublimely gifted Frenchman who faced the onerous task of replacing Lynagh. Penaud, at 29, still had plenty of rugby in him. Although currently out of favour with his international side, he had been capped 30 times by France. He had captained his home club, Brive, to European glory in 1997, but had endured an unhappy season since, in which Brive had moved him from fly-half to full-back.

The three players constituted a handsome triumvirate of signings and Saracens were installed as pre-season favourites for the title, a position that was reinforced by an extraordinary opening victory against much-fancied Northampton. Continuing in the same ludicrously perfect Hollywood vein, Penaud, Coker and Thomson had each scored a try within 26 minutes of the start of the season. 'How's that for three great signings!' bawled the announcer at Vicarage Road. Saracens were 27–0 up after those first 26 minutes, having produced some of the most dazzling rugby many had seen them play. There was a ruthless snap that belied a summer away. Vicarage Road rocked to the sound of music, cheers and a rattling scoreboard. The subtle prompting of Lynagh was already forgotten as Vicarage Road fell in thrall to a new God: this was wild, opulent, glorious rugby.

With the riveting orgasm spent, however, Saracens' second half was less strident, but their 34–7 victory, supplemented by a 43–26 triumph over Sale and a 58–20 thrashing of London Scottish at the Stoop Memorial Ground, raised them to the head of the most competitive league in the history of the English game. When Leicester were then dispatched 22–10 at Vicarage Road in front of a crowd of over 17,000 (the second highest crowd in the history of non-Twickenham club rugby), the league looked over after four games.

Just to rub it in, Saracens had by then filled the one perceived weakness in their armoury. Before the Sale game, Pienaar had phoned Paul Turner, the archetypal Welsh maestro who was the coach of financially stricken Bedford, and invited him to join Saracens as backs coach. Turner attended the Sale game at Vicarage Road, having visited Pienaar at Bramley Road a couple of days earlier. In his office, Pienaar had discussed with Turner the proposition of his coaching the backs in an arrangement that would see Evans withdrawn from the training field to concentrate on his broader brief as director of rugby. Evans had agreed with Pienaar that they should find a specialist backs coach but, when Evans struggled to find one, Pienaar had taken matters into his own hands and asked Evans for Turner's number.

As Turner walked out of Pienaar's study, he bumped into Evans.

'Hello, Tommy [Turner's nickname]!' cried Evans. 'What are you doing here?'

Turner, rather embarrassed that Evans appeared not to know of his visit, explained the outcome of his meeting with Pienaar. Turner and Evans later sat down to arrive at terms for the post. It was another blow to Evans. Having lost his beloved role as head coach the season before last, he was now being removed from the training field altogether.

Saracens had never had a specialist backs coach. Evans was a forwards coach by trade but had ended up coaching the backs in recent years because somebody had had to. He had evolved in that time from a schoolmasterly figure into a more *laissez-faire* supervisor. The previous season, he had overseen sessions that had included significant input from Lynagh and Sella.

Evans had always suffered from the age-old stigma of never having played the game to the highest level, and a common complaint from observers was that the Saracen backs were being coached by a second-team hooker from the old days. Yet while there is certainly no doubt that a coach will immediately command the initial respect of his players if he was a great in his playing days, thereafter a glittering playing career counts for very little. There are no end of popular analogies here: you need not have been a concert pianist to be a piano tuner; you need not have been a racehorse to be a jockey.

Evans's style had always been that of the intellectual analyst slightly removed from the action. Indeed, the more removed from the action one becomes, the less relevant one's limitations as a player become. Evans had a brilliant mind, he was steeped in, and understood, the game and he communicated his ideas with a dazzling clarity. To sit with him during a game was to have that game illuminated, and to hear him in press conferences constituted the most refreshing break from the mind-numbing banality of listening to coaches in any sport (usually football, it has to be said) trot out their weary clichés. 'I thought we played well in the first half, but let them back into it in the second,' one coach might say, while his counterpart might obligingly draw our attention to the fact that his side were poor in the first half before sorting things out in the second. Such observations from experts in their fields could be made by your averagely senile octogenarian granny.

In this department, however, Evans was a pressman's dream, and he loved nothing more than holding court with the press. He describes himself, in his inimitable way, as 'not brilliant at being peripheral'. His affinity for the limelight had caused tensions in his early years as assistant coach to John Davies, who could never understand why Evans was always being quoted in the press when it was Davies who was the head coach. But Evans courted the press and obliged them with lively quotes without ever giving anything away. He had the happy knack of making the party line sound interesting. Most coaches have to be frog-marched into the pressroom after a game; Evans would make a beeline for it.

Nevertheless, as the new Saracen empire was being built all around him, he inevitably found himself superseded in the press's attention by far bigger names. It hurt Evans when Pienaar took charge of playing matters, and with Turner's arrival he was forced to take yet another step back from the pulpit. It did allow him, however, as the season unfolded, to keep his head down.

Paul Turner was also brilliant, but in a very different way. He was a classical product of the famed fly-half factory in Wales that was still operational in the '80s. Many a Welshman despairs of his winning just three caps for Wales in 1989 (Jonathan Davies won the crucial nod over him in 1985), but his magical gifts were to light up English rugby in the '90s as he transformed the form and fortunes of first Sale and then Bedford as player-coach. Whereas Evans was intellectually brilliant, Turner was empathetically brilliant, instinctively directing teams with his feel for the game. Whereas Evans operated as the slightly distant, and often prickly, schoolmaster, Turner liked to operate in the heart of the action as one of the lads. His good-bloke charisma rendered him one of the most instantly likeable characters in the game.

At Sale and Bedford he had been installed as the lynchpin of small outfits and was given *carte blanche* to mould them as he saw fit. He coached the teams and he played at fly-half, enabling him to exert immediate control over the team's patterns. Like Evans, he was hugely competitive. He demanded the highest standards but his powers of communication were less developed than those of Evans. He would become manifestly frustrated when players struggled or even refused to do the things he wanted. At Sale and Bedford this had not been such a problem because, as a player, he did it for them anyway. The 1998–99 season, however, was his first as an out-and-out coach. And when he joined Saracens, for the first time in his life he joined as but one part of an established and complex machine. This was not the fluid and pliable set-up that was his own at his beloved Bedford, but an advanced regime that he was soon to find like a cage.

Turner quickly came to feel that he was little more than a trophy: one of the best backs coaches in the land for the team that had never really had one. He felt his influence to be minimal. In his first training session, in the week between the London Scottish and Leicester games, he was thrown by the presence of Tim Wright, of whose role nobody had seen fit to inform him. 'Who's Tim?' was the immediate question that formed in his mind as another tracksuited figure trotted out on to the training field to supplement the panel of Pienaar, fitness coach Mike Yates and Turner himself. Turner was to be just one more voice chipping in and working around those of Pienaar, Yates and Wright. This was not to be his team to do with what he would. He struggled with life on a panel of coaches and his frustrations soon began to impinge upon his working relationship with some of the senior backs.

The day before that Sunday's game against Leicester, Turner watched his former charges at Bedford pull off an extraordinary victory against Harlequins, who had been leading the match by ten points after 80 minutes. Two dazzling Bedford tries in injury time consigned a shambolic Harlequin team to their fourth defeat in their five opening games. Next week they would have to host imperious Saracens. Few could envisage anything other than a resounding Saracen victory.

There was a lightness in the mood of the Saracen management as they took their seats at the Stoop on Saturday, 17 October. The banter was high between Mike Scott, Evans and Turner, reflecting the breezy mood in the camp and the widespread conviction that the following game would be a formality. Minutes later, there was disbelief etched across their faces as they stared at the grisly massacre unfolding below them. It was the blood of their invincibles, however, rather than that of Harlequins that spilled across the turf in south-west London that afternoon.

Harlequins, the former lords of London rugby, had come out with their eyeballs rolling, furiously intent on assaulting the capital's new premier club. They tore into an abject Saracen defence. 14–0 down after six minutes, 28–0 down after 34, Saracens flapped helplessly in the unprecedented hurricane. They steadied the ship sufficiently to haul the score back to 28–21 shortly after half-time, but the catch-up rugby soon caught up with them and Harlequins finished victors, 41–28.

There was a reasonably calm atmosphere as a stunned Saracen squad gathered in the cramped changing-room in the Stoop after the game. 'Unlucky, boys,' Diprose summoned the composure to say. 'We're not good enough to give a team 20 points and still beat them. Not yet, anyway.'

Pienaar, who had come on as a substitute to make his first appearance of the season after injury, stood motionless with a sympathetic smile and eyed his troops. 'It happens, guys,' he reasoned. 'They played some great stuff. But it's not how you get knocked down, it's how you get up again that counts.'

Thereafter the changing-room reverberated to a deathly silence while outside the Harlequin players danced around the perimeter of the Stoop.

The following Tuesday night, a dazzling second-half display up at West Hartlepool secured Saracens a handsome 50-point victory which seemed to hint at a settling of damaged nerves, but the following weekend's game sent them reeling again. Those other aristocrats of London rugby, Wasps, clearly did not consider the matter closed after Saracens' chastening experience at the hands of Harlequins. And there remained the small issue of the previous season's cup final to avenge. On Sunday, 25 October, Saracens suffered their worst hiding yet. Trevor Leota, Wasps' Samoan hooker, ripped into the Saracen defence and Alex King, Wasps' cultured fly-half, sent his myriad runners scorching through the resultant holes. A final score of 31–17 and the Vicarage Road fortress was in ruins.

This time it was panic stations. To lose at home brought tears to the eyes, and to do it to neighbours Wasps hurt even more. Other than the pre-season friendly (also against Wasps) over a year ago, Saracens had only ever lost once at Vicarage Road, by one point to Leicester.

Pienaar reacted severely. The clamps came down on the squad. Turner, as well, was appalled at how reckless and slipshod the Saracen back division had become. Against Sale and Leicester, although winning, they had failed to close out the opposition convincingly, and a personality clash was beginning to develop between him and Penaud. Both men had very clear ideas of the way they wanted the game played. Turner wanted Penaud to play more like Lynagh, bringing others into the game rather than looking for the gap and hitting the ball up. Penaud, however, equally strong-minded, resented being told to do anything, preferring to rely on his instinctive flair. Pienaar, meanwhile, introduced a curfew on playing the ball in their own half – at one point he insisted that whenever they had the ball in their own half it had to be kicked. Turner, however, was concerned that there was not an adequate kicking strategy at all. Penaud was lavishly gifted, with pace, power, skill and the sweetest of left boots, but he was simply not playing his cards in the right order. He and Thomson were both left-footers, which further restricted the team's kicking options. Moreover, it was not until that week that Penaud discovered that Thomson was left-footed.

An argument developed in training over the optimum defensive strategy. Penaud had been playing a different defensive system from the rest of the team. From fly-half, he was hitting up quickly on the opposition inside centre, leaving his opposite man to the duty of the back row and allowing his outside backs to engage in an aggressive drift defence. Wright, the defence coach, and Turner, on the other hand, believed that each back should press straight up on his opposite number before drifting, and that was the system that everyone else in the team seemed to have been playing. It was clearly essential to get everyone playing the same system: gaps between the fly-half and the open-side flanker had leaked tries against both Harlequins and Wasps. The argument grew to embrace most of the squad. Most agreed with Wright and Turner. Pienaar, however, felt that there was no right or wrong way of defending, as long as everyone was playing the same one. He also recognised the importance of Penaud's peace of mind to the team's success. He felt that it was more important that Penaud feel comfortable than that one defensive system be adopted instead of the other. He therefore backed the Frenchman and the system was changed.

Turner began to wonder why he had been brought in, and some of the senior backs were wondering the same. The likes of Penaud, Thomson and Johnson were powerful personalities with a lot of experience between them and they had been happy looking after the direction of the back play between themselves, under the supervision of Evans. They could not understand the need for Turner's introduction and proved intransigent to his wishes. Having played for years at the highest levels under some of the finest coaches, they were unwilling to assimilate Turner's unfamiliar training methods. Players also felt uncomfortable with Turner adopting such a hands-on role in training, playing a full part in the routines and the games of touch rugby.

Turner, meanwhile, for the first time as a coach, felt peripheral, without a team he could call his own. He rarely had the backs for a complete session but continued to have his sessions within a session interrupted by the contributions and concerns of the other coaches on the training field with their myriad different remits. Professional relationships started to become strained as the pressure began to mount.

There was little respite in sight for Saracens. Both props, Roberto Grau and Paul Wallace, were unavailable because of international commitments and injury, and the next assignment was a trip to Newcastle on Hallowe'en. I am sure I need not voice the obvious metaphor. It was the heaviest defeat of the season: 43–12. Like Harlequins and Wasps, Newcastle had been suffering from poor recent form, but against Saracens they were suddenly devastating.

To compound matters, Jeremy Thomson picked up a serious shoulder injury and Troy Coker was sent off during a mass brawl in the second half for a meaty punch on Newcastle prop Ian Peel. With a characteristic lack of banality, Mark Evans allayed any calls for Coker's internal disciplining. 'There were nine others flapping around too,' he pointed out afterwards to the press. 'Why further penalise the one who happened to land a good punch?'

The dark, dark mood in the Saracen changing-room was to lighten a shade, however, when the news came through that leaders Bath had been surprisingly beaten by strugglers London Scottish. After eight or nine games, this put Bath, Leicester and Northampton on two defeats with Saracens only one defeat behind on three, along with Wasps, Newcastle and Richmond. The top eight teams were separated by four points, and if we ignored Bath, who had played a game more, there were seven separated by two. It was the most exciting league in the domestic game's history. On their day, any given team could beat any other. Even winless West Hartlepool would soon start turning over the bigger teams.

With an October that had staged their spectacular fall from grace now behind them, the Saracen squad gathered with foreboding the following week for a post mortem in front of the video screen. Tim Wright flicked on the overhead projector, but in the split second before he switched it on to the video channel there was a sharp burst of an MTV advert. With perfect timing, an American accent boomed out of the speakers in a mock melodramatic tone: 'Is this the end of life as we know it?'

A wry giggle burst from some of the players, gradually building into several seconds of full-blown contagious laughter as the squad grasped the full irony of the coincidence.

Pienaar fronted up to the squad once the laughter had died down. 'It can't get any worse than this, guys,' he said simply, before taking them through the horror story of the game against Newcastle, berating all and sundry, including himself, for lacklustre performances and wrong decisions. He described it as girls against men. Thomson and Johnson received prolonged trial by video, and Danny Grewcock, a favourite son of Pienaar, was given a sharp chivvy-up: 'Danny, last season I would have hated playing against you. This season I'd love it: you're a pushover at the moment!'

Penaud was hauled up for taking the ball up into contact again and again. The propensity of their principal playmaker to do this was becoming a crucial problem as Saracens regularly found themselves with second-phase ball and no fly-half to use it. In his frustration, Penaud retorted, 'Yes, but if I'm on the floor it does not mean we stop playing!'

Penaud was suffering from the pressure. Comparisons with Lynagh continually rang in his ears. His wife, Vanessa, and young son, Damon, were unsettled in the new country and the English winter was starting to bite. His early form that had won him the Allied Dunbar player-of-the-month award in September had dipped to the moody and fitful and he was now nursing the first of several injuries that would disrupt the rest of his and Saracens' season. Suddenly Saracens looked short of cover. Andy Lee, sharing a testimonial season with Gregg Botterman, had been sent on loan to London Welsh and was called back immediately, but Pienaar decided to move Gavin Johnson up to fly-half and reinstall Matt Singer at full-back for the next match against Richmond. Saracens recorded a heartening home victory but were then stripped of Kyran Bracken and six of the pack for the World Cup qualifiers. An unconvincing victory at Bedford followed before Saracens were required to travel to Gloucester for what Pienaar described as 'our international'.

Before that, however, Coker faced his disciplinary hearing at the East India Club in St James's Square, a full two and a half weeks after his offence. In a lavish high-ceilinged room, ornate with grand paintings, Coker and Evans sat across a long mahogany table from an RFU lawyer flanked by two other officials.

The incident in question, which had been conducted off the ball, had not been seen by the referee. Tony Underwood had just scored the second of his three tries and Penaud had restarted the game. Once secured by the Newcastle forwards, the ball had been moved wide and the referee had followed play. Meanwhile, a fight had broken out between the two sets of forwards. It was thus the touch judge's report around which the hearing was conducted.

Evans and Coker were invited to reply to the report, which described Coker as running 'fully ten yards to punch the Newcastle prop'. Evans took up the defence, explaining that they fully accepted that Coker had punched the player but they took issue with his running ten yards to do it, as they would demonstrate with the video. Evans left the room and Coker was questioned by the officials. He insisted that he had acted in self-defence. He saw the player out of the corner of his eye with his arms flailing in windmill fashion. Coker had merely pre-empted the player's intended assault upon him. The lawyer scribbled notes as the other two officials studied Coker in silence. Coker was then asked some bio-graphical details. He had been born in 1963 (not the 1968 that was recorded in the Saracen match-day programme!) and began his first-class career in Queensland in 1982. He had played for six years in England between 1988 and 1994 as an amateur at Oxford University and Harlequins. He had won 27 international caps for Australia and had played in three World Cups with them, winning the competition in 1991. He had been sent off once playing for Harlequins.

Evans was then called back in and proceeded to play the video. Using the clock in the top-left-hand corner of the Sky Sports pictures, Evans noted the time at which the ball was fielded by the Newcastle forwards and the position of Coker and his victim at that point, barely three yards apart. The camera then followed the action across the field before returning a couple of seconds later to the subsequent brawl. By the time the camera had returned to the brawl, Coker had landed his punch. There was no way, argued Evans, that he could have come from 'fully ten yards' since he had been only three yards away from the injured player just seconds before the incident. The punch had not, therefore, been premeditated, but was a simple case of instinctive self-defence.

One of the touchline cameras, however, had caught the incident, and from what I can remember of the replay it showed Peel engaged in a flurry of punches with another player and Coker wading in from the side to catch him a haymaker and make a grisly mess of Peel's face. I wondered how they were going to incorporate this footage into the defence. It soon became clear that they were not. Without ever alluding to the other footage, Coker and Evans left the room as the officials considered the decision. Outside they waited on the landing.

'What do you reckon?' asked Coker.

'Well, we've only got Gloucester and London Irish in the next four weeks,' reflected Evans, 'so 28 days would be great. But I reckon they'll go for more – 42, maybe?'

'Yeah, they're gonna want games, aren't they?' Coker ruefully conceded.

'Sixty days is the maximum. If we get that, we'll appeal and go down to Sky and dredge up every last camera angle they've got.'

'Isn't it going to harm your defence not to have dealt with the footage of Troy punching the bloke?' I asked.

Evans looked at me with his cheeky smirk. 'I don't think showing that would have helped us in any way at all.'

'Presumably they'll have studied it, though,' I said, nodding in the direction of the closed door behind us.

The glint in Evans's eye continued and he shrugged his shoulders.

'I doubt whether they have,' said Coker. 'And I doubt whether they'll know that I've been sent off plenty of times in Australia. Only the once in England, though. I suppose that's the only one that concerns them.'

Coker and Evans were summoned back in, whereupon Coker was informed of his sentence.

'Mr Coker,' the lawyer began, 'you will be suspended for 28 days with effect from today. You will therefore become eligible to play again on 14 December.'

The day after the London Irish game.

'That you have admitted to the offence,' continued the lawyer, 'has counted in your favour, as has a playing career at the highest level stretching back 16 years and incorporating just one other sending off. You must remember, however, that you are a high-profile figure in the game and, as an experienced international, you have a duty to set an example to others.'

Coker apologised for his misdemeanour and the hearing was adjourned.

'Well, that was a steal!' enthused Evans as the pair skipped down the stairs to the elegant foyer of the East India Club.

'I suppose so,' replied Coker, 'but I did nothing more to Peel than he was trying to do to me.'

Coker's suspension meant that he was the seventh forward to become unavailable for that weekend's game against Gloucester. A minor crisis was alleviated to a degree, however, when Tony Diprose, not in the match-day squad for the England international against Italy, was allowed to join up with Saracens. Nevertheless, the club travelled to the infamous lair of Kingsholm short of nine first-choice players. In addition to Bracken (now out with a back injury incurred during England training) and six forwards, Thomson was still unavailable with his shoulder injury and Ryan Constable had also had to pull out the day before.

After half an hour of the first half, Penaud became the tenth casualty, limping off with a recurrence of his groin injury. Saracens had been abject, leaking tries and spilling balls. When Penaud left the field, they were 18–3 down. Just before half-time, Johnson, now at fly-half, landed a penalty to pull the score back to 18–6 and Diprose, mindful of a paralysing habit that Saracens had developed that season, warned his charges not to concede anything before half-time. From Simon Mannix's subsequent restart, however, the Gloucester forwards secured the ball swiftly and fed Mannix, who scythed through a gaping hole in the channel between Saracens' fly-half and fringe forwards. He fed Richard Tombs for the simplest of tries and Saracens went into the changing-room 25–6 down.

During half-time, Wayne de Jonge, the on-loan Australian playing tight-head prop for the day, became the 11th casualty, withdrawing with a shoulder injury, while Diprose addressed the troops in a now-all-too-familiar scenario. Having expressed his disbelief at their conceding another score before half-time, he asked them to get their heads up and show some pride and spirit. The result was of secondary importance now. Evans urged them to have patience in the opposition twenty-two and to take many phases as it required to break Gloucester down. Finally, a strangely subdued Pienaar could only bring himself to ask that they cut down the mistakes.

The team then pulled themselves together and the second half was Saracens'. They scored three converted tries to none to take their tally up to 27 points with the last kick of the game, but Mannix had earlier kicked a 72nd-minute penalty that gave Gloucester the vital edge in a thrilling 28–27 victory.

A cloud of steam grew from the dank shirts of the players as they linked arms in the away-team changing-room after another numbing defeat. There was a strange air in the room as Diprose thanked his players for the second-half performance. Evans praised the character of the squad for bouncing back from the first-half débâcle and Turner told the players that he took his hat off to them, but it was two points lost.

Pienaar had been standing listening to the various half-hearted accolades for his charges. A seething fury was welling inside him. He had always been animated and aggressive in his addresses, but nothing had prepared the fractured squad for the unprecedented explosion that followed.

Pienaar had had trouble throughout the game with his contact lenses and his eyes were now glowing red with the irritation. Sweat-honed shards of hair grew like angry horns from his head. The steam in the changing-room continued to rise all around. The fevered roar of his voice might have come from the very bowels of Hades itself. Pienaar in this sort of mood is a fairly life-stopping proposition.

'You can all go off on your two-week holiday now, but when you come back, I'm telling you, you'd better show me you want to play for this club or you can fucking get out! I have never in my life played in a worse team than I did in the first half today! I was embarrassed to be a Saracen! Do any of you want to play for this club? There was nothing in that first half. Those are two enormous points we've dropped today, and I wonder if any of you care. I'm telling you, you either come back from your holidays dribbling to play for Saracens or you can fucking pack your bags!'

Pienaar spun away from the group and slammed himself down on the bench. The rest of the squad broke the ring. Some stood dazed, others shook their heads in heat-of-the-moment resentment. Mike Yates stormed out of the changing-room shouting something about team selection and Mark Evans dissolved into one of his smirks; this one, however, seemed to be shaped by awkwardness. Pienaar had never delivered a rocket like that, but one had been needed. Indeed, in retrospect, most felt it might have been delivered earlier. Nevertheless, in the cauldron of the steaming changing-room that late afternoon, the emotions were boiling.

It had been a crippling defeat for their league ambitions. The weekend before, the principal perceived threat to Saracens' league challenge, Leicester, also stripped of most of their team through international commitments, had been thrashed by Wasps, pulling them down to three defeats, level with Saracens. Yet the luck of the draw had meant that Leicester's other fixture on this pair of international weekends was a meaningless friendly against one of the Welsh rebel clubs. Saracens had desperately needed to survive the two international weekends with maximum points. They had fallen agonisingly short and Leicester were now back in pole position. Saracens had fallen to the Kingsholm curse once again.

While players moved around him in uneasy silence, Pienaar sat motionless in the changing-room with his head in his hands, staring at the stone floor. It felt like something had died. Outside, the gaunt figure of Nigel Wray paced up and down the Kingsholm concourse with his long overcoat flowing behind him and his mobile phone pressed to his ear.

The pressure was starting to mount.

13

Pienaar

Every once in a while, there rises a sporting figure that transcends the parameters of the sporting world, a persona that represents far more than the triumph of one competitor over another within the arena of combat. Muhammad Ali springs to mind. So too does François Pienaar.

The image of Pienaar accepting the 1995 World Cup from Nelson Mandela is probably the most famous and powerful image in rugby. The towering Pienaar, complete with blond hair and blue eyes, was bent forward slightly in deference to the diminutive African in front of him, clad in Pienaar's number-six Springbok shirt and about to bestow the glittering gold prize. The smiles on the faces of both men represented to millions the fusion of two previously incompatible peoples whose co-habitation had begotten a desperate and bloody history.

Internationally, it was a powerful moment; in South Africa it was nation-shaping. Those heady six weeks in the Rainbow Nation saw spectacular advances in South Africa's emergence from her turbulent past. By the end of it, blacks, who had never had the slightest care for the white man's game of rugby, cheered the Springboks in their hour of victory as ardently as whites. Pienaar was catapulted to a celebrity status which he could never have conceived even months before. The blacks in the townships adopted him as a new and most unlikely hero. Within weeks he had risen from being the captain of contenders for the World Cup to being a symbol of hope for the nation's future. Mandela himself courted him as the worthiest of allies in their country's development.

It is perhaps difficult to appreciate the esteem in which Pienaar is held in South Africa. When he was dropped from the national squad within a year, by the controversial André Markgraaff, who succeeded the ill Kitch Christie as South Africa's coach, there were television shows and phone-ins to debate the issue. Markgraaff received death threats. Later still, nearly four times as many people in South Africa watched the 1998

Tetley's Bitter Cup final on television as watched it in England. The Twickenham showpiece attracted a bigger television audience in South Africa than the Super-12 games that were going on at the same time. If Saracens had been famous in English rugby for being unheard of, everyone in South Africa knows them now. It's where Pienaar went.

The images of that tumultuous day in Johannesburg were flashed across the globe, securing Pienaar's fame internationally as well as domestically. Not many of us in England had heard of Pienaar before that World Cup, but we were all party to his extraordinary rise over the ensuing tournament. He became an equally astronomic name in sporting circles over here – even more so, in many ways, because of his distance from us. We had never seen Pienaar in the northern hemisphere, or, if we had (he toured Britain with Transvaal in 1992 just after the South Africans had been re-admitted to international sport), we had never noticed him. Suddenly, there was a brilliant star erupting far away over the southern hemisphere. The distance made it seem more otherworldly and awesome.

I remember watching the game on television. I remember watching Pienaar sink to his haunches at the final whistle with his forefinger and thumb pressing fervently into the corner of each eye to hold back the tears before leading his team-mates in a prayer. It was clear from the images that Ellis Park was a swirling cauldron of emotion that day and it was clear from the history books and news footage that South Africa had been a tragically divided nation that was now coming to terms with its past. It was a momentous time in history, let alone sport. I had drunk quite a lot of beer with my mates thousands of miles away. Through my beer goggles the entire spectacle had appeared all the more surreal.

When Pienaar arrived in England in December 1996, a little over 17 months later, to play for Saracens, it was one of the most extraordinary ideas to grow out of the professional era in England. Saracens and François Pienaar – we might as well have had the Sultan of Brunei carrying his luggage.

I could feel that sensation of the surreal descend once more. It closed in further when Matt Singer presented me with the idea for a book on Saracens, and further still when Saracens let us go ahead with it. The dizzying pitch reached its climax when I came face to face with Pienaar on a windswept hill above Bath before a Saracen second-team game. Michael Lynagh had introduced himself to me with characteristic grace, and Pienaar was next to maintain the atmosphere of *bonhomie*, thrusting his hand towards me. Reeling from the shock of having just met Lynagh, I next looked at the expectant figure of Pienaar as a drowning man might look at an approaching tsunami. I wondered how on earth I might possibly secure any sort of purchase on the monstrous meat hook that waited in front of me. It was my only lifeline, however, and the resultant pain of its grip was a small price to pay for the retention of my balance.

Once the initial shock waves had subsided after meeting Pienaar, a deeper appreciation grew of his extraordinary qualities as a leader of men. He truly constitutes a tsunami of passion and energy. When Nigel Wray first suggested to Kitch Christie, Pienaar's mentor, that he would be trying to bring Pienaar over to Saracens, the first thing that Christie asked him was whether the coaches and people at Saracens were strong people. Because Pienaar was a very, very strong person.

With accuracy, one could certainly describe Pienaar as a strong person physically. At six foot four and 17 stone, he is big by anybody's standards, but statistics here are simply not enough. There are more impressive dimensions to be found in the world of rugby. I am yet to come across, however, or even hear of a more impressive presence.

Were the designers of a new breed of superman to inspect Pienaar as the result of their labours, they would be well pleased with the proto-type. The hair is blond and encases a wide and attention-commanding face. The eyes are steely blue in colour and sufficiently narrow in shape to admit to nothing but the most ferocious will. A well-defined crease leads decisively from the edge of each nostril to each edge of the mouth, which is itself straight and unyielding. The face is underlined emphatically by a square and prominent jaw. From there, the neck breaks out into a torso lifted directly from a Greek epic. Rugby players are all muscled impressively nowadays but usually have had to work with unorthodox body shapes. Pienaar's physique is a pure distillation of symmetry. Enormous shoulders career sharply, via aggressive pectorals and a granite stomach, into a narrow waist. And the legs are such that they can keep the above structure operational, which says a great deal for them.

The entire package is more than a little striking. And when combined with the fame, it makes for an extraordinarily daunting first impression. If I found my head spinning when I first met Pienaar, I know there was a collection of similarly dizzy crania that greeted him at the Trocadero the day he was heralded into the English game. Most of the Saracen players were also impressionable young men when Pienaar rose to his heights in

1995. When that faraway icon arrived one day to introduce himself as a new team-mate, none of them knew quite how to react. The net result was that none of them did react. Like Michael Lynagh, Pienaar found the unresponsive reception unfriendly. And when the passage of time demanded from the players a reaction of some sort, the results were sometimes unthinking and hurtful. Pienaar was regularly upset by a perceived attitude towards him that he found as cold and difficult as the inclement weather with which he struggled upon arrival.

Despite the outer aura, Pienaar is driven by intense emotions that are as vulnerable to incoming factors as they are powerful in determining his outwardly reactions. That daunting outer aura, reinforced tenfold by his astronomic profile, thus becomes something of a burden to him. If others can find the aura difficult to break through initially, so too can Pienaar find his own aura an impenetrable shell precisely because of the reticence of others. When his feelings are then hurt, the fires that burn within can sometimes provoke a reaction that serves only to heighten the austerity of his imposing persona.

Pienaar was born and bred in the Transvaal, renowned even in South Africa as the seat of spartan Afrikaan values. It is not a place for delicate souls, and the sons of Transvaal have a reputation for their intense hardness. Pienaar is hewn from the purest of such Transvaal rock. He regularly alludes to the outdoor lifestyle that shaped him in South Africa. We might like to think we are sports-mad and active in Britain, but Pienaar describes the outdoor life in Britain as non-existent compared to that of South Africa. Results on the sports field between our respective countries tend to bear him out. His was a lifestyle devoted to sport. Pienaar not only played rugby to the highest level in the South African schoolboy set-up, but also played cricket. He has a single-figure handicap on the golf course (do not be fooled by the handicap certificate of 12: notice instead the faded and crumpled quality of the paper upon which it is printed) and he was a successful athlete in the high jump and sprints. In South Africa, he explains, everything is geared around the outdoors.

While he is an unwavering champion of the political revolution that Mandela and F.W. De Klerk set in motion in his country, he confesses to thinking little about the issues in his youth. Neither did he think much about why his sporting heroes were denied international competition, and why he himself was denied it as a schoolboy. In South Africa the kids just went out and played; the outdoor life never yielded much scope for reading and reflection. It was only when circumstances granted him an active role in his country's development that he channelled his formidable energies into that area. Pienaar is a man of action rather than philosophy. The idle indulgence of conjecture is not for him, only the decisive performance of deed.

Pienaar's appetite for action, however, is supplemented by a sharp and lively mind. He has a degree in law. He became a central figure in the events leading to the professional revolution in world rugby not just because he was the captain of South Africa. His articulacy and legal know-how made him a powerful mover in the negotiations. Meanwhile, Mandela was attracted to him by more than just a robust physical presence and the shiny World Cup. Pienaar has an intelligence and grace that seems all the worthier for the physical presence from which it emanates.

He speaks with an effortless fluency that, when it pours forth from his mountainous physique, is nourished with the richest charisma. And the cascading stream is laced with the clipped staccato of his Transvaal accent that lends added urgency and drive to the quality of his words. He is the embodiment of charismatic leadership. He has been a captain for as long as he can remember, not because he has ever sought it but because it is irrepressibly natural to him to lead from the front and motivate his team-mates. He has played for South Africa 29 times. He has captained South Africa 29 times. His team addresses in the changing-room are invariably experiences in themselves, playing to shifting rhythms and seizing the attention of his colleagues before hurling it in a single direction. Some are so perfectly timed that they would look well rehearsed were it not for the fact that they are so obviously delivered in the moment. Pienaar seems more entranced during them than anyone. He may start some addresses quietly sitting down, before gradually building to his feet in a defiant crescendo. Sometimes he is a smooth but pressing agent keeping the operation on the boil, other times he stalks the room with the enormous hand at the end of his taped wrist waving a furious forefinger in exhortation. The intangible of galvanising leadership becomes close to tangible in Pienaar. When he asks you to run through that brick wall, you know that he will do it first, if he is not doing it already.

The unique qualities with which Pienaar is blessed invest him with extraordinary powers of character. His eloquence, his passion, his physique, his charm, his pre-eminence – in short, his aura – they all combine to wield enormous influence over those within their compass. When Pienaar talks to you, he devotes every last ounce of his engaging energy to your conversation. It can make you feel like the centre of the world. From a playing perspective, it can imbue players with immense confidence and an inspiring sense of worth. Within a season, players like Danny Grewcock, Ben Sturnham and George Chuter were transformed under Pienaar's guidance into players of international ability. To have a man of Pienaar's esteem and charisma show interest in you is profoundly liberating.

The other side of the coin, however, is that his aura can also wield powerful influence when he administers criticism, even if the criticism in absolute terms is not particularly fierce. When it is dispensed from his mountainous persona, it can hit home hard. The manager in any organisation is a necessarily powerful man and lectures from him are a correspondingly weighty sanction. But Pienaar's critiques carry with them the added force of his unique aura and their impact is thus magnified without any intention on his part.

Pienaar's leadership is largely based on confrontation. He persistently throws questions and challenges in the face of his charges. He defies them to improve. His relentless energy in this regard is fuelled by a restless need to reach perfection. When the team is winning, the balance is perfect. In the cup-winning season, Pienaar regularly exhorted his players in the pursuit of one of his principal quests. It was the search for the perfect 80 minutes. He would not let things lie until they had reached that holy grail. It kept the players bubbling throughout a long season. If there were imperfections in the performances, however slight, he would alert attention to them, but at the same time he found far greater scope that season to use his empowering praise. Any stern lectures were offset by the warmth of his mood. The momentum of the season was spurred on by his examinations, which were effectively cosmetic adjustments to a smoothly functioning machine.

When the operation of that machine went awry in the following season, however, the necessary examination was suddenly of a fundamental nature and far more painful to Pienaar and the players. Neither Pienaar nor the players had confronted that situation before as a group. Some responded better than others, but the classic vicious circle of poor form, tumbling morale, soul-searching and further poor form was quick to start its motion. It would take a mighty heave from Pienaar and the team to arrest the spiral. In the dark days of October and the subsequent fall-out from them, the mood in the camp was prone towards the desperate. The most important factor was that the team started losing, and that, in turn, was attributable as much as anything else to the new desire prevalent in English rugby to beat Saracens. The autumnal form of Harlequins, Wasps and Newcastle had been radically transformed by it and the results were devastating.

Under such grim circumstances, Pienaar's confrontational methods began to disorientate players, suddenly causing disruptive, rather than inspiring, unrest. Players were to nurse wounds to their pride and belief over the season, as well as soreness in their weary muscles from everlonger training sessions. Minutely detailed and grisly reviews of painful defeats fostered ever-darker moods. Even senior players with Super-12 experience felt they might have benefited more by looking positively to the next game and consigning the previous defeat to experience.

Perhaps Michael Lynagh was missed most, following his retirement, for the gentle counterweight that he represented off the field to Pienaar's more exacting approach. Pienaar and Lynagh had formed a balanced double act. Both had achieved the highest honours, yet while Pienaar embodied the virtues of aggressive self-advancement, Lynagh was the softer face of perfection. Lynagh was close to Pienaar and also close to the squad; he formed a link that kept the entire operation as one seamless organism. When Lynagh left, however, the distance between Pienaar and the rest of the squad started to yawn during the bleak winter months. Pienaar also now had a young family that naturally occupied every last ounce of energy and attention that he did not have to channel into Saracens and rugby. Quality time with the players was not a particularly realistic proposition.

Pienaar's overriding aim was always to give the players the opportunity 'to be the best that they can be', to quote one of his favourite phrases. He has been utterly honest in this endeavour. He would stand before them in front of the video screen at Bramley Road and implore them that criticism not be taken personally, that it was nothing other than a means of reaching that goal of perfection that he so ardently sought. As the mood thickened in the face of the defeats, however, the players found it harder and harder to take on the chin. Suddenly the techniques that had worked so well the season before did not seem to have the desired effect. The team had become fragile.

The 1998–99 season was a lonely and trying one for Pienaar. The worst part about it was that his team lost a lot of games, more than any other team he had played in. The defeats against Harlequins, Wasps and Newcastle, and later against Bath at Vicarage Road, were the severest he professes to have experienced. It was a new and agonising experience for him to lose so often. The defeats all registered in him on a profound scale. Pienaar took them personally, too personally, in that the blows to his inner soul were reflected in his outwardly reactions. He struggled to contain the raging competitive fires that drove him. His jaw would tighten and he would retreat into himself, putting further distance between him and the squad.

He was to learn more from that season than any other. After the happy initiation to management that the previous season had constituted, the campaign that culminated in the suitably apocalyptic date of 1999 introduced him to the agonies of the position. Across the board, people are agreed that he overreacted to the defeats in October, and it is a mistake that he acknowledges himself. He soon found himself having to tackle personnel issues rather than playing issues. He racked his brains, for example, to find the best method to keep Alain Penaud ticking (probably the single most important key to Saracens' success that season), and his attempts to keep Penaud happy sometimes offended others.

Every man at Bramley Road felt the pressure intensely when the results ran against the team, but Pienaar felt it the most. With Lynagh and Sella now gone, he was the astronomic name and the figurehead of the club; he was in charge of the first team; he was a key player in the first team; he dealt with the press; he stood as a role model for thousands; he was co-opted on to a working party for the restructuring of the game in the northern hemisphere. It was becoming an unhealthy workload. The pressures were ubiquitous. He was spreading himself too thinly. The players feared that he was undertaking too much without sharing enough responsibility out. He feared that the players were not following the game plan. As the defeats started to kick in and he felt he was losing an element of control of proceedings, he decided to reverse his policy on the issue of the team's captaincy. Despite Wray's long-held view that he should captain the side, Pienaar had always believed, with some justification, that Diprose's tenure lent the operation more balance and preserved the roots of the club's identity. Yet Pienaar was one of the great captains in the game's history and, in the despair following the defeat at Gloucester, he agreed that it might help for him to take over the captaincy as well, if only for a few games, to show Diprose what he wanted. Diprose, again quite rightly, decided that there could be no half measures and ceded the captaincy on a long-term basis. It further set Pienaar up as the all-powerful commander. It probably did more harm than good.

Pienaar is an intelligent man, and when discontent rose to the surface during the fall-out from the autumnal defeats he was quick to take remedial action. He learnt a lot of lessons in the unfamiliar circumstances of defeat. Yet one of his truly outstanding assets is the unique focus of his ferocious desire to win, and he would likely discard all the baggage of fussy philosophy before he would compromise that one burning quality.

'When we lose, I take it very personally, very hard,' Pienaar said to me. 'I don't go, "Oh great, that's just another loss." But I've always spoken to the guys about it. I think people can get a little sensitive in that regard. You can ask my wife; that's my personality. It's not because of any person or any individual. But I take it very hard.

'And, of course, there has been a lot of pressure from Nigel, but nobody has put more pressure on me than myself. I don't care what other people say. I want to win more than anybody in the club. More than the players. More than the spectators. More than Nigel. I want to win more than anybody.'

The bristling body was still as Pienaar looked at me. I think he probably meant it.

14

Fall-out

Those at Saracens who had not witnessed the steamy pressure cooker of the Kingsholm changing-room soon got wind of it. The events of the second half of October had sent shock waves pulsing throughout the Saracen squad. As they lurched variously from defeat to unconvincing victory, self-belief was steadily draining away and the heavy hand of expectation, from above, below and all around, was tightening its grip on every last soul in the camp.

If the steam had scalded at Kingsholm, it was hoped that the two-week break that followed might provide some release. Those excused the rigours of consecutive international weekends took themselves well away from rugby for those two weeks. The overseas players took the opportunity to return home and visit their families before spending their Christmas in north London. François Pienaar and Gavin Johnson returned to South Africa, and Bobby Grau went home to Argentina. Meanwhile, the hours of groundwork that Ryan Constable and Brad Free had endured on the sunbed (with accompanying grief from their pale British team-mates) came to nought as they were greeted on the Gold Coast by the spectacular thunderstorms that saved England's bacon in the first Test of the Ashes series.

Rested, if not necessarily recuperated, the squad reported back to Bramley Road after England's heroic victory over the Springboks at Twickenham on the first weekend in December. A home fixture awaited against London Irish, whose inspired form under the guidance of Dick Best was taking the Premiership by storm. London Irish had become the surprise package of the season.

A more fundamental surprise lay in wait, however, for a Saracen playing squad that was feeling increasingly alienated from the management. Pienaar had told Tony Diprose that, after deliberation, they were considering relieving him of the captaincy. Pienaar, who would take over, suggested that they try it for a trial five-week period and asked Diprose what he thought. Diprose replied that if they had already deliberated over it without him, it was going to happen anyway and he would rather the decision take effect immediately, one way or the other.

Diprose had been the captain of the first team for 30 months, having taken over after the 1995–96 season. He was a talismanic figure at Saracens, truly one of the club's own. He and Richard Hill were now the only survivors from the old days who were permanent fixtures in the first team. Andy Lee was on loan to London Welsh, Gregg Botterman was kicking his heels on the bench, and Steve Ravenscroft was scrapping it out with several competitors for a place in the centre.

Diprose and Hill were from similar English middle-class back-grounds. Off the field, both were deliciously laid back. On it, too, they tended to wear expressions of apparent insouciance as others charged around in the fevered arena of combat. Hill was by now an established international in a swift and skilful England back row, his unflustered look belying a fearsome workrate and tackle appetite.

Diprose's worth in the international game, however, tended to polarise opinion. He, too, was now a full international, but his regular selection was blocked by a posse of the clenched-fist pugilists with which English rugby has always felt more comfortable. Diprose was a sublimely gifted footballer who, in everything other than his six-foot-five-inch, 17-stone frame, possessed the qualities of a skilful three-quarter. Whereas the instinct of most forwards is to tuck the ball under the arm, Diprose looked to exploit space and unpick opposition defences. He could stop a game with a touch of magic and raise the crowd to its feet by the sheer majesty of his handling. One such occasion was to follow in the league game in Bath the next week. The ball was bobbling loose on Bath's twenty-two and, with players rushing in from all sides to secure it, Diprose strode up to the untamed projectile with his long-legged swagger. Without breaking stride, he somehow managed to stoop low enough to scoop the ball up with his right hand and, in the same flowing movement, dispatched it out of the back of the same hand with an imperious flick. All around, onlookers in the crowd, be they of Bath or Saracen persuasion, reacted to the extraordinary flourish. Some shook their heads, some laughed, some swore unashamedly and others just stood up and clapped.

His detractors, however, would point out that while it may have been beautiful to watch, nothing came of it. Pienaar was the recipient of the outrageous flicked pass and he knocked it on, presumably as the last thing he was expecting. Diprose's moment of magic had constituted high entertainment but Bath were awarded the resultant scrum. Such frills are all very well, the argument ran, and can result in the odd try, but it is the grunt and grind of the hard yards that should be a forward's first priority. In this, Diprose always suffered from the stigma of his unusual talent. In the same way that many beautiful women are automatically assumed to be brainless bimbos, so Diprose, because of his obviously extraordinary gifts in one area of the game, was assumed to be deficient in others. Those from the old school of English rugby were suspicious of his talents, dismissing them as the jewellery of the delicate. It was a grossly unfair assumption that ignored the work and drive that he had channelled into the Saracen cause for years. And without Hill, Pienaar, Bracken and Lynagh towards the end of the previous season, he had led Saracens in a series of bloody-minded performances that had kept their hopes alive in the league.

After inevitable awkwardness when Pienaar first took over as player-manager, the power balance in the changing-room that had evolved between Pienaar, Diprose and Evans had functioned productively. Diprose was the players' representative, Evans the analytical brain removed from the heat of the action, and Pienaar the supreme motivator. There had never been any secret or embarrassment surrounding Pienaar's role in the triumvirate. In the changing-room, after the more technical directions of Diprose and Evans, the floor had always been left to Pienaar to provide the clenched fist that is essential to any rugby team's performance. There was never any sense of Pienaar superseding his captain. The arrangement was settled and it was balanced.

The events of the previous six weeks, however, had disrupted any sense of equilibrium in the camp. On the Thursday before the London Irish game, Pienaar announced to the players that he was taking over the captaincy. Players were not doing what they were supposed to be doing on the pitch and in this way he hoped to rectify the situation. As he was to tell the press, it was an attempt to get everyone 'reading off the same page', to streamline the channels of communication. It would also give Diprose a chance to concentrate on his rugby and win back a place in the England squad.

The effect, however, was to enhance the growing feeling of alienation between the players and the management. Diprose, the players' spokesman, was now just another foot soldier while Pienaar, already oppressing many under his spartan regime, had added the captaincy of the team to his positions of authority. As he took over the captaincy, Pienaar asked that Diprose's supporters air any grievances now rather than become stroppy about it. They could thus get any conflict quickly out of the way and move on to the more important issues at hand. It was a strange request, symptomatic of the disunity and suspicion into which the camp was subsiding.

A three-and-a-half-hour training session ensued, during which Pienaar gave George Chuter a torrid time. Brendan Reidy, supremely concerned at the direction events were taking, approached Pienaar on the matter. 'Frankie, you're the captain now,' said the big Samoan. 'You're the coach. You're everything. You can't single out a player like that. There's nowhere else for him to turn now.'

Pienaar thanked him for the advice and took it on board. A festering mood, however, had taken hold, and everything was now to be laid at Pienaar's door. The circle of action and reaction between Pienaar and the playing squad was becoming ever more vicious.

Saracens recorded a much-needed victory against London Irish that weekend, which was noticeable for the emergence of David Flatman, an 18-year-old prop making his debut in the first team for the injured Bobby Grau. Playing opposite Rob Hardwick, a full England inter-national, he formed a seamless part of the dominant Saracen scrummage and claimed a try at the end of the game to crown his first-class baptism. The following weekend, he looked equally comfortable against experienced international Victor Ubogu in Bath.

The 19–11 victory in Bath repaired much of Saracens' broken morale but was a classic expression of the wild fluctuations in form that were plaguing their season. Moments of brilliance from Bracken and Penaud put Saracens in the black, while a couple of moments of madness from Penaud threatened to put them in the red.

Penaud, more than anyone, embodied the Saracens of the 1998–99 season. Sometimes simply brilliant (more so than Lynagh had been), he could nevertheless undermine everything he had done in passages of ill-disciplined pique. And the regularity with which he was picking up injuries was starting to raise eyebrows at Bramley Road. Off the field, his Gallic charm proved extremely popular when he was on good form, but he fell prey to regular bouts of moodiness. He and his family were still unsettled in the prosaic suburbia of north London, and his fierce independence had not taken kindly to the arrival of Turner, somebody who would try to exert an influence over the way he played. Saracens were acutely aware that their fly-half and playmaker needed to temper his individual instincts if they were to establish more consistency, as much as they knew that to tell him so tended to provoke a counter-productive strop. When Pienaar complained in his captaincy speech that players were not doing what they were asked to do on the field, he basically meant Penaud. Players wondered why he did not just speak to the Frenchman rather than overhaul the leadership structure.

The victory at Bath, however, was predicated upon a stern defence and the goal-kicking of Johnson, whose 80 per cent success rate that season was proving an invaluable asset. And the victory raised spirits for the annual Christmas party at Bramley Road that followed that evening. It was a traditionally debauched affair, with some imaginative costumes, but it did not go unnoticed that Pienaar did not attend. He and Nerine had been unable to find a baby-sitter. People were far from convinced, however, that he had even wanted to go.

The next league game against London Scottish at Vicarage Road, however, ripped open the paper that had temporarily concealed the cracks. The day after Boxing Day, Saracens had never looked more disjointed. Not only was this a home game, it was also against one of the strugglers at the bottom of the table, a team against whom they had posted nearly 60 points at the Stoop in September. This return match was not even close. Two tries in the last ten minutes gave the Exiles a 24–7, three-tries-to-one victory. Saracens, however, had once again been disrupted by the kind of fundamental injury crisis that was making it so difficult to settle as a team. Bracken, who had been a source of continuity and creativity throughout the season, was forced to retire with concussion after only five minutes and Penaud retired at half-time with a dead leg. Johnson moved up to fly-half and Singer came on at full-back.

The following week, a severely pressurised Pienaar delivered a stinging critique of the team performance. He had been very poor himself and proceeded to tear apart his own game on the video before tearing apart that of others in the squad. Amid all the fury, though, Steve Ravenscroft was held up as a beacon of tenacity and spirit and Brendon Daniel won man of the match for his dangerous running. Nigel Wray also attended and delivered an impassioned speech, describing the performance as the worst he had seen from Saracens before spurring them on for the rest of the season.

Some positive training ensued that week, in which the great games against Tonga and Bath at Vicarage Road the previous season were invoked to try to restore spirit among the squad. An overriding problem remained, however, in that Bracken and Penaud, the creative axis of the team, were again unavailable for the next game, and Pienaar was also out with a foot injury. Johnson was struggling to fit in at fly-half and he too had developed a resentment towards Turner.

Pienaar was set on Johnson as reserve fly-half and had long since decided that the man who had played fly-half in that Tonga massacre the previous season was not up to it. Andy Lee had been sent to London Welsh on loan. The Saracen management considered him departed. Yet they would need a reserve fly-half for Johnson in the forthcoming home game against Bedford.

In the selection meeting for the Bedford game, the issue was addressed. The idea of recalling Andy Lee was considered, but it was rejected as it would terminate his future availability for London Welsh. Saracens had already started looking for a loan fly-half, and Matt Jones was on his way from London Irish but had yet to arrive. Pienaar, Evans, Wright and Scott looked at Turner. Turner, in the meantime, beginning to sense what the others were thinking, tried to make further suggestions. The selection panel sat as Turner continued to consider other options for cover at fly-half. Eventually, Evans interjected.

'Paul, you don't seem to realise what we're saying here.'

'Oh, come on, boys,' Turner replied. 'It's against my old team.'

'Yeah, but it's an emergency.'

Turner was extremely uncomfortable at the prospect of joining the playing squad, particularly against his mates from Bedford, but he was eventually persuaded to sit on the bench. The 39-year-old would only come on in an emergency.

Saracens registered a comfortable victory over Bedford, but the game was to constitute a watershed in the season. At half-time, they held an uneasy lead. Two prompt tries after the break, however, from Johns (who had come on as a replacement) and Daniel gave Saracens a comfortable 27–6 lead.

In the 51st minute of the game, Singer collected a loose kick outside his twenty-two and, sensing space behind the first wave of Bedford's defence, attempted to chip the ball into it. He underplayed the chip and Junior Paramore was able to reach up and seize the ball on its upward trajectory before cantering in under the posts. Pienaar, sitting in the stands next to Evans and Scott, lost his temper. Minutes later, he slammed his fists on his lap and screamed 'No, Matty!' as Singer played another chip with which he disagreed, and when Singer looked shaky chasing back against Rory Underwood, Pienaar decided to take action. Mike Scott traditionally sits in the stand with Mark Evans. He relays messages to and from the bench through the microphone and headset that wires him up to Tim Wright and Mike Yates at pitchside. Pienaar told Scott to issue a message for Turner to replace Singer as soon as he could be warmed up. Johnson would move back to full-back.

Scott, having passed the message on, relayed the answer. 'Wrighty isn't sure that's such a good idea,' he said. 'It might hit Gavin hard to be moved back from fly-half. And Paul's only supposed to come on in an emergency.'

'Get him on,' insisted Pienaar. 'We're losing control of the game.'

Turner began warming up and stripped off his tracksuit on the touchline. Suddenly Saracens broke out from another loose Bedford kick, Chuter charged on with the ball, Hill was in support and his inside pass found Singer scorching through to the last line of Bedford's defence. A well-timed pass from the full-back released Grewcock and the big second-row galloped under the posts to round off a scintillating try.

Pienaar muttered, half to himself, 'Sing-Song came into the line like a dream there.' But as soon as Johnson was lining up the conversion, the number-15 card was held aloft by the fourth official and Turner trotted on to the field as Singer's replacement. Johnson was told to move back to full-back. Wright had been correct. Johnson was livid at the switch. He and Singer had spent the entire week working at the reserve combination of fly-half and full-back and, with Penaud's injury troubles, would probably have to repeat the formation the following Wednesday night at Wasps. From his point of view, they had just scored a try to clinch the game and to disrupt the combination now, just as he was starting to feel good about it, made no sense at all. He had been working hard at the fly-half role and he interpreted his withdrawal to full-back as a slight on his efforts. And to be replaced at fly-half by his 39-year-old coach, with whom he had had some strenuous disagreements of late, was too much. In the irrational haze of his anger, Johnson felt Turner responsible and soon signalled to the bench that he wanted to come off as well, throwing Pienaar and Evans into a panic without a full-back in the squad.

'Can Matt come back on?' asked Pienaar, knowing the answer too well. Johnson left the field for Jeremy Thomson, Constable moved to the wing and Daniel filled in at full-back. In the last minute of the game, Daniel was forced off with an injury, stretching Saracens' resources to their very limit. Free came on as a makeshift winger and Wallace moved back to the troublesome full-back spot.

The 44–13 victory had been secured, but the team sheet at the end of the game made for chaotic reading. Pienaar, who had run down to pitchside during the chaos to bypass the clumsy communication arrangement with the bench, asked Johnson what was going on. Still fuming, Johnson replied that he would not play in the same back division as Turner and he was furious that Turner had come on for Singer just as they had broken the back of the opposition.

In the changing-room, Pienaar gave his post-match address to the squad before asking all the backs, whether playing on the day or not, to go to the boot room next door. Once gathered, Pienaar shut the door and addressed the company that included Turner and Wright.

'Sing-Song, I'm sorry I brought you off,' he began. 'I shouldn't have done it. I made a mistake.' Having dealt with the individual grievance, Pienaar went on to the broader issue. He spoke with a calmness laced with pressing authority. 'Now, there's a lot of tension between you guys at the moment and I want you to sort it out. You're making our lives very difficult.'

Pienaar's words were greeted with silence.

'You've got to get your eyes back on the ball,' he continued. 'We can't go any further forward until you do. I don't care what all the tensions and niggles are about, I just care about one thing. And that's the emblem you guys are wearing on your chests. And Nigel Wray as well, because he's been good to us.

'I don't care what you all do – go and have a beer or have a croissant, but, for God's sake, *sort it out!* You guys in the backs are the soul of a team – it's always been that way. We forwards, we'll always give our all, but you guys are the spirit of the team, the wit and the intelligence. You've got to sort things out before any of us can get back on track.'

Pienaar left the room and Turner followed him. Johnson stood up immediately and addressed the stunned throng.

'I'd just like to say that I'm fucking pissed off that Matty was brought off and Paul came on.'

With that he sat down and Turner soon returned to the room.

Turner had followed Pienaar out of the room and asked him what was going on. Pienaar replied that Johnson had told him he would not play in the same back division as him. Turner told Pienaar that he was pretty disappointed with that and he thought Johnson should be disciplined for leaving the field.

When Turner returned to the boot room, Johnson asked him why he had come on and whether he was there to coach or to play. Turner replied that he was there to coach. Next, Jeremy Thomson questioned Turner, asking him what the game plan was and accusing Turner of trying to make players play like he used to. The other backs, meanwhile, sat and watched as the explosive personality clashes between the two South Africans and Turner blew wide open. Johnson felt that he and Singer had just started to crack their new combination at fly-half and full-back respectively, and that it had been senseless for that to be disrupted with the game already won. Penaud's injury problems were still a critical factor and they needed to practise the substitute combination as much as possible. Johnson was also deeply offended by Turner's impatience with him in recent weeks as a fly-half. Turner had a habit, when he was angry, of telling players that he was not prepared or was embarrassed to put his name to some of the things they were doing. It had upset some of the players during half-time at the Bedford game in November when Turner had expressed his embarrassment at the way they were playing. And the previous week he had had a blazing row in training with Johnson, whom he accused of doing just whatever he wanted at fly-half, totally ignoring what Turner was asking of him. Again he told Johnson he would not put his name to anything he was doing. Turner, for his part, lamented the loss of Michael Lynagh. He saw Lynagh as the only difference between this season and last – a player who pulled strings and brought others into the game rather than hit it up time and again, something that was a trait of both Penaud and Johnson at fly-half.

If the tension between Turner and the two South Africans was hindering progress, Turner saw Penaud's presence as crippling it. It was a feeling that was taking hold throughout the camp. In the Vicarage Road bar after the Bedford game, comments were passed behind the hands of members of the management team about Penaud's worth to the cause. Evans was taking him out for lunch the next day to have a chat. People felt that he had not been pulling his weight in training, that his injury problems were just getting ridiculous and that perhaps we should have known better if Brive had seen fit to move him out of the way to full-back in his last season there. Turner was in no doubt that Brive were right to remove him from fly-half. His prodigious talents might very well be best employed from the back, where his individualist style of play might find more effective expression. It was a proposition that Pienaar, Evans, Wright and Turner were to consider very seriously in the coming weeks. The key problem, of course, was the lack of alternatives at fly-half.

A backs meeting was organised for the following day at Bracken's house. Pienaar attended to oversee matters and Mike Scott went along to take notes. Pienaar started it off by drawing attention to Johnson's words to him after the Bedford game. Turner had also complained to him about Thomson being a disruptive influence in training and Thomson, in response, had written Pienaar a letter about the state of things. Now was the time for them to sort everything out.

The meeting that followed incorporated more debate between Johnson, Thomson and Turner, but, as it unfolded, the expected grilling of Turner did not materialise. He was more or less in agreement with everything that was said and he emerged from the meeting with a measure of dignity. A black mood had spread throughout the squad on a deeper level with respect to playing matters.

Bracken, acting as spokesman, expressed his concern at the way players were told to do things by the management and were not allowed any feedback. The knee-jerk reactions that had greeted the traumatic defeats in October had stripped the players of much of their confidence. They were not being consulted on playing matters. It was restricting the way they performed on the field. Whereas last season there had been a confidence among players to take things on and to dig their way out of any adverse situations, the attitude this year had become one of fear and inhibition. Bracken was simply not enjoying his rugby at the club. The rest of the backs quickly took up on the theme.

If the mood and equilibrium in the squad had changed from the previous season, the personnel were more or less the same. And the characters, to a man, were honest and entertaining. Bracken, as much as anyone, captured the mould. Regardless of his talent on the field, he had represented the shrewdness of purchase that had characterised Saracens' foray into professionalism. I was a new boy at the Bristol University rugby club when I first encountered the qualities of this club man. Bracken, in his second year, was the first-team captain at the time and was spoken about reverentially in university rugby circles as the star performer in the England Students team. He would take time out to talk to us anonymous freshers to ask us how our holidays had been and how much beer we had drunk. And, as we laboured in the muddy corner of a far-off field for the nth XV, Bracken would often be watching from the touchline. At Saracens, he had immediately struck up a rapport with all and sundry, engaging in various wars of practical jokes. The banter in the Bramley Road dining-room was always high, even at the lowest points, as the characters enjoyed each other's company: Bracken's housemate and terrible twin Danny Grewcock, the Irish contingent of the Wallace brothers and Paddy Johns, the Aussie beach bums Constable and Free, and the mischievous Johnson. (Johnson and his wife Penny lived so close to their local pub that their baby monitor still worked in there. They could thus go for a drink at the pub and not have to worry about a baby-sitter.) These were just some of the new characters that contributed handsomely to the solidarity that had carried over from the old days at Saracens. Off the field, the squad and management to a man had generally enjoyed themselves. That life on the field had now become so burdensome for such characters was not a little worrying.

Turner, also a popular guy off the field, was to speak to Johnson a couple of days later about their disagreement. 'Gav, I thought we'd always got on,' he said. 'We had a bit of an argument last week, but Frankie tells me you never want to play in the same back division as me, and that's why you came off.'

'Paul, I said it in the heat of the moment. I'm sorry,' replied Johnson. 'I was furious. I'd been working all week at fly-half and just as I thought it was going well I'm pulled back to full-back.'

'Yeah, but, Gav, that was for a different reason. Frankie reckoned Matthew wasn't having a good game, dragged him off, and that's why you went to full-back.'

'Yeah, but, Paul, that wasn't explained to me.'

Detecting a therapeutic benefit from the backs meeting, Pienaar then organised a forwards meeting on the same day. Troy Coker, never one to mince his words, set the ball rolling this time. He claimed it was no use Pienaar walking around the club with his jaw round his ankles whenever they lost. It rubbed off on all the players and sent out the wrong signals. His black moods were creating unrest among the camp, with players virtually hiding when they saw Frankie coming.

Pienaar immediately set about making changes and taking steps. A further meeting was held for the players to discuss the game plan from which they felt so ostracised. To Pienaar's astonishment, however, the game plan that emerged from that meeting was the same as the one they were supposed to have been playing all along. On another occasion, after training, Pienaar announced there would be some extra fitness training. Everybody was to be at the Winchmore Arms in 20 minutes' time, and the mother of all piss-ups ensued, spilling on to Eros in Enfield. In addition, a players' committee was set up and, while he was injured, Pienaar shared out the captaincy of the team. Coker, Johns, Penaud, Bracken, Grau and Diprose would all lead the team out in the following months.

First, however, Saracens could only manage a draw at Wasps on a wet, miserable evening three days after the Bedford game. They had exerted massive dominance in the scrum, with Flatman this time taking on England international Will Green, but five penalties apiece left the score at 15–15. In the press conference afterwards, Pienaar and Evans, looking a smooth double act, consigned their chances of winning the title to the bin. 'We'll see the cream separating now,' predicted Pienaar. 'At the start of the season, everyone's a contender and everyone competes for 80 minutes. Now teams who aren't contenders will not be doing that. For us to have a chance, Leicester would have to lose three games now and I can't see that happening.'

Pienaar played the age-old mind game perfectly, and Evans played off him when he mischievously attempted to plant the relevant seed of doubt in Leicester's mind. Their only chance was if Leicester found themselves with a backlog of games at the end of the busy season and a team of exhausted players to play them.

The mood was still subdued but now peaceful, and Saracens started to build a new momentum over the coming month with two easy away victories in the cup against Morley and Lydney and two inspired home victories over Cardiff and Swansea. A new swagger was developing on the field. Bracken was masterful in both Welsh games and his 19-year-old housemate Rob Thirlby emerged as a genuine option at full-back.

The away fixture at second-placed Northampton on the first weekend in February was absolutely vital to Saracens' lingering hopes of the title. They would have to face it without Paul Wallace or Paddy Johns, who were playing for Ireland against France in Dublin.

It was an extraordinary game. A brilliant break from Penaud in the first half had led to a scorching Daniel try, but the boot of Paul Grayson gave Northampton a 12–10 lead at the interval. Keen to extend more responsibility to his players, Pienaar invited Penaud to contribute to the half-time team-talk in the changing-room, and the Frenchman responded with a passionate speech.

Passion was the order of the day, and she was to prove a torrid mistress. In the second half another penalty from Grayson stretched Northampton's lead before disaster struck for Saracens. Piling on the pressure in the Northampton twenty-two, they had secured ruck ball under the opposition's posts, but Andy Blyth, Northampton's centre, tackled Penaud before the ball had even emerged from the ruck. In his frustration, Penaud lashed out at Blyth in one of those borderline gestures that is either a punch or a push, depending on which team you support. The linesman drew the referee's attention to the incident and Penaud was sin-binned for ten minutes. Utterly flabbergasted at the decision, Penaud hurled a tirade of protest at the linesman while Yates and Wright frantically dragged him away. Two minutes later, Pienaar was also sin-binned for use of his boot. Phil Ogilvie had moved into the backs and Saracens were obliged to play the next eight minutes with six forwards. Their response was heroic. They restricted Northampton to one penalty and when Penaud and Pienaar returned they promptly scored a second try to haul back five of the eight points by which Northampton led. Two Johnson penalties then gave Saracens the lead before Grayson missed three long-range penalties (the last hitting the crossbar) to give Saracens the most invigorating win.

Arms were thrown into the air in euphoria. As they had done in the cup semi-final a year ago, the Saracen players crossed the Northampton pitch to pay tribute to the befezzed fans who had been rocketed into an unfamiliar state of jubilation. With the 18th birthday of Nigel Wray's daughter, Lucy, to come, the players looked forward to a long night of lavish (and complimentary) celebration.

A 48–27 victory over West Hartlepool on Valentine's Day, featuring a man-of-the-match hat-trick for Tony Diprose, kept up what pressure Saracens could exert on Leicester at the top of the table the following weekend. But Saracens' thoughts were now turning elsewhere. On the other side of the next round of Five Nations matches awaited the most daunting of challenges. If league success was out of their hands, the cup was still theirs to retain. In their current form, Saracens were installed as favourites for their quarter-final. Despite it being an away tie at Newcastle.

15

Drifting
___

'The first time I met Matt,' Pienaar once said to me, 'I thought he was a newspaper man. He always had the newspaper. He would turn up to a meeting five minutes late and wouldn't think it a big deal. He was like a student, very laid back. "I'd rather read the newspaper than listen to what's being said" seemed to be his attitude.

'Training-wise, he always put in an effort, although I think he suffered a bit in the first season, like everyone else, because the intensity was quite hard. As a player and a person, he progressed really well. He has got the highest mark for a player in a game so far and that was his game against Northampton on the first day of this season.

'He has actually become a utility player, where he can play in three positions, but he hasn't really excelled in one. The reason is that he lacks that cutting edge to his game, be it speed or power. I think it's because of Matt's personality. He's not a selfish person and sometimes you need a bit of selfishness in the game to go to the next level. He needs to be full of confidence to be playing well and he needs to be boosted a lot of times.

'He's a lovely guy, a wonderful guy. I like him a lot. He's a team man through and through. He has done so much good for the club set-up and the team set-up. It's tremendous to have someone like that on board. It's very important. You sometimes take people like that for granted – I don't. I know what effort he puts in.

'I also want to see him excel. Because it's such a tough game and it's the professional era, people are battling to get to grips with it and I think Matty's one of those guys. It's not a dog-eat-dog world, but it is a tough world. You have to be selfish. You have got to have a cutting edge to your game and your whole approach to being the best, to being top of the list when the renegotiations come.

'But he battles to get to grips when he has made a mistake. He sees criticism as a threat. It's not. He should see it in a constructive light. But not everybody can do that. That's why you've got to handle each person differently. Everybody's got a hot and a cold button. Matty's hot button is confidence, his cold button is criticism, so you try to push the hot button more.

'But he's also an intelligent guy. You can't fudge over the issues. I won't. And people would see that as favouritism. Why don't I shit on Matty, when I do with another guy? There's got to be a balance.

'Where Matt goes is in his hands. He's got the ability. I don't know where his best position is. I think he's a full-back, but sometimes I don't, sometimes I think he's a wing. He doesn't have the pace that I want in a deadly wing. But then he did in the semi-final last season – he was tremendous, he scored two tries, we called him super-sub, and he was walking on water after that. In the training sessions before and after that, he could do no wrong. He was miles above the others.

'And that's where I want to keep him.'

Matt Singer started the 1998–99 season very selfishly.

After the bitter disappointments of the preceding campaign and the crippling news that he would have to face another season in Gavin Johnson's shadow, Singer was blinded by the proverbial 'fuck-them' attitude that has inspired any number of celluloid heroes. *Year of the Fez* had been a triumph for him that had been heartily acknowledged by the marketing department and the likes of Mark Evans at Bramley Road, as well as Nigel Wray himself. The result of his labours and that of the boys at TPW Press, Saracens' programme producers in Rickmansworth, was a smart glossy brochure (he had been advised to steer clear of labelling it a magazine). He could not wait to put it before the public on the opening day of the season.

His blinkered excitement for the project seemed to rub off on his game. He had shone in a pre-season schedule that had been noticeably less arduous than that of the season before. He duly won selection on the wing for the first game of the season against Northampton at Vicarage Road.

The performance was to be Saracens' finest of the season and Singer excelled. An aura of confidence cloaked his body. He seemed to have control of high balls before he had caught them, to stop players in their tracks before he had tackled them and to leave the Northampton defence in pieces before he had cut through them. It was a new level of perform-ance for him.

Apparently, it was a new level of performance for a Saracen player full stop. Singer was fêted by the management in the post-match video analysis. He was awarded a mark of 88 per cent. Pienaar had introduced the system of awarding marks to individual players after each game. Michael Lynagh had occasionally got into the low 80s the season before, but Singer was entering new territory here.

Yet, as well as Singer had played, he had done no more than shine within a magnificent team performance. He was a worthy man of the match for that game (in the face of some pretty serious competition), but he had not redefined the art of back play. In awarding him the unprece-dented mark (at the time of writing, his mark has still not been approached), Pienaar was pressing Singer's hot button and in the short term the desired effect was achieved. Singer was certainly buzzing at the time. But, as the season disintegrated, for Saracens as well as for Singer, the 88 per cent mark would grow to feel more of a millstone than a spur. A high-water mark had been set for him on the first day of the season. Thenceforth, he could only fall short of it.

Without ever quite hitting the heights of that first game, Singer's form continued in his integral contribution to Saracens' strident opening to the season. As a wing, full-back and centre, he was nigh faultless as Saracens set the pace for the rest to follow. But, like that of the team, his bubble was to burst in the aftermath of the Stoop Memorial Ground massacre.

With Johnson injured, Singer moved back to full-back, where he had a quiet game amid the flying bullets. He was seriously criticised after the débâcle. He had called Paddy Johns off the blind side of a ruck to tackle Thierry Lacroix and help defend a potential overlap. Yet, despite Johns' tackle on the Frenchman, Singer tackled Lacroix anyway and provided Jamie Williams with the overlap that he was trying to prevent. It was Quins' first try and the rest is history.

Singer was dropped, although Johnson's recurring injury earned him a reprieve for the next two games. After the Wasps defeat, however, he was out.

Feeling something of a scapegoat, Singer approached Pienaar for a talk, which was conducted in the doorway of Pienaar's office at Bramley Road. Richie Wallace, Brendon Daniel and the newly arrived decathlete Brian Taylor all suddenly seemed to be ranked above him on the wing and selection issues in the centre were regularly pushing Ryan Constable out wide as well. Where had the confidence in him gone that only six weeks earlier had inspired a mark of 88 per cent? Pienaar told Singer that he lacked the raw athletic edge that frightened defences; he needed to develop his pace and power so that they became threatening weapons in his armoury.

It was a valid point. Constable had been the fastest sprinter in the squad for over a year before the arrival of Taylor, who was a specialist athlete. Wallace and Daniel were not far behind. Daniel, at the time, was one of the most elusive wingers in England, with his sinewy strength and pace. Singer, meanwhile, was equipped with superior footballing qualities and a smooth intelligence. Around such quandaries, however, do selection issues revolve. In this case, the prevailing view was against Singer.

Once again, Singer could feel his mood plummeting into freefall. The heady days of September seemed far away. But it required an eye-bulging gulp to stomach this latest rejection. The team had produced some inherently flawed performances in October, and of the various reactions that they had incited from the management, the first looked to be a loss of confidence in the ability of Matt Singer, one of the form players in the early part of the season. As he was playing most of his rugby on the wing at that time, it was difficult to see how he could be responsible for the violent upheavals that had so suddenly shaken the team's on-field composure. Yet his rivals were bigger names than him and/or more threatening propositions in attack. The selectors felt safer returning to their more obvious gifts.

Singer was now condemned to a life on the bench, only to be released on parole whenever Alain Penaud was injured – which was in fact becoming an increasingly regular pardon. But even when the home internationals were away on pre-Christmas international duty, Singer did not benefit. Kyran Bracken aside, Saracens' home internationals were all in the forwards. Hence he was still sidelined for the two league games that Saracens had to negotiate with only half a team.

One of them was a dour Sunday-afternoon game at Bedford. I was sitting next to Singer on the Saracen bench. An early box kick went up on Brian Taylor, which he struggled to field and eventually fumbled into touch. Feeling the need to boost the obviously flagging morale of my friend, I nudged him.

'Hey, Matt Singer would have had that!' I chirped up.

'No,' replied Singer, slumped into his chair, staring at his comrades moving across the heavy turf to the resultant line-out. 'He's not powerful enough.'

Singer had always had a nice line in sardonic humour. The ebullient enthusiasm, however, against which it had characteristically been offset was rapidly waning. Singer had never known his motivation to be so low. Throughout the season, as he drove to training, he would speak into a dictaphone about life at Saracens to help me with this book. Playing the tapes back, I would hear a voice far removed from the 'Sing-Song' chimes that used to resonate throughout our house at university. A long, ghostly drone would emanate from my speakers, occasionally punctuated by forced explosions of jollity as he tried to conjure up the enthusiasm that had been such a familiar companion through his life. He felt like he had spent the entire week before the Bedford game holding a tackle bag. 'Defend, defend, defend,' he drawled into his dictaphone. Looking about him, he could see no future for him at Saracens. David Thompson was coming back from injury and another precocious talent in Rob Thirlby was forcing Singer on to the wing in the midweek team. He knew he was only ever to be considered as a handyman who could fill in whenever there was an injury. He started to think about looking for another club, a place where he felt wanted and where it might be him for whom they waited, were he to be out with injury.

He might not have the choice, of course. Mark Evans had reminded the squad during the week that 19 contracts were up for renewal come the end of the season. There was a strong sense of impending change in the air. The legion of players in the midweek team were mindful of a proposed regime for the next season, under which Saracens would jettison most of their squad and fill the substitutes' bench with the associate professionals (youngsters who were paid a small retainer to play for the club). It would be cheaper to pay them five grand each to sit on the bench than to pay a full-time professional twenty-five grand to do it. Evans's reminder had been intended as a chivvy-up, but most of the squad realised that it constituted their death knell.

Playing in the midweek team is a fabled phenomenon and the scourge of every sportsman's peace of mind. But the widespread fame of its debilitating effects does not render life in its clutches any easier. Every club or tour has its pet name for the midweek team. At Saracens they called themselves 'the drift'. It was an evocative nickname that neatly captured the mood among the squad players.

The second-team circuit in English rugby is pretty shambolic. Some clubs in the professional era have disbanded all teams below the first team, while the fixtures for those with second teams are irregularly scattered throughout the season and can be cancelled at the drop of a hat. Inevitably, most of a club's energies are channelled into the first team. There are, however, only 15 men in the first team at any one time and the unwieldy mass of squad players supporting them are subordinated to the prime directive of maintaining the first team's form. It becomes soul-destroying.

Of course, most of the problem was directly related to the poor form of the first team and the black mood that it had cast over the club. A vicious circle started to turn. When your first team are losing, soul-searching sweeps throughout an institution and the atmosphere darkens. The heavy and desperate minds focus more and more ferociously on fixing the problems in the first team, and the midweek team, depressed anyway by the first team's form and the consequent mood in the camp, are increasingly neglected. A flat and motiveless midweek team, perhaps even more than a stuttering show team, then serves to drag the morale of the club still further into the mire. The form of one cannot necessarily be said to shape the form of the other, but one can rest assured that the form of both teams in any one season will be broadly similar.

The drift served as a pretty accurate barometer of the feeling in the camp at Saracens. After a typical second-team training session, the showers at Bramley Road would ring out with the galley songs of the unwanted. Kris Chesney and Craig Yandell came up with a beauty to the tune of 'D-I-S-C-O' that ran 'D-R-I-F-T', and other songs would grow from the communal banter in the shower. To the tune of 'Sailing', the drift would sing:

We are drifting,
We are drifting,
Throughout the season,
Without a game.
We are drifting,
No one knows us.
We are drifting,
We are shit.

Morale was low.

Singer, meanwhile, was drifting with the best of them. Off the field, he kept himself busy as social secretary, organising golf for the players, a Christmas lucky dip and Christmas gifts for the management and helping to organise the Christmas party. The Matt Singer Sports Quiz that he used to organise for the players at Bramley Road would test even the knowledge of Tony Diprose.

On the field, he was in and out of the first team with a regularity that exactly mirrored the fitness or otherwise of Penaud. When Penaud came off, Johnson would step up to fly-half and Singer would come on at full-back. He would be a bundle of nerves. He was now resigned to a life on the bench: his motivation had been reduced to working to make the bench each game so that he could collect his match fee and his win bonus, where applicable. Whenever he came on he made mistakes, and he was duly lashed for it in the post-match analyses. Sitting on the bench was no longer intolerable because he was not playing but because he was worrying so much about the possibility that, at some point, he might have to. His confidence was shot, and when he was brought off in the home game against Bedford in the New Year (a change that required Paul Turner to come off the bench), he knew his career at Saracens was in pieces. The midweek team, the only avenue of release for the squad players, continued to stumble from one shambolic farce to another.

In his acute frustration and despair, Singer scribbled a letter to Pienaar on 15 January. He detailed how he had had all enthusiasm hammered out of him by the lack of feedback from the management on his performances in recent months. In the last nine matches in which he had played, he had not received a word of praise for the good things that he had done. He had received what he felt to be an unnecessarily poor mark against Bedford and in previous matches had not even received a mark, despite having come on and played longer than other players who had been given one.

'In each game I have done some very good things,' he claimed, 'but there has not been a word of praise from *any* coaching/management member. However, a mistake against Bedford, which gave them the try from a poorly executed chip, has become fair game for anyone and everyone to mock me.

'It is not the actual percentage marks that have raised such anger inside me (I was the highest achiever when I was dropped in October, so my faith in that particular system is understandably low). It is because I have received so little encouragement or explanation in the last two and a half months that I have had to resort to this method of communication.'

In his letter, Singer also complained about the lack of support for the midweek team. During Christmas week, Singer had asked Pienaar to address this situation, yet the following week's game against Northampton, one of the strongest second teams on the circuit, was cancelled, despite Singer's personal attempts to raise a team.

'Sensing the complete lack of enthusiasm from the management to get a team together,' Singer complained, 'I contacted my contacts at Cambridge University. I filled the two vacant spots with the Cambridge captain at loose-head and another Cambridge Blue in the centre. Two players who would not only cope, but excel in the surroundings. No video had been prepared for pre-match analysis and there has been absolutely no feedback from the last *four* midweek games. I was left to organise a think-tank meeting to simplify the game plan, considering we had our fifth new fly-half in succession in the midweek team.

'Up until now I have explained it all away – it's the first team that matters, so all focus must be on sorting out their problems. The players in the midweek squad won't be needed next season, so why bother with them (you intimated at this during the weeks surrounding the Harlequins/Wasps/Newcastle games). But now that my motivation has reached rock bottom, I feel I must make my feelings known. You *will* need the also-rans before the end of this season, whether they are needed for next season or not.'

Singer had complained about the management's lack of communication through the 'points for consideration' facility that the players had been invited to use to voice any queries to the management. The fact that none of the management had replied to his points for consideration, or addressed the issues raised, had prompted him to write his letter. While he was composing the letter, however, Tim Wright had taken the time out to explain his omission for the forthcoming Cardiff friendly.

'Once again,' wrote Singer, 'I had assumed the reason, but it was very kind of him to take on the potentially difficult task of explaining the decision. What concerned me was that he did not know whether anyone else had spoken to me, so perhaps each member of the management assumes another will be talking to players.'

Singer received a characteristically swift and decisive reply, which dealt with the issues under separate bullet points.

Matt,

- On the 'points for consideration' feedback to the management, I saw the note but thought it was sarcastic, tongue in cheek. But I have made a judgement error and will look into it.

- It is difficult to remember the time you came on to the field for a substantial period and were not awarded a score. It is a valid point and I will take more notice of it and explain why we have not awarded a score.

- It is unfair to say that you are not praised when you do a good thing. You have received the highest score this season for your game against Northampton, the biggest praise anyone has got. Maybe you don't want to remember the praise I gave you for that, but just the criticisms?

- MY DOOR IS ALWAYS OPEN. Although I would like to talk to each and every pro on a regular basis, it is difficult playing, coaching, analysing, etc., etc. Therefore I appreciate it when a player initiates conversation or invites me for a drink.

- The midweek game against Gloucester was approached in the same fashion as a first-team fixture. Pre-match meal in hotel followed by discussion groups, etc. It is impossible to compile footage of opposition second teams and it amazes me that a guy of your intelligence would raise such a petty criticism.

- What did we learn from the Gloucester game by playing several players out of position and others that didn't know the game plan?

- I appreciate your appetite for playing strong teams and thank you for your commitment in organising the back-up players from Cambridge. But combine this with more players out of position and what will we achieve? Do you appeciate that some of these decisions – hopefully all – are for the benefit of our squad and not the other way round?

- The midweek squad will always be needed and to have one is *vital* for the professional era. How it will operate next season is being planned.

- If you want to see yourself as an also-ran, that is your decision. I have a dream to build something special and there are a lot of open seats on the boat.

- If you assume something, you more often than not will make an ASS of U and ME. Talk, my door is open.

- I have been in a similar situation before and things that worked for me won't necessarily work for you, but my motivation comes from within. The external factors are very important, but it is your ability, body and mind that have produced some exhilarating stuff on the rugby pitch.

- Some players wait for things to happen, others make it happen – your choice.

Singer absorbed Pienaar's words and went to see him the following day. He, like most of the western hemisphere, had the utmost admiration for Pienaar's ferocious self-motivation and acknowledged that his own motivation was at an all-time low – a problem he would have to address. Nevertheless, from his point of view, he had suddenly been dropped, despite being one of Saracens' form players at the start of the season, and on a hiding to nothing as a stand-in player he had since felt like a criminal whenever he came on the field. The downward spiral had been relentless, as low morale had led to poor performance, which had led to criticism, which had led to further anxiety, which had led to poorer performance, and so on. Singer could foresee few opportunities at Saracens for him to reverse the decline.

Like so many of the players, the end of the season loomed as a foreboding horizon in Singer's life. With the recent birth of professional rugby, an unfortunate clock had been set ticking which now saw a host of contracts reach simultaneous conclusions. It created a thorny dilemma for the club, with the future of so many players in the balance at the same time, and proved not a little unnerving for the players. Handling this crescendo with a minimum of disruption and offence would require some neat diplomacy from Saracens.

Singer's was one of the contracts up at the end of May and he was far from confident that it would be extended. He and Steve Ravenscroft had each arranged to meet Mark Evans in the third week of January to discuss their futures. Although contract talks were scheduled for the second half of March, Ravenscroft was keen to garner an early indication so that he might inform Lovell White Durrant, his law firm who had thus far entertained his double life as a professional rugby player and lawyer, of his future commitments.

Singer, meanwhile, was just keen to know where he stood. He had already decided that he would like to do more than just play rugby next season. If Saracens still wanted him, he would be keen to involve himself in the development of the associate professionals and to help them manage their way into professionalism, to act as an intermediary between the youngsters and the management.

The meetings that he and Ravenscroft had arranged with Evans fell on the day after a midweek victory over Blackheath. Singer had consequently had the morning off and had carefully shaved and groomed himself for the discussion. He arrived at Bramley Road where the first-team squad were eating lunch, having spent the morning training.

Singer joined them but was soon called away by Evans, who took him and Ravenscroft to one side. Evans apologised but told them that he wanted to deal with all of the contract issues in one batch. He would see them in the second half of March after all. In the meantime, however, he pointed out that no one had said they could not speak to other clubs.

It was not an episode to inspire confidence. Moreover, for the first time in his 18-month professional career, Singer was not in the first-team squad for that weekend's game against Swansea. Barry Lea, the Australian winger on loan from Queensland, would start on one wing with Brendon Daniel on the other, and the young Rob Thirlby would take Singer's place on the bench after an impressive showing against Cardiff the weekend before. Singer sensed the end drawing near.

A further development had rendered concern for the future all the more pressing. Saracens, enjoying an upturn in form after the Welsh friendlies, had just triumphed in heroic circumstances at Northampton in the league and the feeling prevailed that the title challenge was still alive. After the game Singer had, at the last minute and rather presumptuously, asked me for a lift back home to Shenley. Allison had been ill and was in hospital, so he wanted to get back home quickly. The team bus, meanwhile, would be returning to Bramley Road before the squad descended on the Wrays' house to help celebrate the 18th birthday of their daughter, Lucy. Having waited the standard hour or so for him to banter, shower, banter, change, banter and emerge from the players' tunnel bantering, I drove him down the M1. In the car Singer spoke to Allison on the mobile phone and then, having completed the conversation, turned to me.

'Allison's pregnant.'

Narrowly averting a minor pile-up on the M1, I swiftly re-established my grip on the steering wheel.

They had learnt of the news in January, prompting Singer to request an early contract discussion. They were, however, keeping the news private. Allison was still in the period most susceptible to miscarriages and her illness, although not serious, was unusual and was causing mild concern among the doctors. Singer had kept Mike Scott at Saracens informed of the situation, but otherwise they were waiting for Allison to be cleared of any doubt before they announced it generally. At the end of the following week Allison was out of hospital and Singer announced the news to a delighted and congratulatory squad.

Singer's life now had a focus that provided welcome relief from the bleak depersonalisation of life in the Saracen reserves. His rugby career was providing little in the way of inspiration. He was now either on the bench or not involved at all, with Rob Thirlby superseding him. A game at Vicarage Road against Bath in the Cheltenham and Gloucester Cup (the competition conducted between the top clubs during the Five Nations) was built up as a chance for the midweek players to put down a marker for inclusion in the first team. Singer was included at full-back. The team, however, had long since stopped believing in the 'this is your big chance' line and their subsequent first-half performance was dire against a Bath outfit starting to find its feet again after a miserable winter. Singer was desperately nervous again, fluffed his goal-kicking duties and was substituted in the second half.

The following weekend the first-team squad left for Newcastle without him and were sent crashing out of the cup at the quarter-final stage. Singer, at home with his family in Porthcawl, felt like any other fan when he heard the news. He was gutted but he felt distant. The clock was ticking down to his meeting with Evans when he would be informed of his fate. In his heart he knew what the outcome would be, but the mind cannot help constructing happier scenarios. His morale, like that of other squad members at the club, was boosted a fraction with the news that the league next season would be played throughout the World Cup. Saracens would need a big squad to cover the loss of most of their first team during that period, a realisation that encouraged the fringe players to believe they had a future at the club. Yet there pervaded a sombre, nervous atmosphere among the squad as the majority awaited their respective contract talks with the same relish with which the condemned await the firing squad.

Singer had made sure that his appointment was among the first and had booked the 10.30 slot on Friday, 19 March. Steve Ravenscroft was before him at ten o'clock, and Singer joked that he would probably be greeted with tears as Ravenscroft, the faithful and emotional servant, took his leave. At quarter past ten, I pulled into the driveway at Bramley Road as Ravenscroft drove out. With a terse flick of his wrist, the normally cheery centre acknowledged me before speeding off. I feared the worst.

Singer arrived soon afterwards and we sat together in the dining-hall, cracking anxious jokes. A few minutes later, Mark Evans came out of his office. The sparse needles in his angry haircut bristled with characteristic attitude, but the big, homely glasses on his nose adorned a pale face drawn with emotion.

'Well, Matt,' he said with a weary smirk, 'shall we do it?'

The pair adjourned to the same wood-panelled office in which Rob Cunningham had so rudely greeted Singer upon his arrival at Saracens a little over three years earlier. Singer placed himself on the brown office chair in front of Evans's desk, while Evans threw himself into the high-backed swivel chair behind it. He looked at Singer through his thick glasses.

'There's no easy way to say this,' he began. 'We're not taking you on next year.'

Singer did not flinch, but started playing with his loose-fitting wedding ring below the enormous broken knuckle that secured it.

'Now, feel free to talk to me about it next week if you want. I'm happy to take you through all the whys and wherefores, but I realise it won't make any difference to the way things stand or the way you feel. I know you'll be gutted. And so am I, to be fair.'

There was a pause. Singer, sitting straight, held his head high and continued to play with his wedding ring.

'Well, I suppose I knew . . .' he stammered. 'I mean, what . . .?' He took a long, thoughtful intake of breath. 'You've got some good young-sters coming through.'

Evans took up the baton.

'You're in your mid-twenties, Matt. You're not going to get any better than you are now. If you were 18 or 19, we could work on you, but you've been unlucky with the timing of professionalism. If you'd have been caught at a formative age, things might have been different, but you're not going to be a Test player now. And you're not young. Next season the squad is coming down to about 25 and, basically, if you're going to be in it, you've got to be an international or a young-ster.

'Another issue is that we've got Rob Thirlby and he's a goal-kicker. And Rob and Thomo [David Thompson] are younger and cheaper. The wages have got to come down and that means that guys like you, who aren't internationals but are in your mid-twenties and cost a bit of money, are going to suffer. And we'll be moving Ryan [Constable] back to the wing next season.

'Look, please feel free to come back and discuss what you want to do next. But if you want my opinion . . . I think rugby is in fucking chaos and I'd get out now and build a career. Unless you're an international and are gonna make a fortune, I'd go. You are a very good club player, but you're not going to be a Test player. Best scenario: you'll get another three-year contract. That'll take you up to the age of 29, then what?

'I have to say – I haven't talked to anyone about this, so I don't know – but you have done so much for this place on and off the field and it has been so much appreciated. If you made it known that you were going to go for a career, I wouldn't be surprised if someone came in with some pretty good work for you.'

Singer, in a last act of constructive input and no doubt fishing for a bit of work already, voiced his fears to Evans about the young players and the way they were treated. The future of young schoolboys coming into the game is possibly the most critical issue facing professional rugby. Although rugby is still sufficiently close to its amateur roots to retain some welfare provision for its saplings (in that they are generally allowed to go to university, even if it has to be local), the wheels of the rugby factory are turning. The future of the players after rugby is clearly of secondary importance to the development of their immediate assets as players. The logical conclusion of this trend towards a professional future is the situation facing footballers, whom the football industry appropriates at tender ages and then turns out into the real world when they are spent. Rugby is still a long way from that, and Saracens have an outstanding youth set-up that Evans himself had been instrumental in building, but the future is heading towards that scenario, not away from it. These are issues, of course, that would require a book in themselves, but Singer was here concerned with the immediate handling of the younger elements within the actual playing squad.

'I think, Mark,' he said, 'that there's a lack of work on the associates. I don't think the 18- and 19-year-olds are being catered for enough. You know, they play in friendly games against Cardiff or Swansea or someone, and then are discarded for the next one. No one talks to them about it and they think it's because they're shit.

'You need someone who is there to liaise between them and the management and to help them with motivation and life skills. Matt Cairns [the young hooker] has a bad day throwing in, nobody takes him aside to talk to him about it and he has to go off and practise by himself. The Brunel [University] boys slog it up to training from university, it takes them an hour and a half to get here and then it's, "Where have you been?" And then you've got someone like Dave Flatman who has to remember to smile and remind himself that he's living his dream or he just gets miserable.'

Evans nodded throughout and scribbled notes, thanking Singer profusely for his input and saying how he had only recently advised Nigel Wray that he felt they were understaffed at Bramley Road.

Having made his points, Singer got to his feet and, with a shake of Evans's hand, left the room. I sat down opposite Evans.

'This has been the worst week in my life,' he said. He was sitting back in his chair, emotionally drained. His glasses were large and thick, but I thought I could see a tear welling in each of his eyes. 'I've got about 20 of these to get through. Ches [Kris Chesney] is next and his is good news, otherwise they're all "no"s today.'

'How was Ravers?' I asked, assuming Ravenscroft had been administered the bullet.

'Not good. We've fudged his a bit, actually. We can't decide between him and Kevin [Sorrell], so I've told him the jury's still out. It's the only one that's kept me awake at night.'

'Well, you've known him for about nine years now,' I reasoned.

Evans looked at me with another weary smirk and nodded.

So, Ravenscroft had a stay of execution, although that was not much good to him with his legal commitments. Singer, meanwhile, had taken up position on one of the sofas in the players' lounge. He chatted with a sympathetic Ryan Constable (who had another year to run on his contract), while Kris Chesney entered the lion's den and Craig Yandell arrived for his turn. Chesney came out with the news that he had been offered another year. Yandell emerged a few minutes later nursing his bullet wound. He took his seat next to Singer and, with a strange mixture of disappointment and relief, the pair wondered what they would do next. Alex Bennett, who also had another year to run, had joined them in their philosophical ruminations. Bennett's season had been disrupted by injury, but he had become a stalwart of the drift and he was about to leave for Warrington Wolves, Peter Deakin's rugby league club, on loan for the rest of the season. Yandell voiced a desire to return to his roots in the West Country, while Singer mulled over the quandary facing him with a baby on the way. The lifestyle of full-time professional rugby was ideal for raising a child: apart from the healthy salary, there was plenty of free time. He was keen, however, to go part-time and have something else to employ him.

'You've got to stick with it, Matty,' suggested Bennett. 'At the start of this season, we all thought you'd be playing for England.'

Bennett then took his leave. He was off to Warrington and was not sure when he would next see them all. It was breaking up. The catalogue of the departing unfolded over the next few days.

Troy Coker left his one-year contract early under a cloud. Gavin Johnson could not wait to return to the plains of his beloved Africa, where he was retiring to a life running a safari lodge in Zambia. This time there was not even the slightest hint of a change of mind. Paddy Johns was returning home to Ulster, where he intended to finish his playing career.

The roll call continued. Brendan Reidy had already learnt of his fate through his agent, who had earlier spoken to Evans because Reidy could no longer bring himself to do so. Many have been offended by Evans's fitful moods. If you are flavour of the month he is scintillating company, but he can brusquely pass over those who do not fit into his immediate frame of reference. Some attribute his fickle attention span to a free-ranging intellect, others to a ruthless disregard for anything he considers peripheral, and others to the short man's need to assert himself. If he considers your conversation over, he will move on to another. Reidy and Evans were to sort out their differences before the season ended, but a lot of disjointed noses have been left in Evans's wake. The loyalty of those who are close to him, however, is fierce.

By the end of March, Richie Wallace, Adrian Olver, Andy Lee (who had already moved into the marketing department at Watford), Gregg Botterman (who was bought out of the final year of his contract), Brad Free, Marcus Olsen, Brendon Daniel, Yandell and Singer had all been advised of their imminent departures.

Daniel's departure caused a major outcry among the Saracen fans. The news came as a complete shock to everyone, not least Daniel him-self, and it was one of those decisions that did seem a little difficult to explain. Although acknowledged by Evans as a decision that might return to haunt them, the feeling was that they might be better served by a more complete footballer with a higher workrate. Yet he appeared to satisfy most of the criteria for a renewed contract: he was young, he was supremely gifted and, if his footballing skills were a weakness, they were improving rapidly. Daniel seemed to take the news in his stride, however. When he scored a typically dazzling solo try in the defeat by Harlequins a few weeks later, he leapt into the crowd in true showbiz fashion and milked the cheers of his adoring public. Daniel was a colourful character. To shake his hand was to become tied up in an elaborate brotherhood variant of that simple greeting. He had earned the nickname 'Cuzzy Bro' from his team-mates because of his tendency to call everyone 'cuz' or 'bro', and, with his guitar never far away, he had become a popular member of the squad.

The already-fractured team morale inevitably continued to dissipate after the contract talks. Another development unfolded the following week that sent the management spinning with worry and compromised the contract talks still further. Nigel Wray phoned Evans on a Tuesday night to inform him that the clubs had agreed in principle to the introduction of a wage cap. It was news that sent Evans deeper into depression. Everyone, including Evans, was in favour of the idea, but it was the timing and severity of the measure that concerned him, both of which had yet to be established. Earlier that same day he had success- fully negotiated and signed an expensive new three-year deal with one of his leading players, which would threaten to become a millstone should a draconian and immediate wage cap be introduced. In a panic, he had been forced to put on hold the contract negotiations that he was con- ducting with Paul Wallace, Richard Hill and Tony Diprose. Until they knew the exact details of the wage cap, Evans felt they could proceed no further. Hill's and Diprose's contracts were not such pressing issues, since they didn't expire until December, but Wallace's was up in May and, as the squad's only specialist tight-head over the previous three years, he was arguably Saracens' most indispensable player.

Despite the crushing blow upon morale that the contract talks had dealt, it had been an honourable measure on Saracens' part to resolve them before they expired. There was a delicate balance to strike here. It was clear that players would lose all commitment to the club if they knew that their careers there were over. Only personal pride and the need to impress future employers would motivate them to perform in any future opportunities that season. Yet to turn around at the season's end and tell players then that their contracts were terminated would leave them in limbo. Evans had felt it important that the issue be broached with the relevant players a couple of months before the con- tracts were due to expire. Pienaar was not so sure but agreed to it. Amid all the simmering ill feeling that had brewed throughout the season, the players were grateful to Saracens for resolving contractual issues early. Other clubs were not doing this, and Saracens, embroiled in a desperate fight for a place in Europe, were compromising their chances of qualification by giving the players notice with several crucial games still to follow.

Singer's adventure with Saracens, however, was now over. He would not play again for the first team, although he was required for bench duty in a crucial league game at London Irish. He had put out feelers to other clubs through David Powell, the lawyer who acts as Kyran Bracken's agent. Stade Français showed an interest but concrete offers were quick to come in from Neath and Narbonne, the two first-class clubs that had previously experienced the benefits of Singer's membership. Narbonne came in with a deal that represented a marked improvement on Singer's current contract. Neath's offer was similar to his Saracen contract but with little in the way of win bonuses or match fees. The Narbonne offer was tempting, but a move to a foreign country might prove trying with a baby on the way. Singer also wanted to be employed by his future club as more than just a player. Conferring with Tony Copsey, who had moved to Llanelli to head their marketing department as well as play, Singer informed Neath of his desire to fill a similar role. He travelled down to Wales to discuss the situation with the club and they arrived at a revised contract. Singer would become commercial and marketing director at Neath as well as playing full-back.

The move was perfect. Singer's parents were thrilled at the idea of him and Allison moving back to the area, where they might cast a watchful eye over their new grandchild as he or she grew up. And the staff at Neath were delighted at Singer's return. 'We'll have you in that Wales shirt yet!' promised Lynn Jones, Neath's coach with whom Singer had got on so well in his former days at the club.

The force seemed to be with Singer once more as he wound down his commitments with Saracens and prepared for the new challenges that lay ahead. He and Allison managed to sell their house in Shenley immediately for a very tidy profit and encountered similarly little difficulty in buying a four-bedroomed house in Porthcawl. Leaving Saracens, meanwhile, would cause little in the way of distress. Singer had developed some close friendships in the four years that he had spent at the club and would miss the people to a man. He had also formed a rapport with many of the fans and was touched by messages and gifts of good will. But there were too many difficult memories to render his parting from Saracens anything other than a relief.

That chapter, however, was now closed. With the same excitement with which he had greeted his new life as a professional rugby player two years earlier, he returned to the land of his upbringing with his pregnant wife. He looked forward to the birth of a new Singer.

16

Run-in

The memories of that dreamy May day at Twickenham still registered profoundly within the Saracen camp. If much else had failed during the season to date, they could still describe themselves as the holders of the Tetley's Bitter Cup. And they could still win the 1999 version.

For that to happen, however, they would have to do what no other team had managed in nearly three seasons. They would have to win at Kingston Park, the spiritual home of Newcastle.

Saracens had only had one home draw in winning the cup the season before and that was against Leicester. They had not been given one in the 1999 event. Their first two ties were away draws against relatively straightforward third-division opposition, although a trip into the infamous Forest of Dean to take on Lydney had caused some palpitations, particularly when Paddy Johns was assaulted during the game by a member of the West Country crowd. Saracens' draw for the quarter-final, however, was as formidable as they come and rekindled the intense rivalry between the previous season's front-runners.

The conditions in the north-east on the last day of February were characteristically miserable as a persistent drizzle was whipped across the featureless outskirts of Newcastle in which Kingston Park is situated. The few hardy Fez Boys who had made the long journey from London huddled together on the exposed terraces.

Playing into the wind in the first half, Saracens looked the more likely try-scorers, coming close on a couple of occasions, but a penalty from Jonny Wilkinson had earned Newcastle a three-point lead at the break. Pienaar, who was having a forthright game, worked on the team morale at half-time in between the lung-dredging fits of coughing that had been troubling him for a day or two. With their captain and talisman sounding like he was fast approaching death's door, Saracens returned to the ever-worsening conditions outside in an ominous silence.

The decision to play into the wind in the first half backfired. The elements performed an abrupt about-turn for the second half. The wind intensified and blew viciously into and across Saracens' faces, rendering any sort of kicking game farcical. The ferocious figure of Va'aiga Tuigamala then proceeded to peddle his own brand of biting inclemency. The Pacific Islander burst through the Saracen defence to score two tries as the visitors' composure waned alarmingly in the deteriorating conditions. Sitting as high in the stands as they could in order to escape the rain that was blown under the overhang, Evans and Scott watched helplessly. With tears welling in the eyes of native Geordie Mike Scott, Saracens' hands were slowly prised free from the Tetley's Bitter Cup. A 15–0 defeat rendered the long train journey home that Sunday night a voyage back to painful emptiness. There would be no trip to Twickenham this year. A desolate Pienaar sat in the café at Newcastle station with a beer in his hand, surrounded by Evans, Turner, Wright and Yates, and described it as the worst season in his career.

Pienaar was to close himself off again in the aftermath of the defeat. The following Wednesday there was a second-team game at Richmond which saw Saracens register an uplifting victory. The conditions were even more appalling than in Newcastle, affording Brendon Daniel the opportunity to indulge in countless belly slides across the sodden pitch.

In the Richmond bar after the game, Pienaar stood watching the closing stages of Manchester United's European Cup clash with Inter Milan. He sipped quietly from a pint of Guinness. His black leather jacket stretched cavernously across his broad shoulders as his players filtered into the bar and drank together in small clusters. Turner, who still felt distant from him, approached Pienaar.

'You all right, Frankie?' he enquired.

'Yeah, I'm okay.'

'Well, you haven't looked it. You need to come and speak to us.'

'You've got to understand, Paul, I'm different to you guys. I take it pretty hard.'

'So do we. But we're supposed to be a team. Where I come from, we take it on the chin, and we live together and get pissed together, and we sort it out.'

The pair proceeded to have a few beers in the Richmond clubhouse.

Now out of the cup, Saracens' hopes of winning the league were surviving by the most precarious of margins. In third place, they were one point behind second-placed Northampton and had a game in hand over leaders Leicester, who themselves were seven points ahead of Saracens. Leicester had lost three times, Saracens five times with one draw. Essentially, they could not afford to lose again and they had to hope that in their remaining seven or eight games Leicester would lose three times and Northampton once. It was not inconceivable. The next round of league matches would see Leicester visit Northampton and the Tigers still had away trips to Bath and Newcastle to negotiate, as well as a contest against Wasps. Saracens would also be paying a visit to Welford Road in April.

The defeat in the cup, however, had hit hard. Pienaar advised the squad of the importance of ensuring second place in the league. It was the first time that anything other than the prospect of triumph had been entertained. Perhaps it had been the actual removal of the prospect of triumph in the cup that had invoked the lowering of ambition. Or perhaps the gloomy words of Pienaar and Evans after the draw at Wasps had been genuine and not just the playing of mind games.

After a passing alleviation during the Welsh friendlies and the victory at Northampton, the black, black thrall that had shrouded the squad for much of the season settled once again in the wake of the cup defeat. Unrenewed contracts were due for review in the coming month and a heavy burden of pessimism weighed upon a sizeable majority of the squad. And there was no longer the glamour of Twickenham to spur them through the rainy days of late winter.

Further ill feeling was to arise in the aftermath of the cup defeat. In the video review, there was a rare examination of Steve Ravenscroft's performance. And he was not even present to defend himself. The following day, Tim Wright took him through the video review, and Ravenscroft, in the privacy of Wright's office, countered the criticism with the plausible justifications for his actions in the game. Ravenscroft had felt that he had had a reasonable game but was philosophical about the criticism. In a game as grey and open to interpretation as rugby, one can take most pieces of evidence and work it to suit one's line of argument. He had also been praised on other occasions for things that he had thought pretty standard.

At training two days later, Ravenscroft was duly relieved of his place in the starting line-up for the game at Sale. A slightly sickening feeling quietly oozed throughout the squad. Ravenscroft was a rock and had become one of the unshakeable points of reference around which the Saracen empire had been built. He was the life and soul of the club, having joined from school nine years before. Everyone in the squad honoured him with the utmost respect and affection. And, throughout all the turbulence, he had been one of the players of the season, with his emotional commitment and rational balance. It had become a source of some amusement that in the post-match allocation of marks throughout the season, Ravenscroft invariably picked up the same assessment from Pienaar: 'Ravers. Sixty-nine. Solid.'

His ejection from the starting line-up was viewed disapprovingly. Nevertheless, Kev Sorrell, who took Ravenscroft's place, had been pushing hard and the coaches had long known that the youngster was deserving of a few starts. There were other changes too. Danny Grewcock picked up a nasty knee-ligament injury in training and was replaced by Kris Chesney in the second row. Gavin Johnson, meanwhile, was also dropped. Kev Sorrell and Jeremy Thomson, returning from long-term injury, formed a new centre partnership, pushing Ryan Constable on to the wing, from where Rob Thirlby moved back to full-back. Johnson's response to the prospect of sitting on the bench was characteristically dry. 'I hope I don't have to come on,' he said during one session of banter with the boys. 'It will be very cold up there.'

It was, indeed, to be a cold day for Saracens. Nigel Wray had made comments in the week about the inadequacy of Sale's facilities for a first-rate professional rugby club and the home team, along with their frosty supporters, took great pleasure in their subsequent 32–24 triumph. Saracens had more than enough of the game to win it, but the midfield pace, power and guile of Shane Howarth, Chris Yates and Jos Baxendell tore their defence apart. Leicester beat Northampton. The door to the title was finally slammed shut.

Immediately after the game, Turner and Wright left for Natal, where they spent 11 days of reconnaissance studying the methods of Natal and Otago, who were meeting in Durban in the Super-12 competition. Meanwhile, back at Saracens, wheels were turning.

A fortnight later, Saracens entertained Bath on the first day of British Summer Time on an appropriately sunny afternoon. The news had come through that there would be a place in the European Cup next season for the top six teams in the Premiership. Saracens' ladies won the Bread for Life Cup in scintillating style in a curtain-raiser that, along with strident rock music and supple dancing girls, had created another carnival atmosphere among the 14,000 crowd.

While the sun sparkled and the crowd rocked and the Sky Sports cameraman leered ever closer at the grinning, bikini-clad dance troupe, ominous overtures were making their presence felt. Turner and Wright had returned from South Africa the day before and nobody had asked Turner how the trip had gone, bar a few jokes from the lads enquiring after his holiday in Durban. Turner, who had noticed Wright take a few phone calls from Mike Scott while they had been away, sensed that something was afoot.

Despite an extraordinary atmosphere reminiscent of the cup final the previous season, Saracens were cut apart by a rampant Bath and an inspired Iain Balshaw, who claimed a hat-trick. Evans and Turner snapped at each other in the East Stand as they argued over who had been at fault when Bath sliced open the Saracen midfield. Penaud was off again by half-time, requiring young Billy Stanley from the youth squad to make his debut, while his partner at half-back, the fourth-choice youngster Matt Powell, was the only fit scrum-half left in the squad. Another cruel injury crisis meant that Saracens had no cover for him on the bench. When he went down with cramp towards the end of the game, the physio worked frantically. Powell simply had to stay on.

After the final whistle had consigned Saracens to a 34–14 defeat, the home-team changing-room was drained of life. The players could not even summon the motivation to link arms. It was the first time in my experience that they had not greeted the changing-room get-together with a huddle of solidarity. Evans delivered a desperate speech as the new carrot of Europe, now proffered, suddenly looked like slipping away.

'We're in serious trouble, guys,' he implored them, stalking the room and looking up into each player's eyes. 'We've got to work at this! No heads down! Everybody's got to put their hand on the table and say, "I'm in!"'

With Evans's exhortation complete, Pienaar stood still at the back of the room.

'I've got nothing to say,' he almost whispered. 'I'm very disappointed.'

The following morning, Turner arrived for training and Pienaar called him into his study.

'Paul,' he said, 'Mark's going to be speaking to you.'

'What about?'

'We're going to be parting company. Mark's going to be coaching the backs.'

'Well, where does that leave me?'

'Mark's talking about paying up your contract to the end of the season.'

'Oh, okay. I'd better talk to Mark then.'

Despite the sting of rejection, Turner's initial reaction was one of relief to be out of the uncomfortable set-up at Saracens. He nevertheless felt let down by the management; he had felt cruelly so over the Bedford substitution affair. He was certain that Pienaar had done nothing to fight his corner and he had never felt anything other than coldness from Evans. His influence over the team had been marginal. He had struggled to adapt to life as one of a panel of coaches, having always been the chief architect at previous clubs. There had been problems within the squad when Turner had adopted a hands-on role in coaching. Only recently retired as a player, Turner could not resist stepping in during training to play at fly-half and this had represented a radical break from the detached supervisory role that Evans had filled before him. Many of the backs disagreed with the training drills that he had tried to introduce, further undermining his position. As his time at Saracens progressed, he had had to grow into a clipboard-and-stopwatch mode of coaching with which he never felt comfortable. He had wanted to be able to take the backs off for a day every now and then, but he rarely had them for more than about half an hour a session, and much of that would be disrupted by the contribution of other coaches. He was the wrong man in the wrong place at the wrong time, and he was hugely disappointed that that should have been allowed to happen.

But it was the lack of support from Pienaar and Evans that had really galled him. It seemed that neither had ever wanted him there. The pair would meet fortnightly with Nigel Wray to discuss recruitment matters and Turner had never been invited. And he knew that neither had moved mountains to defend him when the time had come. Pienaar himself had been caught in an awkward situation, with his close friend Johnson, his principal playmaker Penaud and his fellow coach Turner all struggling with each other on the training field. He had felt unable to take sides.

Turner and Pienaar expressed their mutual admiration for each other as men. On a social level, the relationship had always been amicable, but it had never settled professionally. Pienaar then expressed his deep regret at the situation that had evolved. Turner had often wondered why he had been brought in. One theory was that the tension that had simmered between Evans and Pienaar had led to his recruitment, so that Evans might be removed from the training field.

'You know and I know the political situation between you and Mark,' Turner said to Pienaar. 'I would have thought you'd have sorted it out long ago. It would have saved all this hassle. I'm very disappointed. My hands and feet have been tied behind my back since I arrived here.'

Turner took a training session that morning with the midweek squad and saw Evans in the afternoon. Over the next 48 hours he and his lawyer arrived at a settlement, in which he was bought out of his two-year contract. A suitable press statement was arrived at that did not impinge upon Turner's record as a coach. A 'rationalisation' of the coaching structure had led to his departure.

'It's sad, really,' Turner said after the event. 'You only seem to make money in sport when you're sacked. When things are going well, they just tick along quietly.'

The squad were generally sorry to see Turner go. The players had liked him and several rang him with their condolences the following week. He also received a phone call from his friend and assistant coach at Bedford Rudi Straeuli, who had played in the same back row as Pienaar in 1995 to win the World Cup for South Africa. 'I'm really disappointed for you, Paul,' he said with the regret of one whose two friends have not got on, for whatever reason. 'I'd hoped you and François might form a double act like you and I did.'

'So did I, Rudolph,' replied Turner, 'but there's no double act with François.'

Back at Bramley Road, Evans emerged from his office back on to the training field, where he endeavoured to restore some peace and harmony among the troubled back division.

Saracens, meanwhile, suddenly had a desperate fight on their hands to make the promised land of Europe. Having been firmly ensconced, despite their troubles, in third place throughout the year, the defeat to Bath, together with the blow of being knocked out of the cup, left them in a serious position with morale not exactly sky high. Contracts had been terminated and, with Leicester and Northampton safe, the next seven teams were playing for four remaining places in the tightest of struggles. Richmond, with ominous question marks hanging over their continued existence, soon fell out of contention for Europe, but the race among the rest became fevered. Kyran Bracken and Danny Grewcock were doubtful for the remainder of the season and Paul Wallace was definitely out.

After the Bath defeat, however, there was a break in the fixture list for the Saracens players, with the cup semi-finals and the final round of the Five Nations accounting for the following two weekends. Pienaar encouraged his charges to indulge in a few parties to help foster the necessary spirit for the final push. On the Thursday before Good Friday, Bramley Road hosted a day of basketball, volleyball and pool competitions among the players. Later the next week, the players and their families would meet for a picnic on Hampstead Heath and the Matt Singer Sports Quiz would further focus the minds, as would the consumption of alcohol.

On the morning of Good Friday itself, Ravenscroft, Diprose, Chuter and Nigel Roe, the physiotherapist, met again at Bramley Road. The mission was to leave for an as-yet-undecided location for 'a hefty drink up' over the Easter weekend. Bringing their passports was one of the requirements, but Ravenscroft had his sights set on a visit to his native Yorkshire. His parents were away, so they could leave for the Dales and spend some time in the bracing air and rather more time drinking some good old-fashioned ale. He thus turned up at Bramley Road having packed a few jumpers. The others, however, did not harbour such affection for Yorkshire. Chuter arrived at Bramley Road with nothing more than a wash bag, a change of party shirt and a big lilo. Diprose was similarly light. Roe was from Australia. They clearly did not intend to spend the weekend walking in Yorkshire. Much to Ravenscroft's distress, they left for Stansted Airport and asked at the desk what they had in the way of flights for four blokes on 'a hefty drink up'. The result was a hefty drink up in Copenhagen. Constable and Free, meanwhile, spent the weekend in Biarritz with similar objectives.

They all returned to regale their delighted team-mates with stories of their antics. The mood in the camp was beginning to lighten again and an improvement in form would follow, although a corresponding upturn in results still remained elusive. The storm was yet to lift. In April, Saracens lost narrowly at Leicester before losing again to Harlequins, this time at home.

The situation became critical. It was their fifth consecutive defeat and they also lost Pienaar for all but the last 20 minutes of the season. For the first time in 18 months, Saracens dropped outside the top six at the most crucial of stages.

Finally, the inevitable came to pass. Penaud, with his wife and son still unable to settle, announced that he would be leaving Saracens to return to France at the end of the season, one year into his three-year contract. He expressed his regret, vowing to do everything in his power to help Saracens make Europe, where he would hope to face them the next season. But he had to listen to the wishes of his family. Saracens did little to stand in his way. Off the field, where he oozed Gallic charisma, he had been popular, but it had become clear to his team-mates as the season's problems had unfolded that he did not want to be there. His injuries were viewed as somewhat convenient, and while most thought Pienaar's training regimes spartan and lengthy, Penaud simply extricated himself from them with suspicious regularity.

Pienaar had despaired at trying to make Penaud tick but had long since realised that Saracens needed a new fly-half. For all his extravagant gifts, the Frenchman was as far removed in temperament from Pienaar's ally, Michael Lynagh, as one could conceive. Penaud had suffered intolerably under the shadow of Lynagh and the pressure to escape it – not to mention that of his lionised compatriot Philippe Sella. And the more he had suffered, the more unreliable he had become. His rampant form in the first month of his sojourn had proved an ornate bubble that burst at the Stoop Memorial Ground, along with that of his team. Technically, Penaud was as talented a player as there was in the world. Pound for pound, he was the strongest player in the Saracen squad, yet the lightness of his touch could bamboozle defences. His left foot was sweetness personified. The technique was immaculate. It was its application that proved problematic. Flashes of supreme brilliance regularly lit up his stay in England, although they could blind even his own team-mates. But it was to prove difficult to build a consistent game plan around him. His adventure in England had misfired and Penaud was eager to return to his homeland.

That week, the issue of Brendon Daniel's future also resurfaced. Daniel, Saracens' leading try-scorer by some distance, was in devastating form during the run-in. He had scored two tries in the second defeat to Harlequins, one brilliant, and his stock had never been higher in the eyes of the Fez Boys. Yet his services had been dispensed with during the March contract meetings. Pienaar, who had not thought the March contract meetings constituted final decisions, called Daniel in at lunchtime on the Friday after the Harlequins game and told him Saracens wanted to renew his contract. Daniel replied that he had been offered a deal by Harlequins. Playing with and for Zinzan Brooke, his fellow New Zealander and Harlequins' player-coach, was an attractive prospect. Pienaar asked him to give him until Monday to come up with a new deal.

Daniel phoned later in the afternoon to inform Pienaar that he would be taking the Harlequin offer regardless. Nigel Wray himself then put a lucrative deal in front of Daniel with money up front. But his mind was made up. He had felt offended by the initial decision to reject him and he was happy to join the ranks of his departing team-mates. Saracens had meanwhile secured the signature of Harlequins' England wing Dan Luger. The two clubs would effectively swap.

Despite the squad's imminent break-up, the crisis on the field had to be addressed with four crucial games remaining. Anything less than victory in all four would seriously jeopardise the chances of qualification for Europe. The first was a testing journey to Sunbury for the last league game at London Irish's old ground. The Exiles had announced their intention to play their first-team games at the Stoop the following season and they were desperate to host European opposition there. They were three points clear of Saracens at the time and in third place, but with only one more game to follow, at troubled Bedford, they would have to sit tight and anxiously await their fate if they failed to beat Saracens.

In the hot sunshine that greeted the month of May and the first day of the bank holiday, nearly 7,000 spectators – a record for the place – crammed into London Irish's Guinness-fuelled home. The weary and injury-struck Saracen team stumbled to a flattering 20–3 half-time lead, with Penaud playing as if a weight had suddenly been lifted from his shoulders. A spirited second-half fightback from London Irish set the nerves jangling, but a drop-goal from Penaud and a penalty from Gavin Johnson, now reinstated at full-back, served to buffer Saracens against London Irish's resurgence and they held on tenaciously for a vital 26–21 victory.

It was a life-saving triumph against the odds. Saracen players embraced each other on the field in tired relief as members of the ever-vociferous travelling support scurried this way and that across the old pitch. It was a victory that moved them, if only for two days, back into the fabled top six. Harlequins leapfrogged them again with a win over Richmond on Bank Holiday Monday, before Saracens responded with another uninspiring but gutsy win over Gloucester the following Friday night at Vicarage Road. Bracken, returning from injury earlier than expected, was on fine form and Daniel stole the show again with another solo try, to the delight of his audience who chanted his name into the Watford night air. Saracens now needed two points from their remaining two games to enter Europe the following season.

Their next assignment was at the futuristic Madejski Stadium in Reading. Richmond, now desperately fighting for their very existence after Ashley Levett had withdrawn his financial backing, stood between Saracens and an international adventure. It was a peculiar Wednesday night. A persistent drizzle grew heavier throughout the game. Penaud skipped through the Richmond defence for a solo try, and Johnson and Sorrell both touched down before the break to give Saracens a 19–3 lead at half-time. The cheers of a measly crowd of 2,500 echoed throughout the cavernous stadium, while Richmond's beleaguered announcer tried to invoke what he referred to as 'the Thames Valley roar'. The second half was worse. A fractious game staggered to its limp conclusion: a 25–18 victory to Saracens. It meant that they had made it into Europe.

The realisation lent the atmosphere in the changing-room an appropriate accent of relief, but it had been another desperately mediocre performance. The season had reached the stage, however, where the quality of performance was of little consequence. They had limped over the line for Europe and were grateful for it, but there was no celebration. One more home game now waited, against none other than Newcastle on the Thursday night of the following week. Newcastle would have to win to stand any chance of qualification for Europe. But Newcastle had beaten Saracens to the league the previous season, administered their harshest thrashing of the current campaign and knocked them out of the cup of which they were the holders. A pledge was immediately made in the changing-room deep in the Madejski to gain revenge.

Higher up in the Madejski, John Kingston, Richmond's exhausted director of coaching, held weary court with the assembled press at 11 p.m. It had been a long day for him and a long, long month. He was fighting feverishly alongside his directors to preserve the future of Richmond, one of the oldest clubs in rugby and a founder member of the RFU. Richmond had been in administration since Levett's withdrawal and EFDR, the representatives of their fellow professional rugby clubs, were threatening to buy Richmond out and then close them down. Kingston was as sick with disgust at the heartless cynicism of the proposal as he was with exhaustion at trying not only to fight it but also to warn other Premiership coaches of such a desertion of honour from their noble game. 'I will be doing everything in my power over the next few weeks to preserve the future of this club,' he said flatly with his head cocked downwards amid the shame of it all. 'Then I shall have to decide whether I want to stay in an industry that can countenance this sort of thing.'

Outside, the drizzle had developed into a pervasive deluge.

EFDR had, in the meantime, arrived at £1.8 million as the wage cap for the next season. It was not as restrictive as it might have been, and Evans, Pienaar and Wray set about drawing up their strategies. Paul Wallace was offered a new contract, which he signed. Ravenscroft was offered a modest contract and the benefits of a testimonial year, which he too accepted. Meanwhile, Pienaar called in Diprose, Hill, Bracken, Grewcock, Grau, Constable and Thomson, the seven highest earners in the following season's squad, to ask them to join him in taking a pay cut. They agreed.

The final scene of a long and difficult season was played out at Vicarage Road on the night of Thursday, 20 May. Newcastle arrived having lost to Wasps in the final of the Tetley's Bitter Cup the previous weekend. Bath's 70-point hiding of London Scottish on the same day meant that Newcastle would have to beat Saracens by more than 30 points to claim the last remaining place in Europe. It was never likely.

Saracens produced a spirited performance against a weakened Newcastle team to win 40–26 and deprive their arch rivals of a place in Europe while securing themselves the highly respectable position of third place in the league. A hearty crowd of 7,000 turned out for the meaningless midweek fixture to show their continuing enthusiasm for the Saracen venture. Pienaar took the announcer's microphone at the end of the game to thank them. Third was not good enough, he said, and the situation would be addressed next season. It would be his last season as a player.

The entire playing squad, blazered or otherwise, gathered in the changing-room after Daniel had been presented on the pitch with his supporters' player-of-the-year award (he had won 44 per cent of the vote on the Internet). They linked arms in the traditional way. Mark Evans stood on the changing-room bench outside the ring and rested his elbows on the shoulders of Ryan Constable.

'I've got a lot of respect for Newcastle as a team,' he said to the players. 'Probably more for them than any other. To put 40 points past them is really not a bad way to finish. We asked for four wins to end the season and you've given us them.'

Evans's voice began to crack with emotion and his eyes inflamed as he continued. He bade farewell to those players who were departing, thanked them for all their efforts over the years and wished them the best of luck for the future. The next day, Evans would inform the players at

Bramley Road, just before the players' court session, that he would also be leaving the playing department. He would be moving to the Watford offices as director of corporate development. The players responded to the news with a simple round of applause for him.

It lowered the curtain on a labour of love that had occupied nearly half of Evans's life. He was finally to leave the rickety walls of Bramley Road that had been a second home to him for the best part of the last 20 years. The professional tension that still simmered between him and Pienaar had become intolerable. If, before Pienaar arrived at Saracens, Kitch Christie had asked Wray if the personalities were strong at Saracens, the reply would have been resoundingly affirmative in the case of Evans. He was strong to the point of stubbornness. The walls of Bramley Road had creaked with the presence of the personalities of Pienaar and Evans. It had been painful for Evans to lose his beloved role of head coach two years earlier and he had struggled to sit on the sidelines ever since. He had become fiercely protective of his position as director of rugby and the concomitant responsibility of player recruitment, and lack of communication between him and Pienaar in this department had started to impinge upon playing matters. It had led to the loss of Ben Sturnham at the start of the season and the half-baked conditions under which Paul Turner was recruited. Towards the end it had cost them Brendon Daniel. Evans had tendered his resignation as director of rugby before the end of the season but, recognising the value of his intelligence and perception, Wray offered him the new position developing the Saracen project from Watford, which he accepted.

After Evans's words to the ring of players in the Vicarage Road changing-room, Pienaar rounded the season off with some characteristically honest words of reflection. 'Guys, when we set ourselves goals in life,' he said, 'we have to work hard to achieve them. It's never easy. If you could do it without work, life would be a breeze. Everyone would be happy. It's not like that. It's hard work. But it's worth it. We've finished with four wins out of four and we're in Europe, which is great. But we could have done so much more.

'This place means a lot to me. I'd say Saracens means as much to me as Transvaal, my beloved Transvaal, where I've played all my life. I want to see Saracens be the best and I will carry on pushing for that, believe me. And guys. Let's have more parties and fewer meetings. Winners have parties; losers have meetings.'

All that remained was for Bracken to present the departing Johnson with a farewell gift. Bracken had taken a collection for him and had bought him what he described as a gazelle's hoof, although it looked just a little bit like a horseshoe.

'Hey, Kyran,' cried Thomson as Bracken left the changing-room after the grinning Johnson had received the gift and taken the accompanying applause. 'I thought you said a tenner a head!'

Bracken laughed back as he made good his escape. 'Yeah! I'm all right!'

A season that had started with such extravagant promise for Saracens but had subsided into the fractured and fitful thus ended in high spirits. What had, at times, felt like a desolate campaign now concluded with Saracens standing defiantly in third position. There could be no greater measure of their progress since the dark ages of Bramley Road than to feel such intense disappointment during a season in which they were the third best team in the land.

Nevertheless, the third season of professional rugby drew to its close beneath the gathering clouds of uncertainty and pain that so many had predicted for the fledgling industry. The future of some clubs was a subject of intense concern as the financial realities started to bite and the laws of natural selection whirred into life. The profile of rugby continued to burgeon spectacularly, but the economics of the game were still lagging behind. Further evidence of the game's high profile would emerge the following weekend, when the tabloid press paid the sport the perverse compliment of its attentions, cynically framing the England captain on the eve of potentially his greatest adventure. The crowding insecurities haunted every last player.

They left Vicarage Road that evening and went their various ways into the Watford night, some to adventures in foreign fields, some to adventures with new clubs or in new jobs, others to holidays before the season's cycle began again in little more than a month.

The hopeful promise of the waxing World Cup glowed red on the horizon. But in British rugby the night was still black.

17

The Fez Boys

You put your left hook in,
Your left hook out,
In, out, in, out,
You shake it all about.
You do the Danny Grewcock and you turn around,
That's what it's all about.
Oooooooohhhhhh! Danny Grewcock!
Oooooooohhhhhh! Danny Grewcock!
Oooooooohhhhhh! Danny Grewcock!
Fists clenched, scrum down! Rah! Rah! Rah!

The Fez Boys.

On Sunday, 9 March 1997, Saracens were playing Bristol at Enfield. Six fans, likely lads to a man with the healthiest respect for the emancipatory benefits of beer, decided they needed to add further spice to their support of Saracens. Some kind of appropriately Middle Eastern attire was in order for the forthcoming match.

The fancy-dress shop did not have any curly-toed slippers with bells on, but there were a few fez hats. Perfect. Cheeky. Ostentatious. Red and black. The Fez Boy was born.

A month later, on the away trip to Leicester, Patsy and Maggie joined to make the Fez Boys eight in number and vaguely correct in policy. Patsy and Maggie could now be Fez Boys too. The clan grew steadily, until 40 hardcore Saracen fans had adopted the headgear as their uniform and lively, beverage-fuelled banter as their stock in trade.

Saracens, armed for the Watford years with an intuitive and pervasive marketing department, were not slow to recognise the iconic potential of the fez. It was promoted as a supremely simple symbol with which Saracen fans could identify. And identify they did. A piece of red felt shaped like a hat with a black tassel stapled on top. Saracens sold them for five pounds apiece. Eleven thousand were bought in the build-up to the 1998 cup final alone. Saracens had found the perfect marketing hook.

With their fez hats now battered with wear, plastered with stickers and drenched in beer, the Fez Boys meanwhile gathered together amid the thousands of brand new fez hats. They found a little niche in the West Stand at Vicarage Road from where rang out their myriad songs. The door to the members' bar was but a few rows behind and a steady stream of beer flowed through it to keep the spirits soaring and the vocal chords lubricated.

Almost upon formation, the Fez Boys had crowned their favourite player. Tony Copsey was King of the Fez, the big man developing a natural affinity for the Fez Boys' boisterous sense of humour. And their drinking habits. He was the first player to don a fez and was adulated by the Fez Boys for the rest of the Enfield year and the season that followed. Copsey retired to Llanelli at the end of that season, and while Lynagh and Sella bade farewell to the game of rugby by parading the cup at Vicarage Road, Copsey stood tall in front of his adoring Fez Boys and gave his own valedictory salute. The desperate search for his replacement began. Kyran Bracken was alighted upon, having been the second player to don a fez. He had been the first to buy the Fez Boys a round of beers. They had not forgotten. They had nicknamed Bracken 'Nice But Dim' for his pains, but conferred the noblest of honours upon him in succession to Copsey. The Errol Flynn of rugby (or 'Kyran Broken', as young Christopher Johns, son of Paddy, would refer to him) was next to be crowned. But only as Kyran, Prince of Fez. The Fez Boys would rather pig-headedly insist that the King was not dead, although sightings of Copsey during one of Saracens' subsequent excursions to Wales suggested otherwise.

If Copsey was King and Bracken Prince, Michael Lynagh was always God. When he lined up his kicks for goal, the Fez Boys would try to reach out to him and transmit their positive vibes. The only time a Fez Boy could be found without a beer in his (or her) hand was at such a point. Even alcohol had to be put down when Lynagh was kicking for goal. Rocket Ron would lead the way and the Fez Boys would hold out their arms in front of them and wriggle their fingers in empowering reverence while Lynagh completed his goal-kicking ritual. It was a communion that soon caught on across the Vicarage Road clientele, and the ranks of murmuring fingers sprouting in their thousands from a backdrop of red felt constituted one of the more extraordinary spectacles at Twickenham in recent years.

The serious business, however, took place after each game in the members' bar, where sweat would add its lustre to the other ingredients of wear and tear, stickers and beer. The Fez Boys would stand in the centre of the 50-yard-long room and announce the entrance of each player with the appropriate ditty. All those assembled in the bar would know as and when a player had completed his duties in the sponsors' boxes and descended to the bar for sustenance. The roar of the Fez Boys would greet each one, sometimes an embrace, always a tune:

[To the tune of 'The Addams Family'] 'His name is Alain Penaud, he probably drives a Renault, he plays at number ten-o, right next to Nice But Dim . . .'

[Batman theme] 'Nananananananananananana, FLAT-MAN!'

[Reeves and Mortimer chant] 'George Chu-TAH-TAH-TAH!'

['Go West'] 'Ooooo aaahhh François Pienaar, ooooo aaahhh François Pienaar, ooooo aaahhh François Pienaar . . .'

['Bread of Heaven'] 'Nothing rhymes with, nothing rhymes with, nothing rhymes with Botterman (Botterman), nothing rhymes with Botterman.'

The Fez Boys were warmly received at each ground and developed a healthy reputation for bringing the party with them. Their singing was hearty, their banter was witty and their love for Saracens deeply entrenched. They revelled in the new-found celebrity of the fez that was conferred with the move to Watford. Clinging on to their trusty wholesome originals, they watched through their revelry as thousands of mass-produced fez hats grew up all around them. The merchandising machine appropriated their little gimmick. As well as the proliferation of tacky replicas, befezzed toy camels were manufactured, a plethora of coffee mugs percolated through the system, a glossy 'brochure' was unabashedly named *Year of the Fez*. The image of the fez was suddenly ubiquitous among the explosive orgy of consumerism that seized Vicarage Road. Everybody wanted a piece of the fez.

The Fez Boys drank on. They followed their team to the ends of the country. They belted out their songs from Bath to Newcastle, from victory to defeat. They were ferocious in their commitment, unshakeable in their integrity. They loved their beer, they loved their Saracens and they loved their rugby, in no particular order. While the showbiz carnival gathered pace around them, they continued unchecked in their long-observed traditions. Indeed, they formed the very bedrock of that showbiz carnival. Without them, the carnival would be rootless.

Without it, the Fez Boys would drink on regardless.

18

Reflections

When rugby union turned professional in 1995, opinion was pretty sharply divided among rugby folk between the nostalgic and the revolutionary. The former loved the game as it was and loathed the possibility of it becoming a big, corporate industry. The latter recognised the absurdities that had crept into the high-profile game at the top level. Players were expected to be professional in all respects other than the vital one of getting paid. Rugby was evolving in such a way that ever greater demands were being made on its players and expectations placed at the door of its coaches. Not remunerating them all for the consequent sacrifices was intolerable. The game was poised for a revolution of some sort. Money had long since started to change hands and television companies had recognised the potential for rugby's marketability. In turning professional, rugby was effectively coming clean.

At the time, I was certainly in the nostalgic camp. I cannot really explain why, other than to say that I loved the game as it was: simple, honest and earthy. I abhorred the prospect of rugby becoming an American football jamboree. I still harbour serious reservations on that front, but my attitude to professional rugby has since changed, along with the game itself. There is certainly an element of resignation in my changed approach. It has happened now and we must just get on with it and make the most of it. But I have also seen new benefits in the professional game. The last two years at Saracens have probably done more than anything else to change my mind in this regard.

Even if I had always loved the game for its simple image, I nevertheless grew excited as other people outside rugby showed an interest. As the game's popularity increased on the back of the World Cups of 1991 and 1995, I thrilled at the idea of more and more people appreciating the joys of rugby. It was almost a case of wanting to say 'Come and enjoy what we have been enjoying'. It still is. I think the excitement of seeing the game I love grow in popularity has now super-seded the regret of watching its subtler charms pass. I now accept, and enjoy, dancing girls, steel bands and rock music as part of the package (although I sometimes wish the stadium announcers would take it easy).

I think we can say that Saracens have succeeded more than any other club in bringing rugby to a new audience. The statistics speak for them-selves. Happy with 1,000 at a game in the old days at Bramley Road, to raise the average gate within three years to a little short of 10,000 is an astonishing achievement. In this respect, Saracens have hinted at the possibilities open to rugby and have gone some way to realising them. Being at Vicarage Road on match-days was an unfailingly uplifting experience in the first year, and even during the troubled second year it was often exhilarating. The build-up to the heavy defeat when Bath visited in March 1999, for example, boasted the most extraordinary atmosphere. Even in view of the subsequent defeat, it constituted a great day out. The bouncing energy of the 14,000 crowd, fuelled by smiling faces, strident music, dancing girls and the sunshine, lent the occasion a quality of universal appeal, whether one understood the tackle laws or not. Every time the team ran out to the thumping strains of 'Men in Black' and the exultant cheers of thousands, the hairs on the back of this once-sceptical observer's neck stood on end.

It is not appropriate to be sceptical about the move towards a carnival atmosphere in rugby. While it is important to retain the good old-fashioned values of the sport, a departure for more populist pastures must be recognised, apart from anything else, as essential to the game's survival as a credible institution. Some complain that, underneath all the razzmatazz and excitement, rugby is now driven by money. Of course it is, like most things in life – but, as in life, we should not always seek to look beneath the surface. When that surface is a glittering spectacle that brings joy to thousands and, even more, an intimate relationship between heroes and community, it should be welcomed as the noblest manifestation of revenue maximisation. Another crucial point to recog-nise is that rugby is maximising revenue not to extract extortionate profit from the enterprise but simply to survive and stand on its own two feet.

One of my principal regrets in writing this book is not affording sufficient attention to the work of the Saracen marketing department in generating such excitement and hope. The same applies to the extensive and highly productive youth system at the club, under the guidance of Bob Crooks and John Davies, and the extraordinarily successful women's section. Each of these departments might require a book in itself. The constraints of time and space have caught up with me, though, and for that I apologise.

This book has, however, been intended as a study of professional rugby from the perspective of the players. Professional rugby is necessarily a very different proposition for them. It is not entirely the dream profession that many outside the game presume it to be. Despite the impressive carnivals that can be enjoyed at Vicarage Road, rugby in general is in critical financial straits, and nowhere is that uncertainty felt more keenly than in the playing department.

The transition from amateur to professional has affected the players more than anyone. Suddenly there is no longer the luxury of margin for error. Suddenly the game ceases to be a hobby and becomes a job. Suddenly there is little scope for escape from rugby. Hobbies are vital avenues of release for us all. Sport starts life as a hobby for anyone who plays it at whatever level, but when it suddenly graduates to become a job, the necessary adjustment can be disconcerting, particularly when the sport in question has no lengthy culture of professionalism to inform it. Intense pressures start to close in. You are getting paid to be excellent and are devoting every last ounce of energy to that one end. Should imperfection ever blemish your excellence, it plagues your conscience, not only because you have always wanted to be the best but because you now have a duty to be the best. Pressures close in from the outside world too. The media may minutely scrutinise your performance (and your personal life) with the justification that you are now getting paid for it. The growing interest from the public and the love for their respective teams exact ever-higher expectations. While thousands enjoy the pre-match carnival outside, the echoes reverberate down to the quiet changing-rooms deep within the stadium.

Then there is the issue of contracts and livelihood. How long can the fledgling industry afford you? How long will it want you? In professional rugby during the 1998–99 season, these issues were more painfully applicable than in any other season in any other sport. When rugby's Big Bang gave birth to the professional era, three-year contracts were set in motion, conceiving rugby's equivalent of the millennium bug. Numerous contracts ticked down to simultaneous conclusions some way off in 1999. When the time came around, rugby clubs across the country were faced with an acute dilemma and rugby players with a tumult of uncertainty. The same scenario will not be allowed to happen again.

Set against this backdrop, life at Saracens in the first three seasons of professional rugby has constituted a roller-coaster of emotions. Honest and honourable men have been thrown together in a high-intensity crucible. Sometimes the ingredients and conditions have mushroomed into a glorious crescendo, other times they have exploded into fractious discord. Inevitable teething problems beset the first year in Enfield. From there, the chemistry was perfect for the first year in Watford: second in the league, swaggering victors in the cup, 20,000 people, the fez, Lynagh, Sella and Pienaar. The images were bold and hopeful, but with them came the pedestal. For all the retrospective theorising over the relative fall from grace, the biggest difference in the second season at Watford was that suddenly everybody wanted to beat Saracens. Harlequins, Wasps and Newcastle had all suffered from abject form before their respective games against Saracens in October 1998. The prospect of playing Saracens, however, was the common theme that seemed to galvanise all three into producing astonishing performances. Saracens had only to be slightly short of excellent to be exposed.

Once the doubt sets in, however, it is fiendishly difficult to reverse, and domestics inevitably ensue. I found the character of man at the club to be nothing other than of the finest calibre, just continually beset by various and shifting pressures. There is rarely such a thing as one person who is right and another who is wrong, just different characters and different perspectives meeting together under trying circumstances. In the crucible, anything can, and does, happen. Sometimes it clicks, sometimes it falters. At times, the third season of professionalism at Saracens felt bleak and desperate. It is a tribute to the characters there from top to bottom, and the standards that have been set by François Pienaar, that for most of that time they were actually still in contention for the league and eventually finished the season in third place. It is also a tribute to the unremitting competition of the Premiership that they could have done all that while losing as many as nine games and drawing a tenth.

Professional rugby's bloody struggle continues. We always knew that the early years would be painful and messy. Nevertheless, expecting it and coping with it when it happens are two entirely different things. When the game turned professional, people estimated it would take about three to five years to sort itself out. I think the actual figure will be nearer ten. Three years have now passed and there is likely to be a lot more suffering yet. The number of clubs in the top flight will have to come down, players will have to accept more pay cuts and redundancies, clubs will have to combine resources. The further changes will upset the nostalgic among us, but they are very necessary before the game arrives at something close to stability.

In the meantime, the game relies implicitly on the goodwill and drive of the owners. Saracens are blessed in having in their hot seat a man like Nigel Wray, who genuinely loves the game, seems utterly committed to the cause and channels his money into the right areas. Saracens can look forward to continued success as long as that remains so. The promotion of Watford Town FC to football's top flight will mean Premiership football at Vicarage Road into the new millennium as well as Premiership rugby, and that will help Saracens and Wray enormously as they continue to work with their co-tenants to promote sport in the area.

Rugby, however, is still a long way from viability. It is gradually getting closer but, until it gets there, the future of the game rests in the hands of those men good enough to lend it their financial support. Without them, the noble old game so many of us love would collapse into ruinous, and possibly terminal, chaos. It is quite a responsibility.